IF YOU WEREN'T A
HEDGEHOG...
IF I WEREN'T A
HEMOPHILIAC...

If you weren't a hedgehog...

If I weren't a hemophiliac...

232 cartoons by

a.weldon.

**Andrews McMeel
Publishing, LLC**

Kansas City

For information, write Andrews McMeel Publishing, LLC, an Andrews McMeel Universal company, 1130 Walnut Street, Kansas City, Missouri 64106.

Originally published by Allen & Unwin, Australia, 2006.

09 10 11 12 13 TEN 10 9 8 7 6 5 4 3 2 1

ISBN-13: 978-0-7407-7971-8
ISBN-10: 0-7407-7971-0

Library of Congress Control Number: 2008938042

www.andrewsmcmeel.com

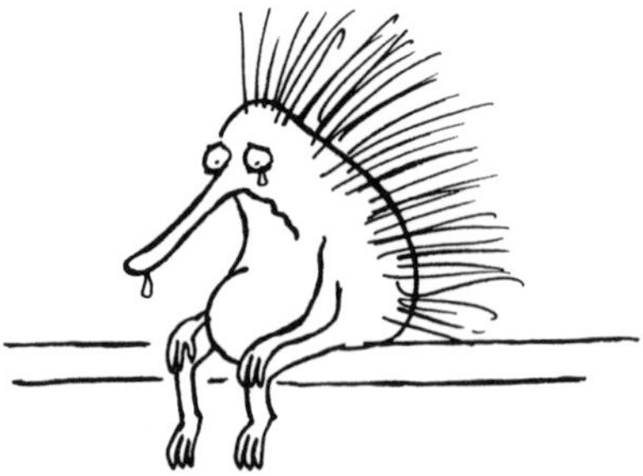

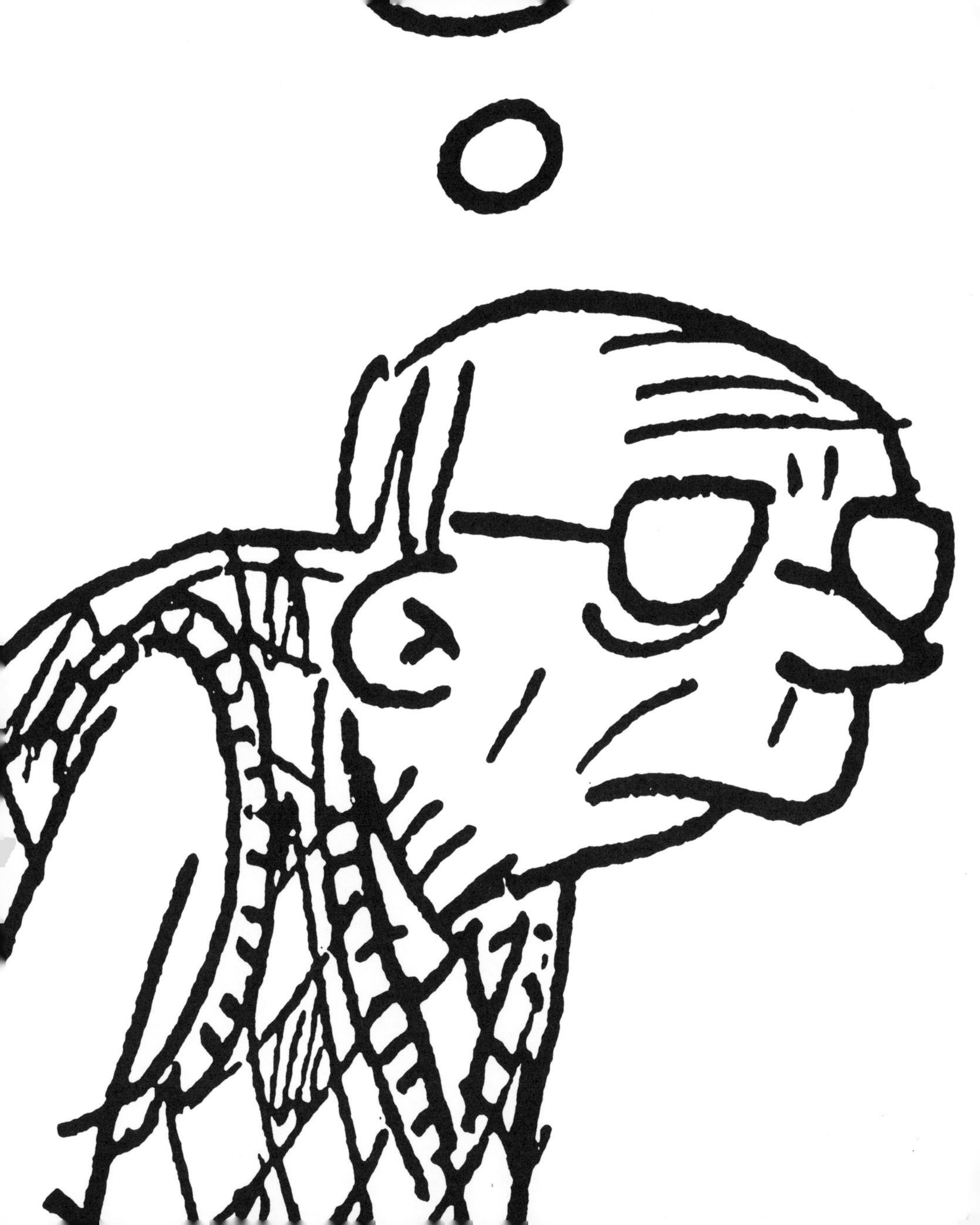

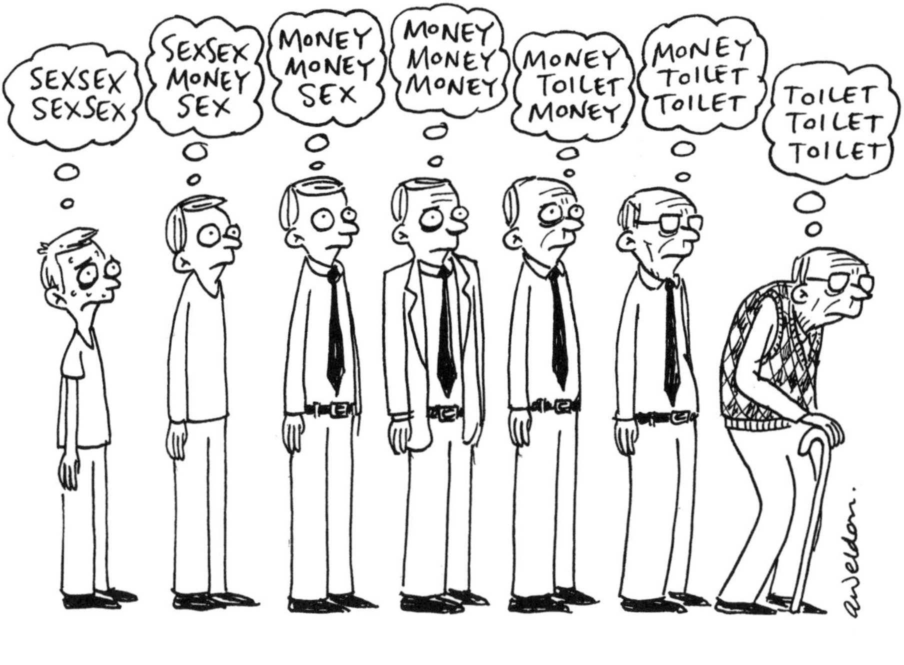
SEXSEX SEXSEX
SEXSEX MONEY SEX
MONEY MONEY SEX
MONEY MONEY MONEY
MONEY TOILET MONEY
MONEY TOILET TOILET
TOILET TOILET TOILET
a weldon.

SHE WAS GETTING THIS **HUNCH** AS SHE GOT OLDER, SO I GOT THE DOCTOR TO HOLLOW IT OUT AND WE USE IT AS SORT OF A 'TRUNK'.
aweldon

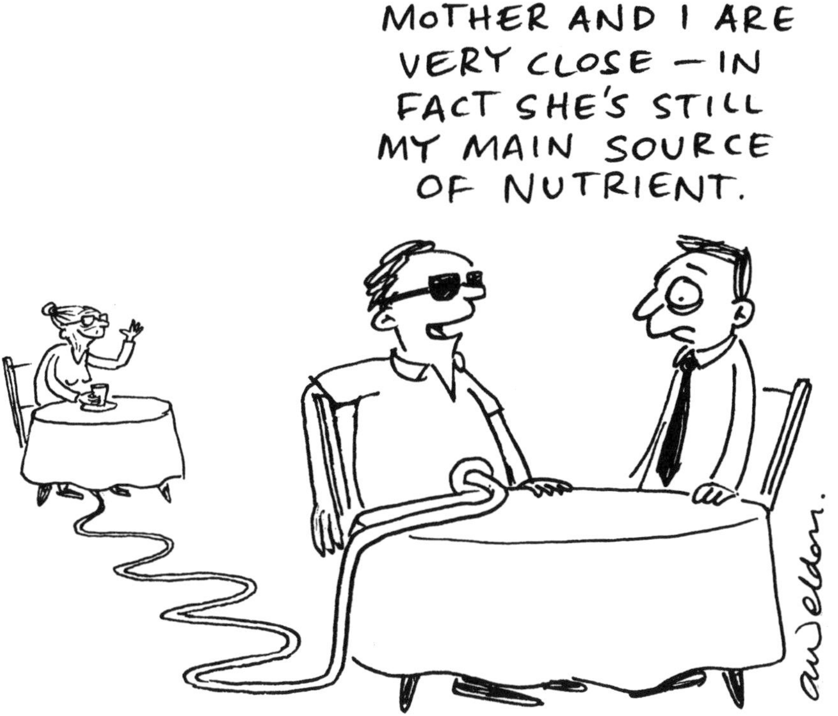
MOTHER AND I ARE VERY CLOSE – IN FACT SHE'S STILL MY MAIN SOURCE OF NUTRIENT.
aweldon.

I ALWAYS SWORE THAT WHEN I GOT RICH I'D BUY MUM THE BEST OF EVERYTHING. THIS IS FROM THE LATEST JEAN PAUL GAULTIER CATWALK COLLECTION.

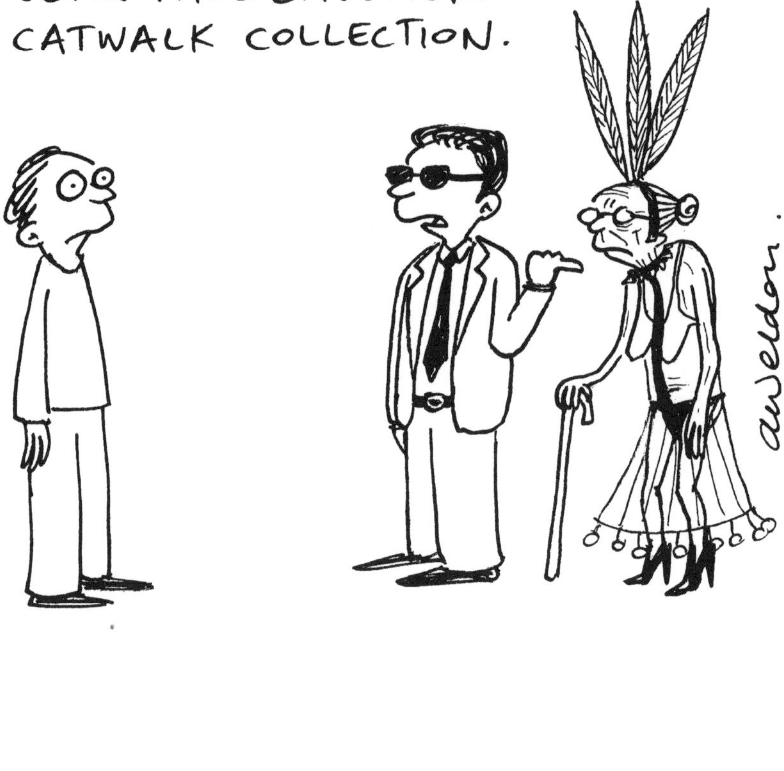
aweldon.

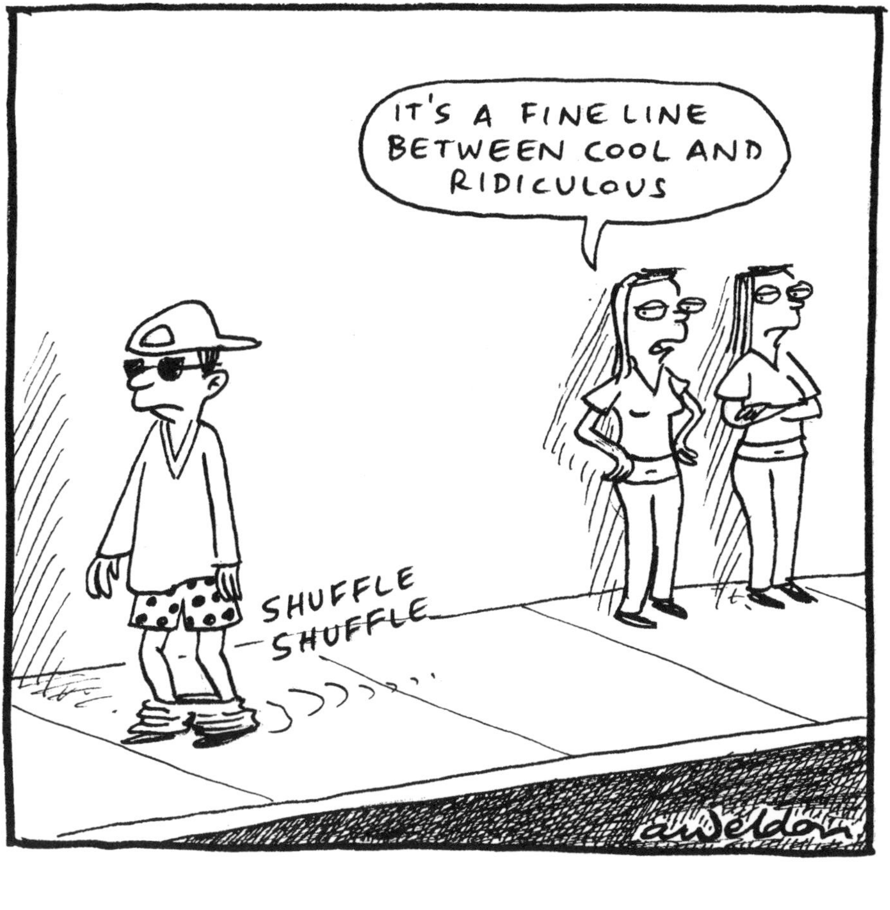
IT'S A FINE LINE BETWEEN COOL AND RIDICULOUS
SHUFFLE SHUFFLE

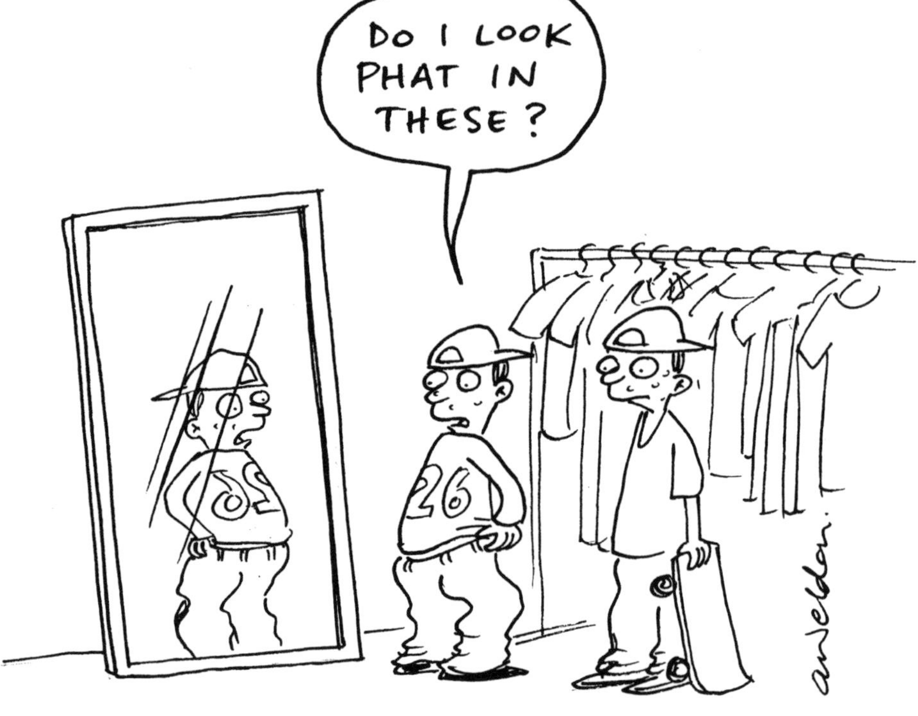
DO I LOOK PHAT IN THESE?
26
anweldon

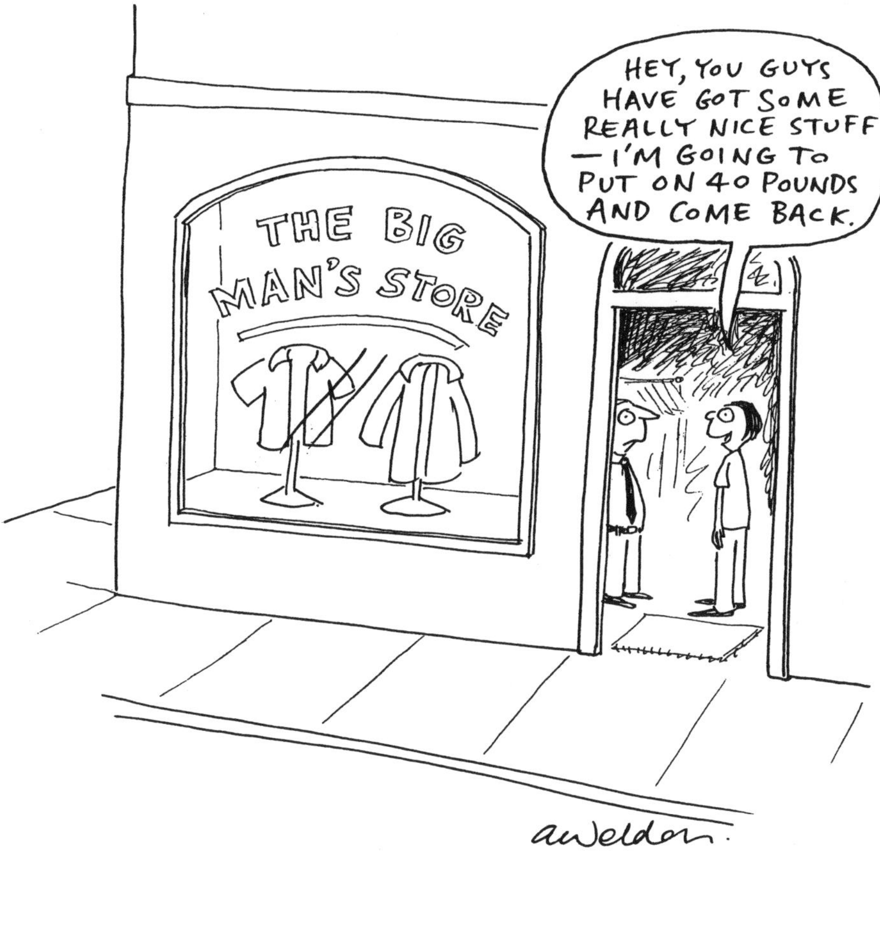
THE BIG MAN'S STORE
HEY, YOU GUYS HAVE GOT SOME REALLY NICE STUFF —I'M GOING TO PUT ON 40 POUNDS AND COME BACK.
a weldon.

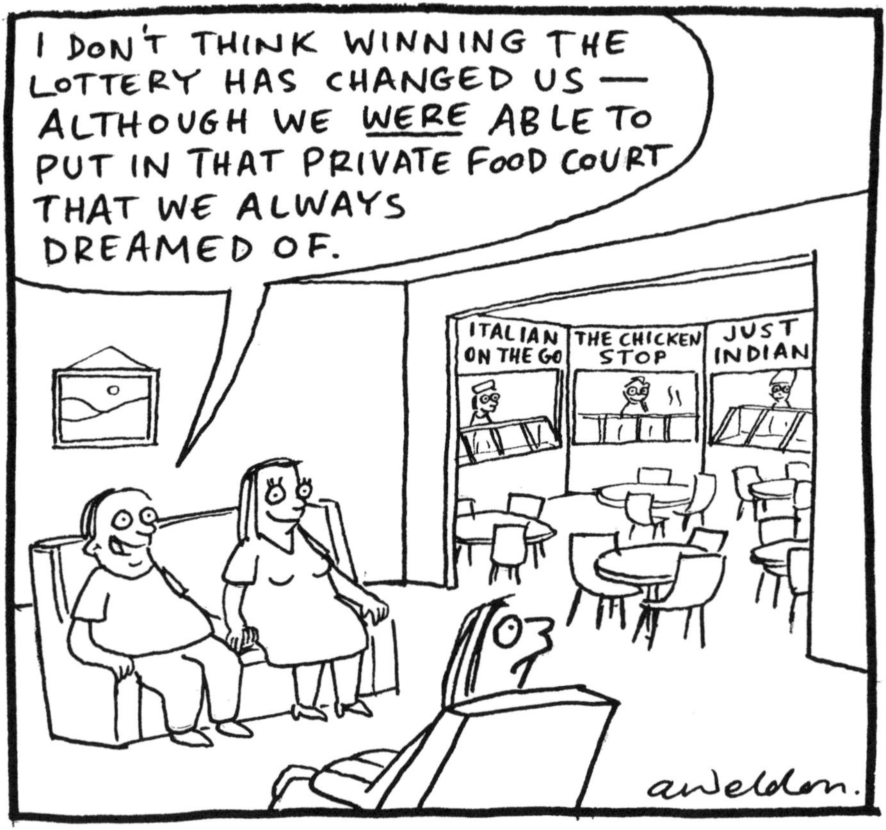
I DON'T THINK WINNING THE LOTTERY HAS CHANGED US — ALTHOUGH WE WERE ABLE TO PUT IN THAT PRIVATE FOOD COURT THAT WE ALWAYS DREAMED OF.
ITALIAN ON THE GO
THE CHICKEN STOP
JUST INDIAN
a weldon.

HAVE YOU
LOST WEIGHT?

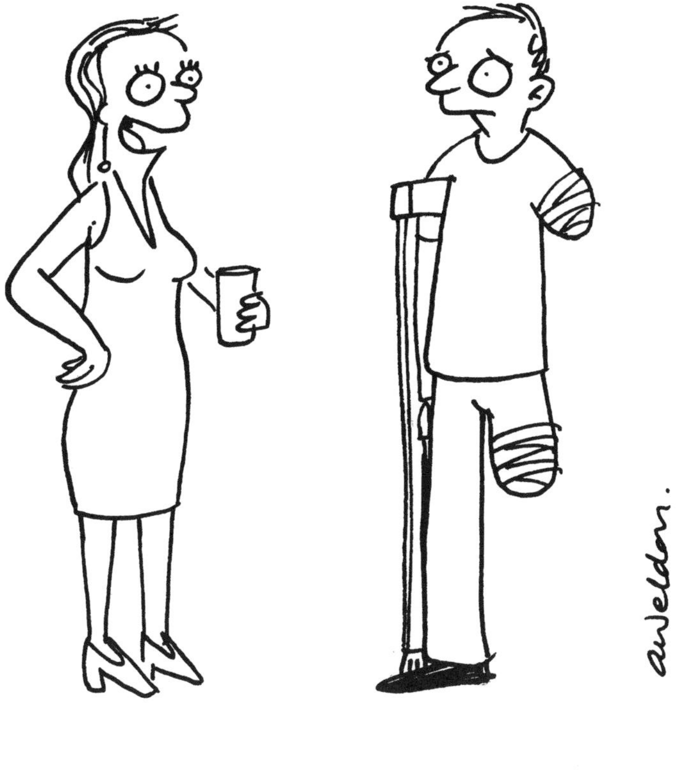
aweldon.

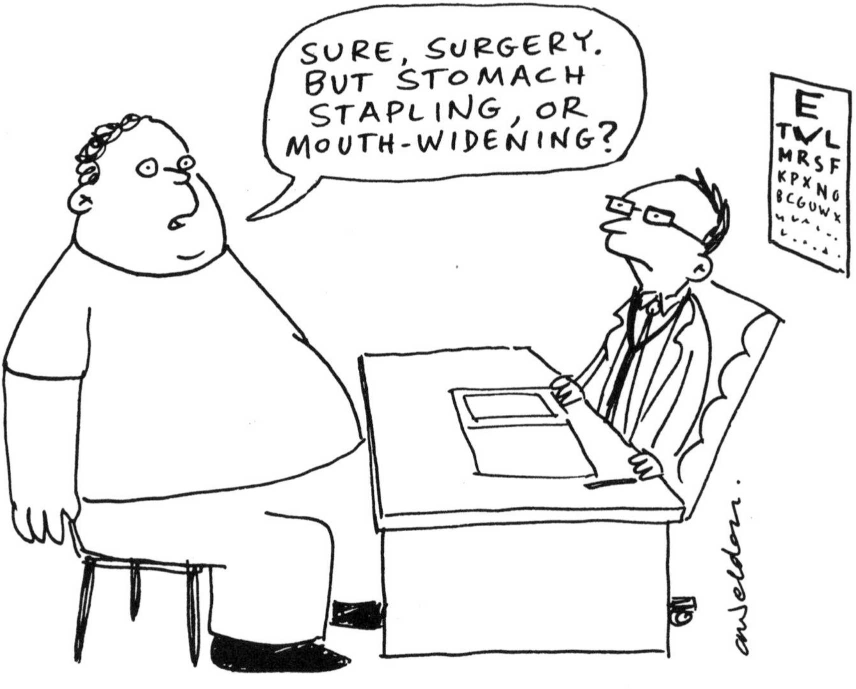
SURE, SURGERY. BUT STOMACH STAPLING, OR MOUTH-WIDENING?

ADVERTISEMENT
DOCTOR HAPPY'S STAINLESS STEEL
SMILE BRACE
GUARANTEED SMILES NO MATTER WHAT YOUR MOOD!
ACTUAL SIZE.
PERFECT FOR:
★ DEPRESSIVES
★ THE SURLY
★ RETAIL WORKERS
BEFORE
AFTER
ONLY $29.95 IN STORES NOW!
a weldon.

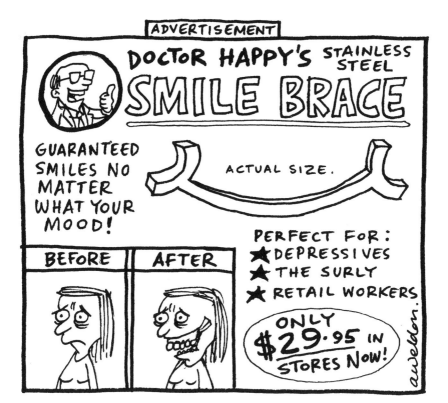

AH! IT'S TRUE, WENTWORTH, I AM BLESSED WITH AN EXTRAORDINARY INTELLIGENCE. BUT I WOULD TRADE IT ALL FOR ONE DAY WITHOUT THIS ACCURSED CRANIUM SCAFFOLD!

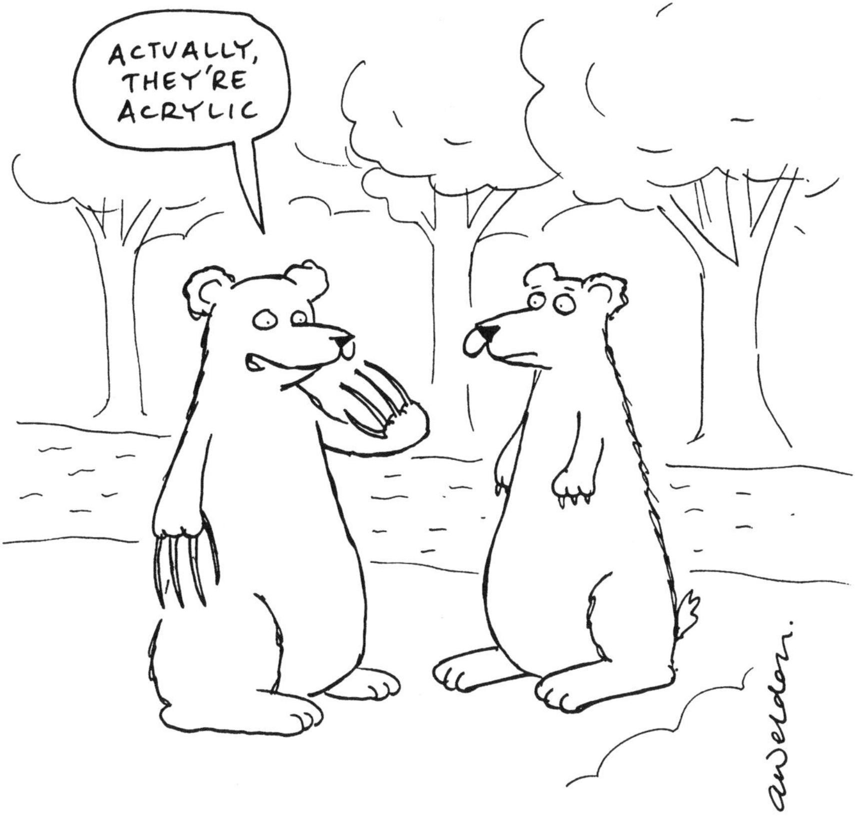
ACTUALLY, THEY'RE ACRYLIC

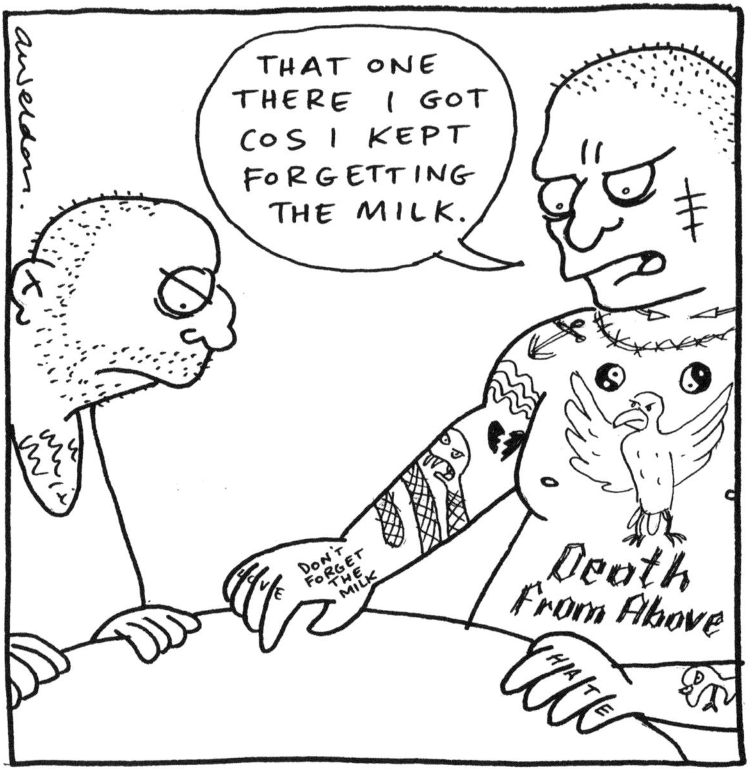
THAT ONE THERE I GOT COS I KEPT FORGETTING THE MILK.
DON'T FORGET THE MILK
LOVE
HATE
Death From Above
aWeldon.

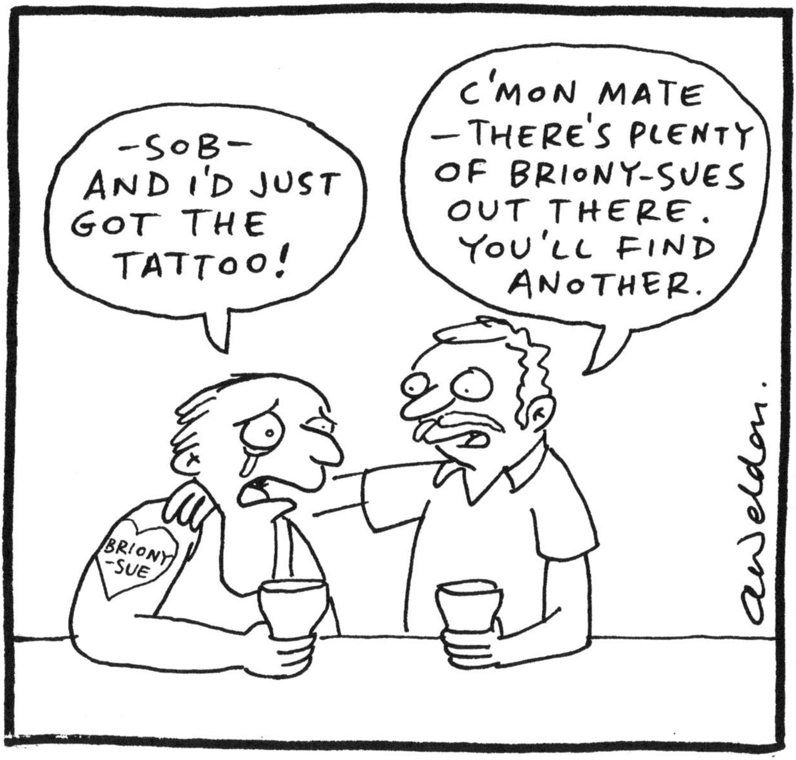
-SOB- AND I'D JUST GOT THE TATTOO!
C'MON MATE —THERE'S PLENTY OF BRIONY-SUES OUT THERE. YOU'LL FIND ANOTHER.
BRIONY -SUE
aweldon.

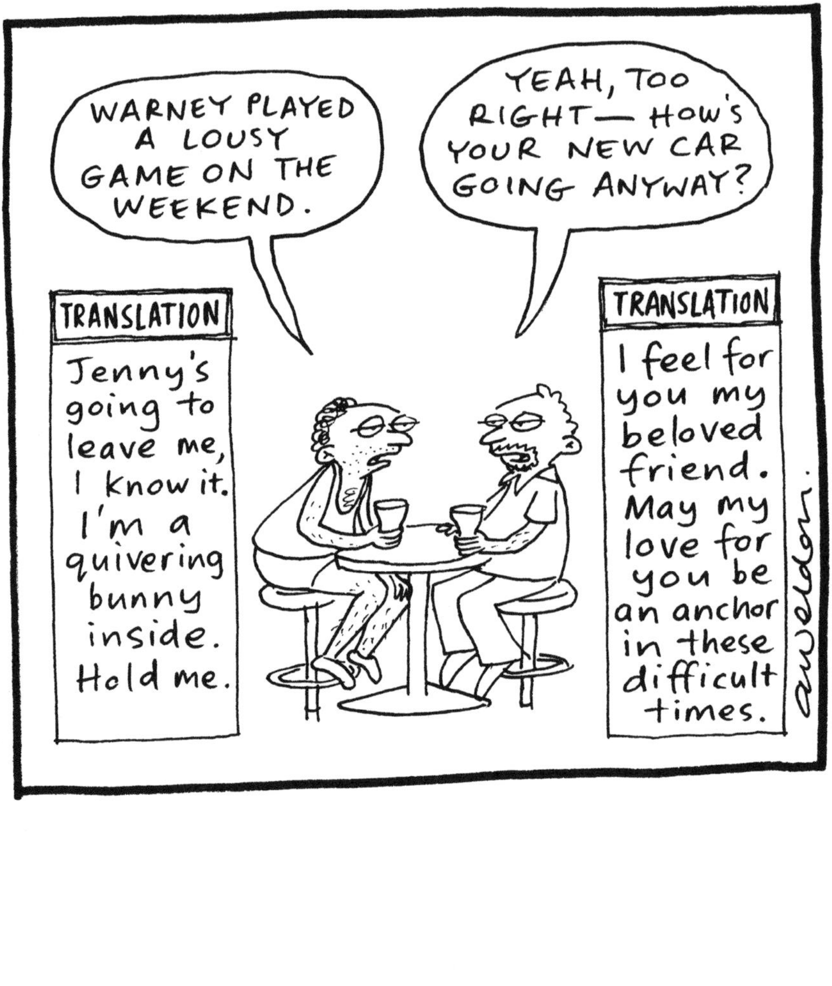
WARNEY PLAYED A LOUSY GAME ON THE WEEKEND.
YEAH, TOO RIGHT— HOW'S YOUR NEW CAR GOING ANYWAY?
TRANSLATION
Jenny's going to leave me, I know it. I'm a quivering bunny inside. Hold me.
TRANSLATION
I feel for you my beloved friend. May my love for you be an anchor in these difficult times.
aweldon.

HERE COMES TROUBLE!
aweldon.

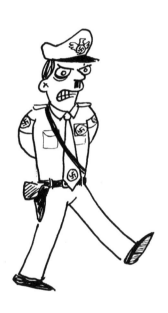

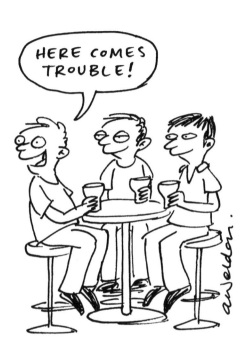

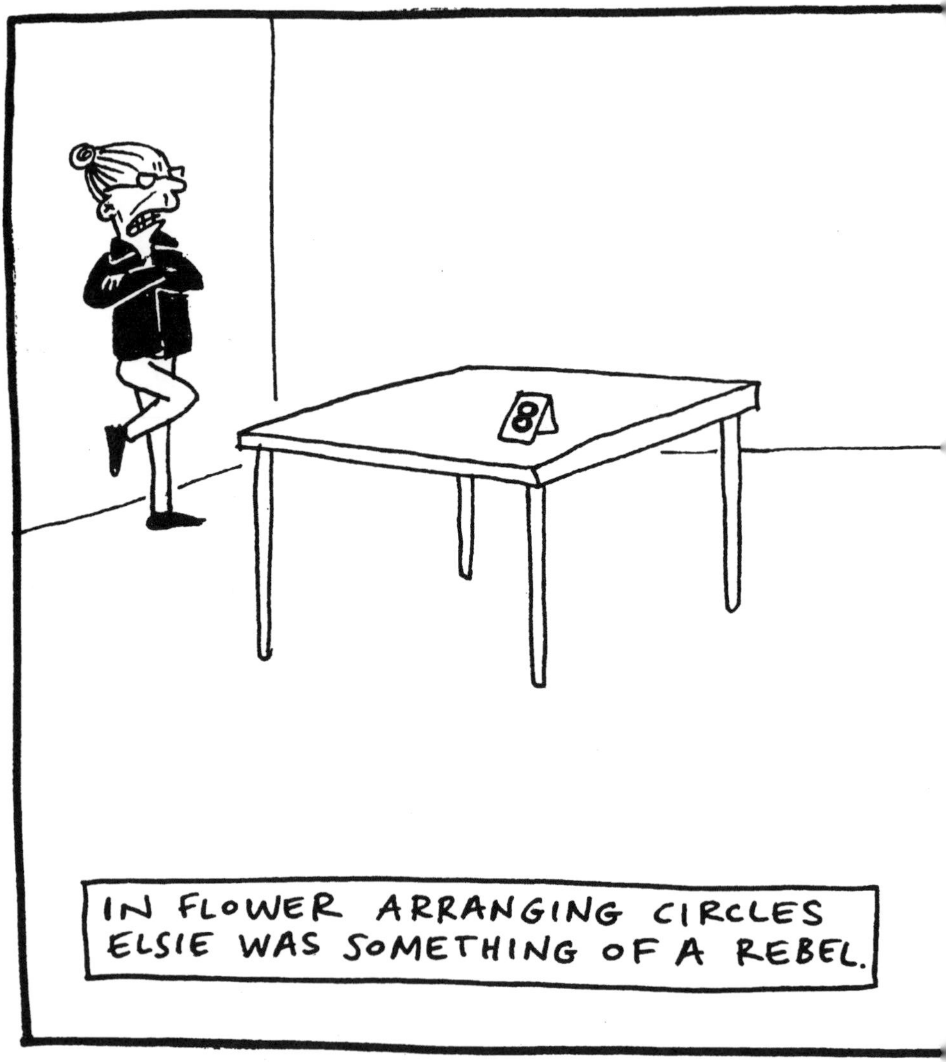
IN FLOWER ARRANGING CIRCLES ELSIE WAS SOMETHING OF A REBEL.

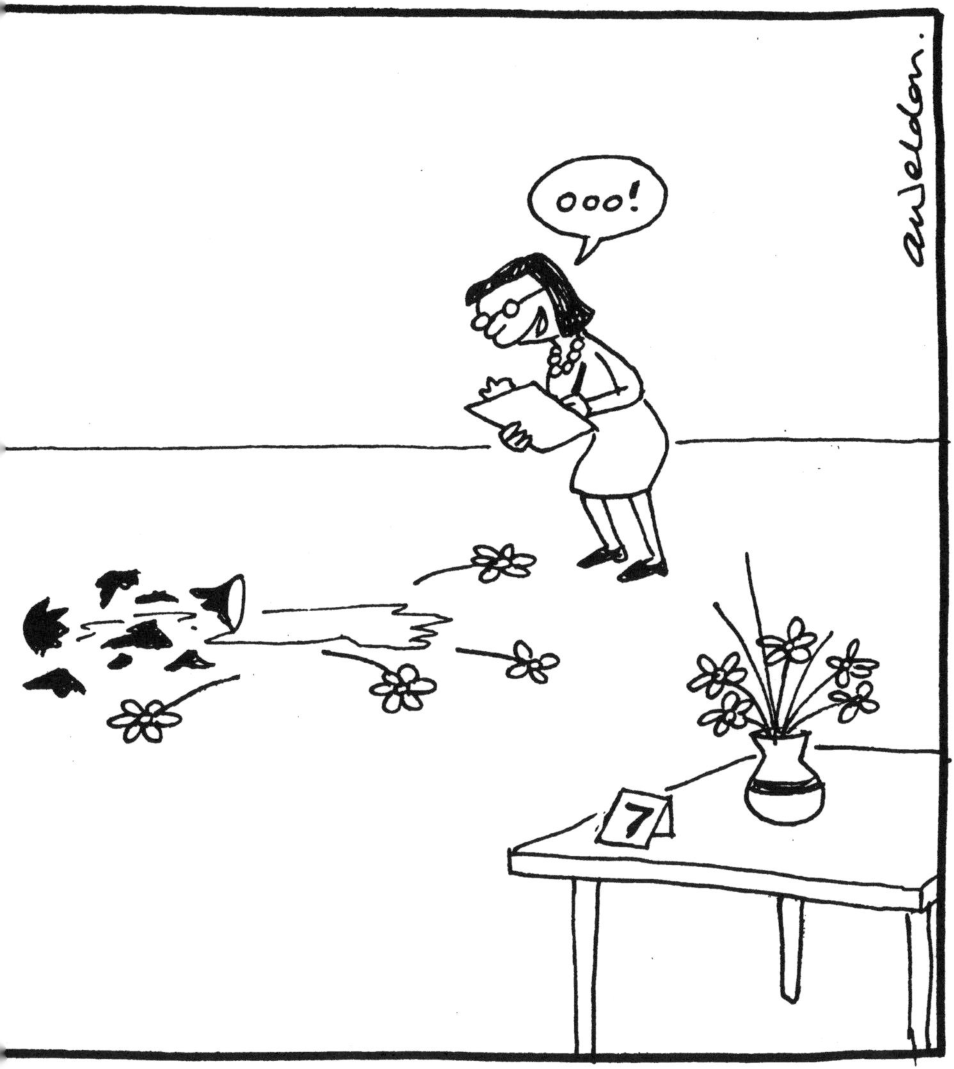
ooo!
7

SOME GANGSTERS.

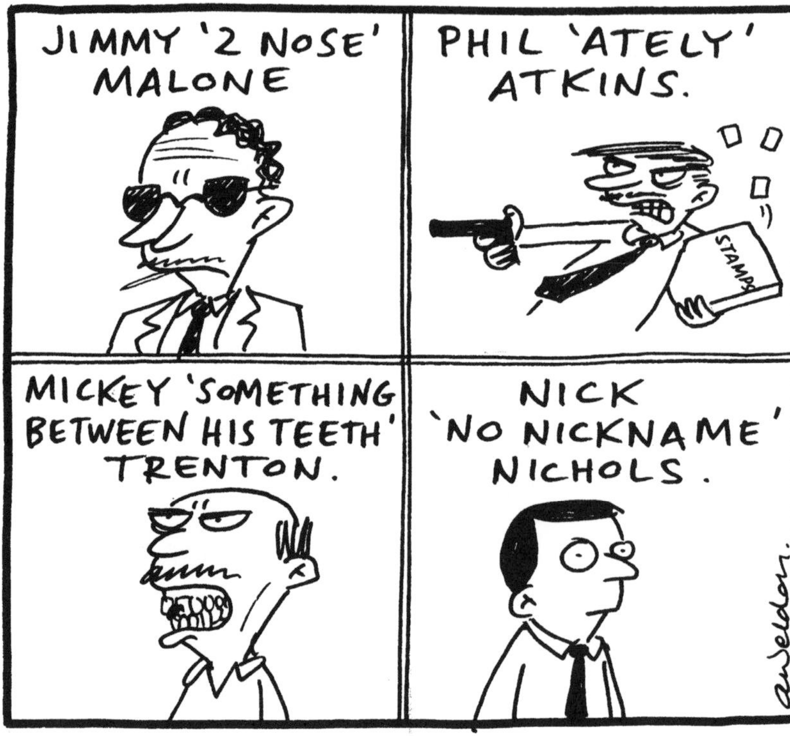
JIMMY '2 NOSE' MALONE
PHIL 'ATELY' ATKINS.
STAMPS
MICKEY 'SOMETHING BETWEEN HIS TEETH' TRENTON.
NICK 'NO NICKNAME' NICHOLS.
aweldon.

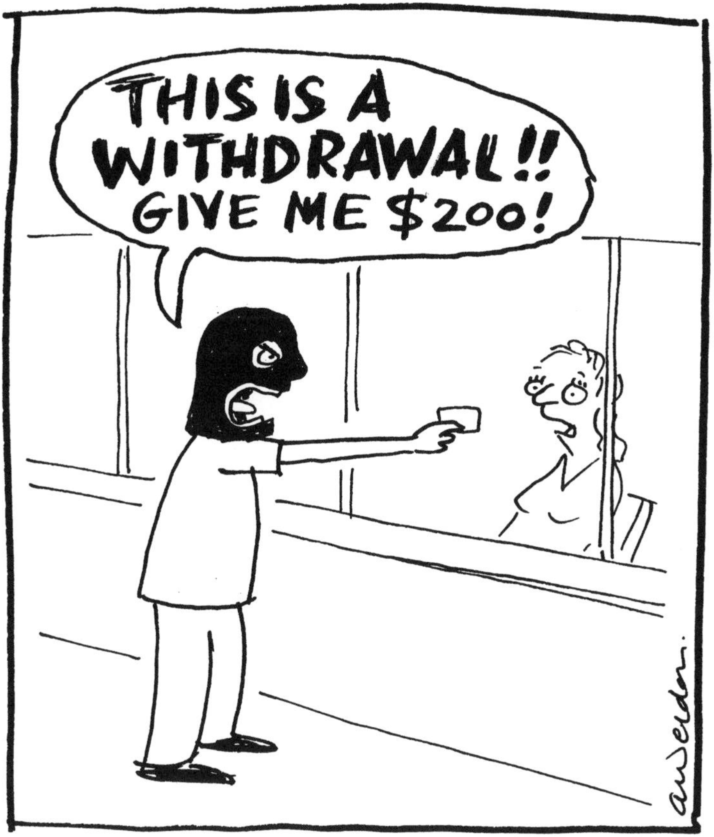
THIS IS A WITHDRAWAL!! GIVE ME $200!
awelden.

REFORMED BANK ROBBER.

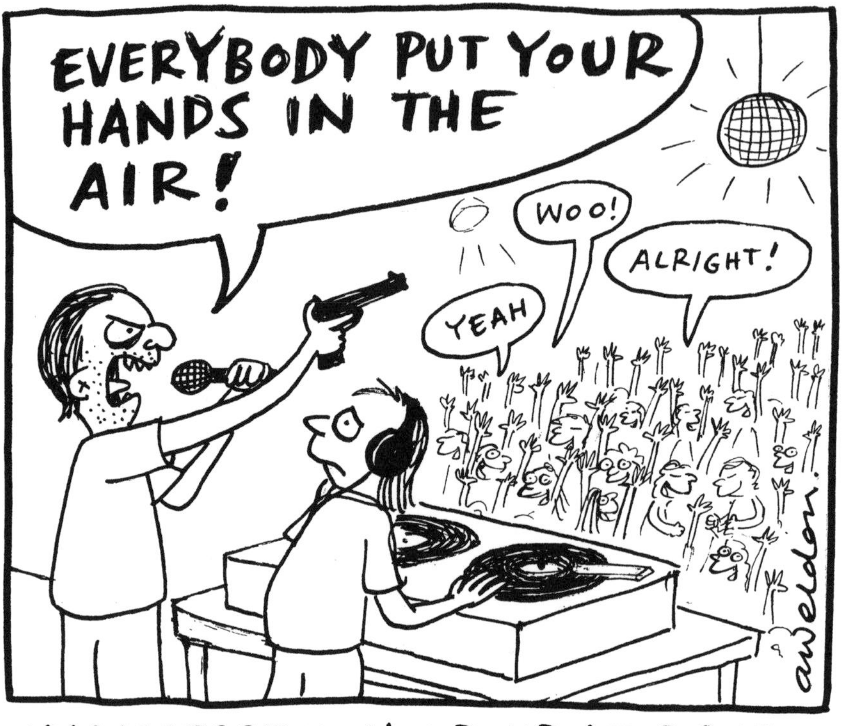
EVERYBODY PUT YOUR HANDS IN THE AIR!
WOO!
ALRIGHT!
YEAH
aweldon.

UNSUCCESSFUL HOLD-UP AT RAVE.

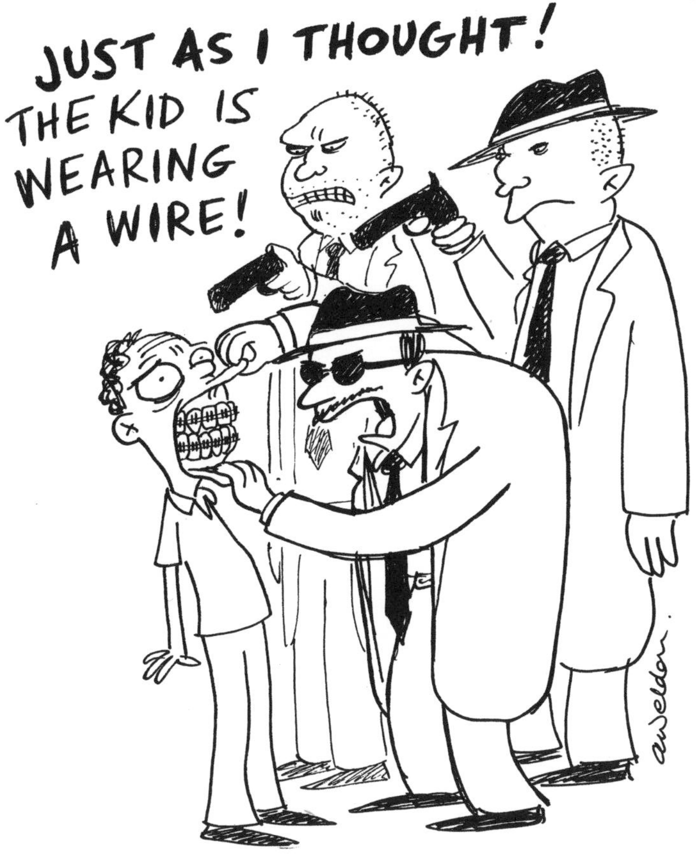
JUST AS I THOUGHT!
THE KID IS WEARING A WIRE!
aweldon

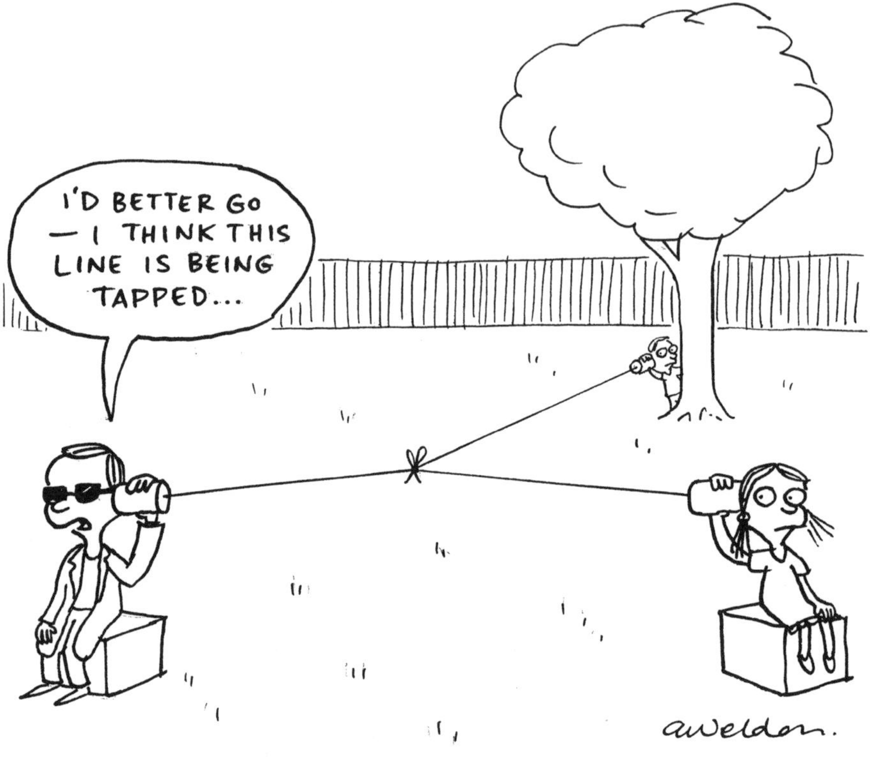
I'D BETTER GO — I THINK THIS LINE IS BEING TAPPED...
aWeldon.

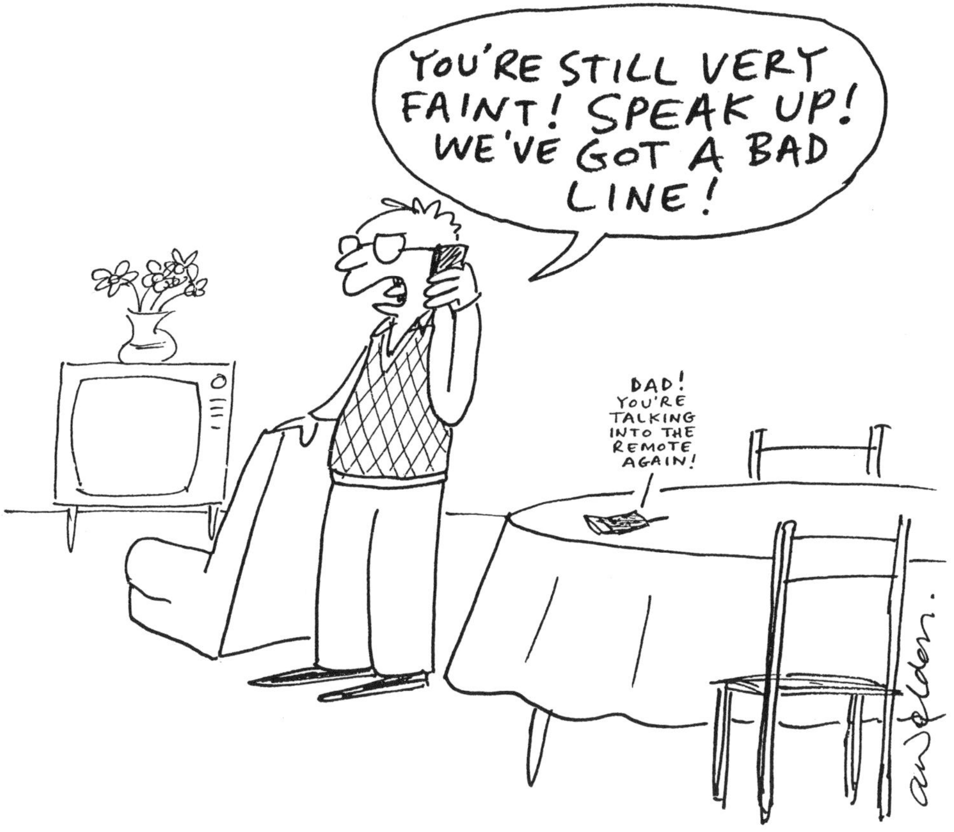
YOU'RE STILL VERY FAINT! SPEAK UP! WE'VE GOT A BAD LINE!
DAD! YOU'RE TALKING INTO THE REMOTE AGAIN!

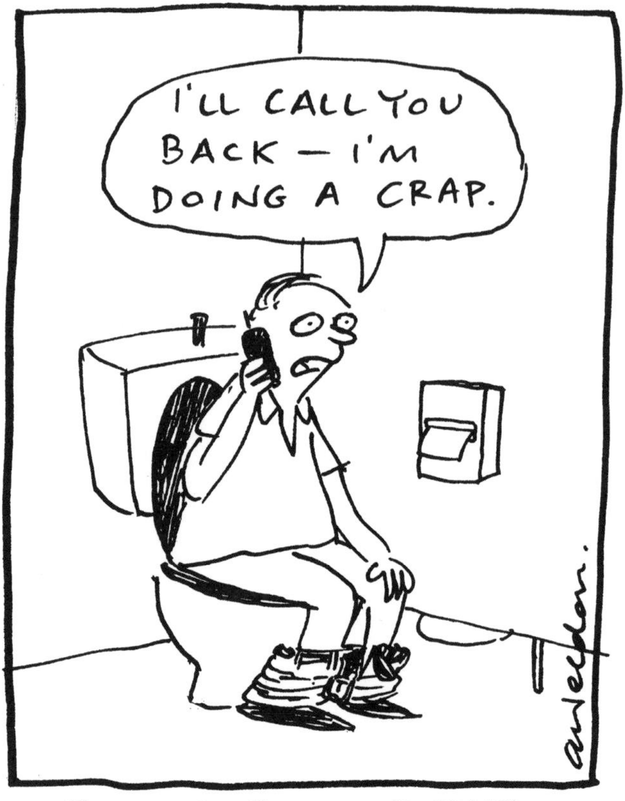
I'LL CALL YOU BACK — I'M DOING A CRAP.
awdeldon.

PLEASURES OF THE MOBILE PHONE ERA #1

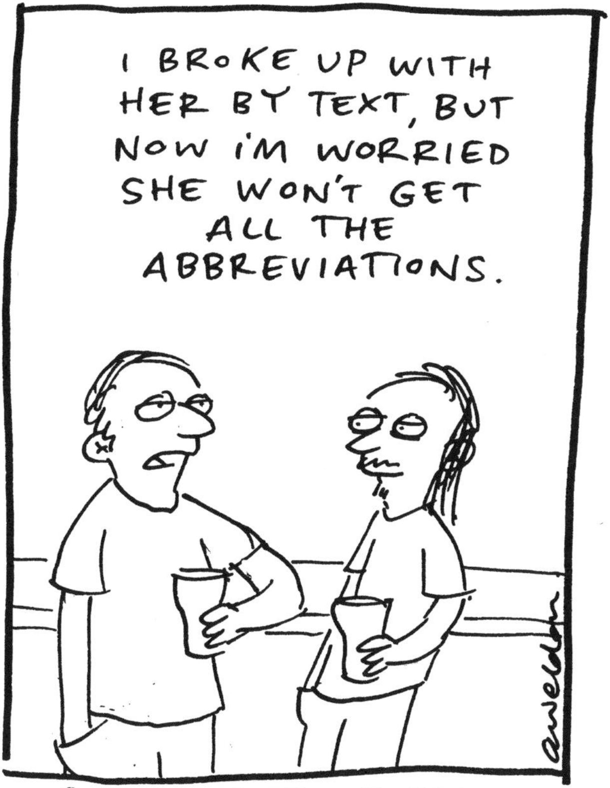
I BROKE UP WITH HER BY TEXT, BUT NOW I'M WORRIED SHE WON'T GET ALL THE ABBREVIATIONS.
aweldon

PLEASURES OF THE MOBILE PHONE ERA #2

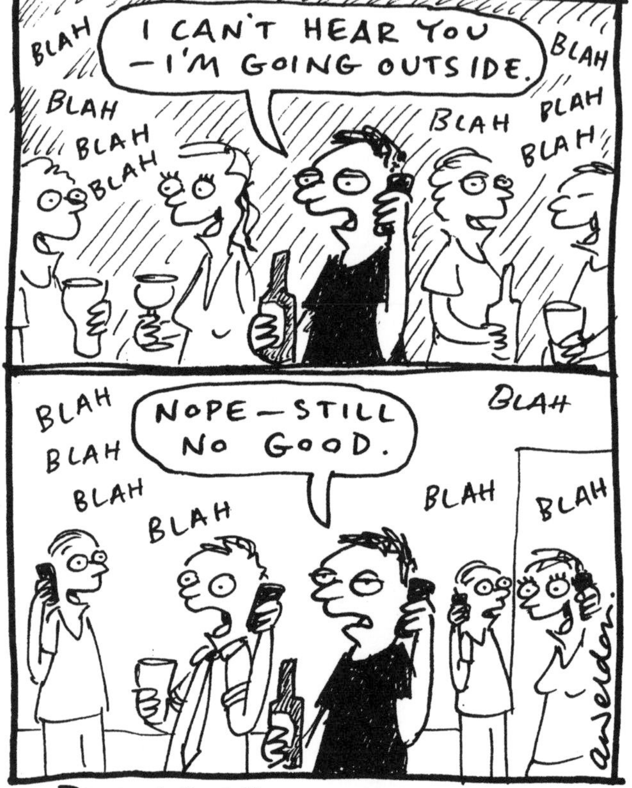
BLAH
I CAN'T HEAR YOU —I'M GOING OUTSIDE.
BLAH
BLAH
BLAH
BLAH
BLAH
BLAH
BLAH
BLAH
BLAH
NOPE—STILL NO GOOD.
BLAH
BLAH
BLAH
BLAH
BLAH
BLAH

PLEASURES OF THE MOBILE PHONE ERA #3

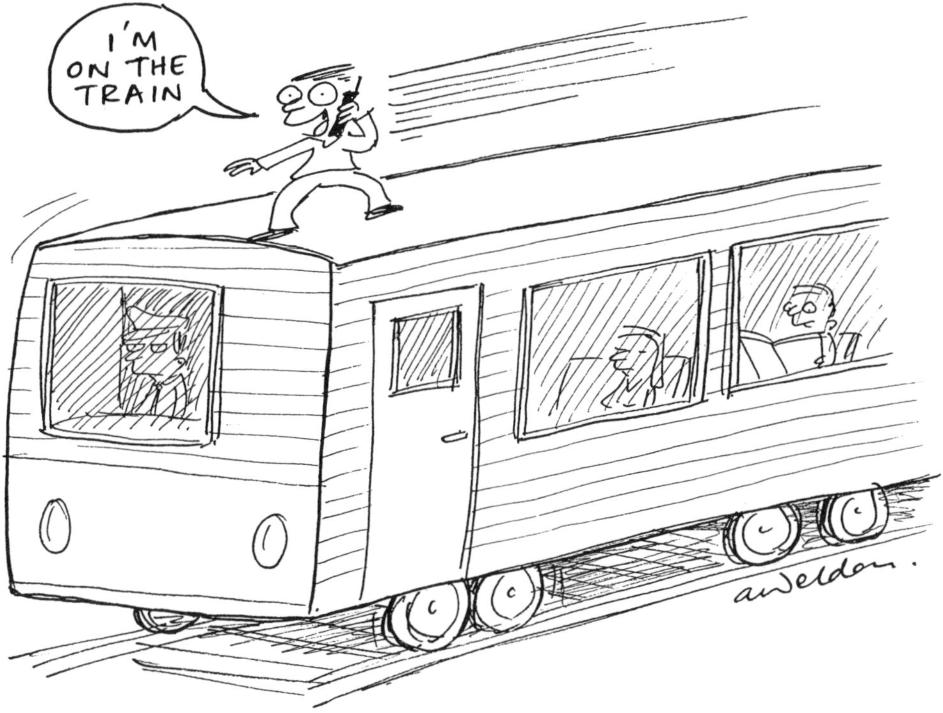
I'M
ON THE
TRAIN

"STOP" — NO, NOT YOU. I WAS JUST
READING SOMETHING.

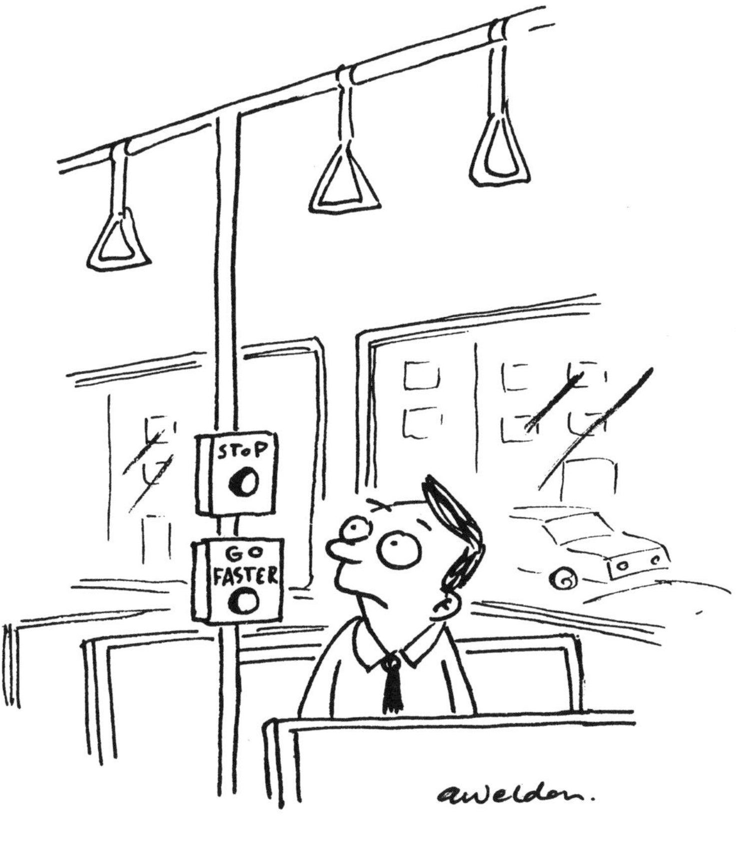
STOP
GO FASTER
aWeldon.

THE FIRST ROLLERCOASTER.

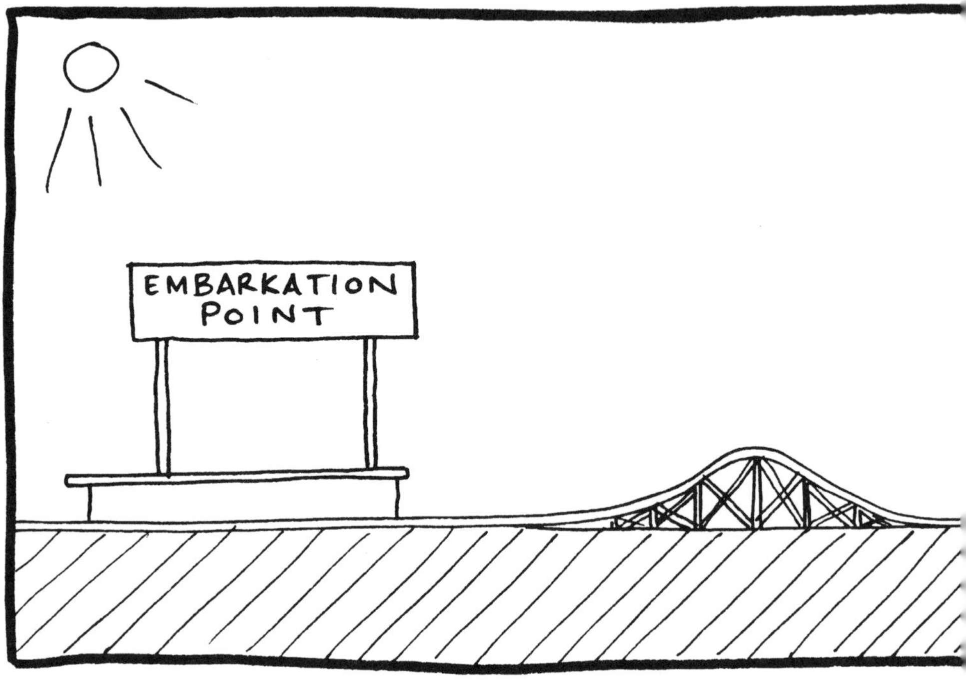

EMBARKATION POINT

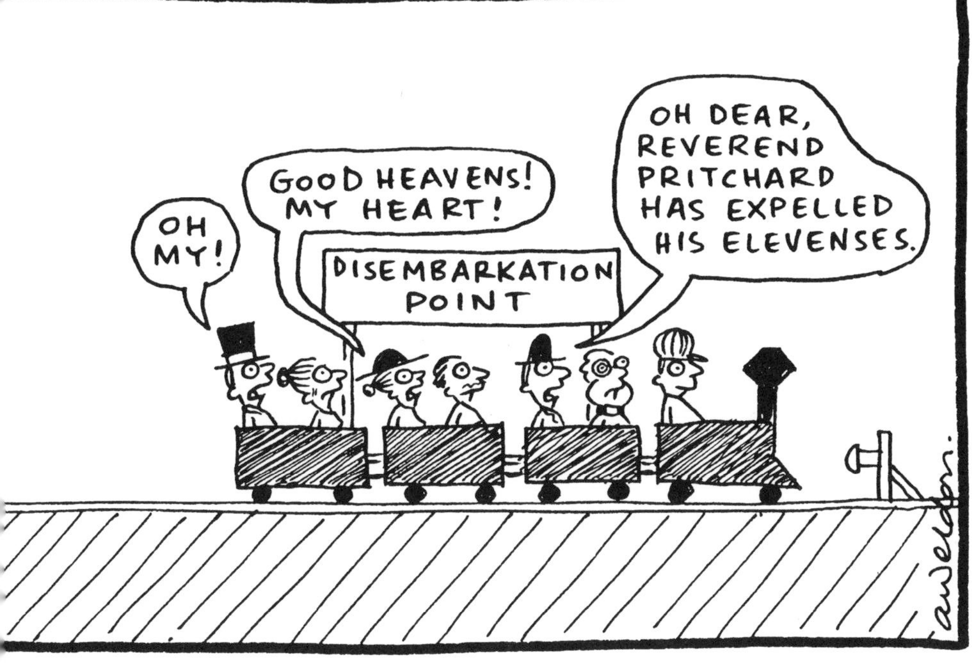
OH MY!
GOOD HEAVENS! MY HEART!
DISEMBARKATION POINT
OH DEAR, REVEREND PRITCHARD HAS EXPELLED HIS ELEVENSES.
aweldon.

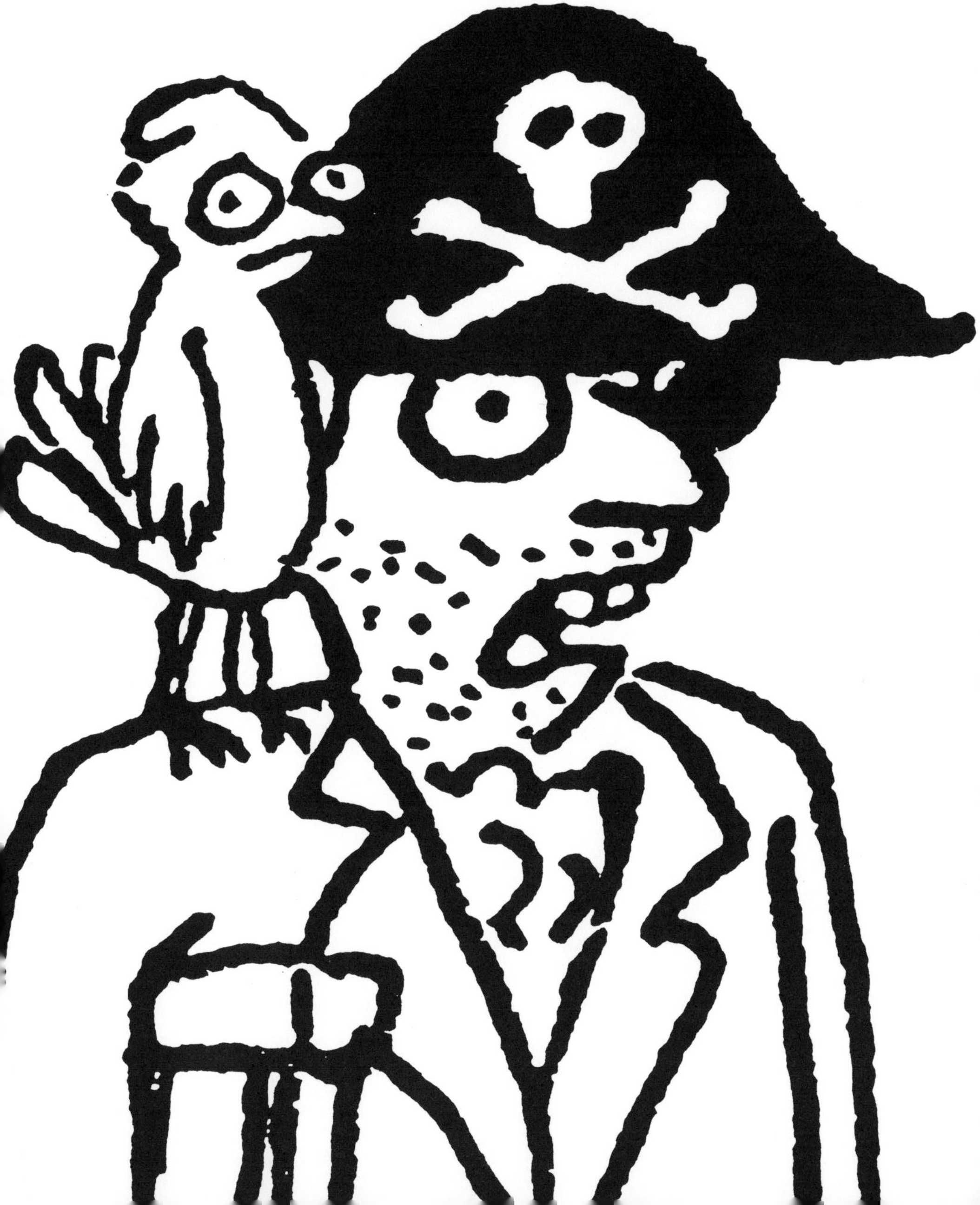

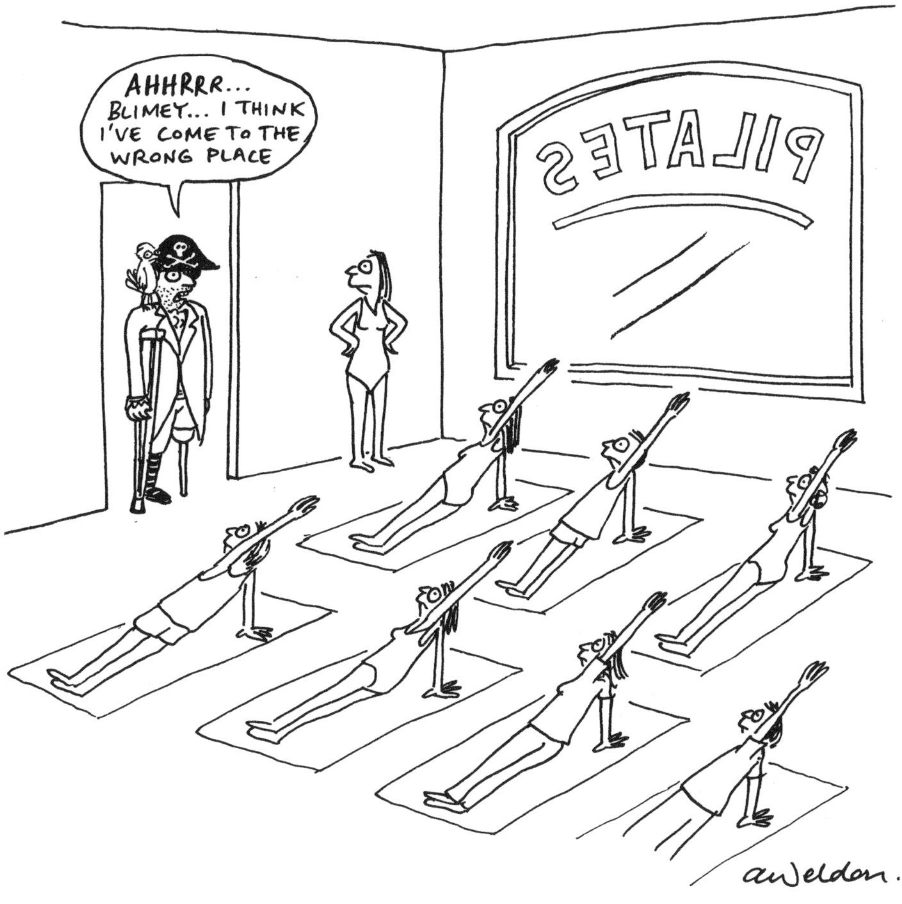
AHHRRR... BLIMEY... I THINK I'VE COME TO THE WRONG PLACE
PILATES
aWeldon.

PROSTHETIC TONGUES

'OL' STUMPY'
TRADITIONAL
MAHOGANY

'THE CAPTAIN'
LONG-LASTING
STAINLESS STEEL

'SUPER-ABSORB'
FREE-RANGE
SEA SPONGE

'THE OX'
BOVINE-SOURCED
IMPLANT

aWeldon.

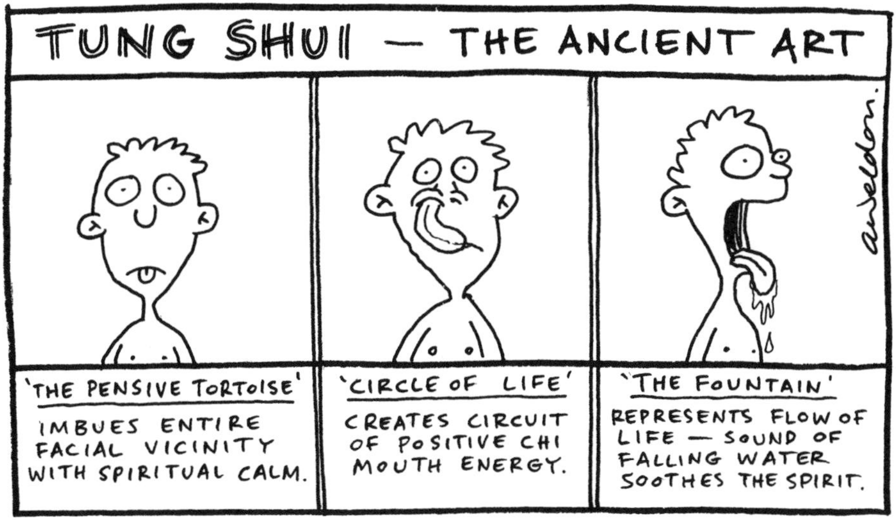
TUNG SHUI — THE ANCIENT ART
'THE PENSIVE TORTOISE'
IMBUES ENTIRE FACIAL VICINITY WITH SPIRITUAL CALM.
'CIRCLE OF LIFE'
CREATES CIRCUIT OF POSITIVE CHI MOUTH ENERGY.
'THE FOUNTAIN'
REPRESENTS FLOW OF LIFE — SOUND OF FALLING WATER SOOTHES THE SPIRIT.
a weldon.

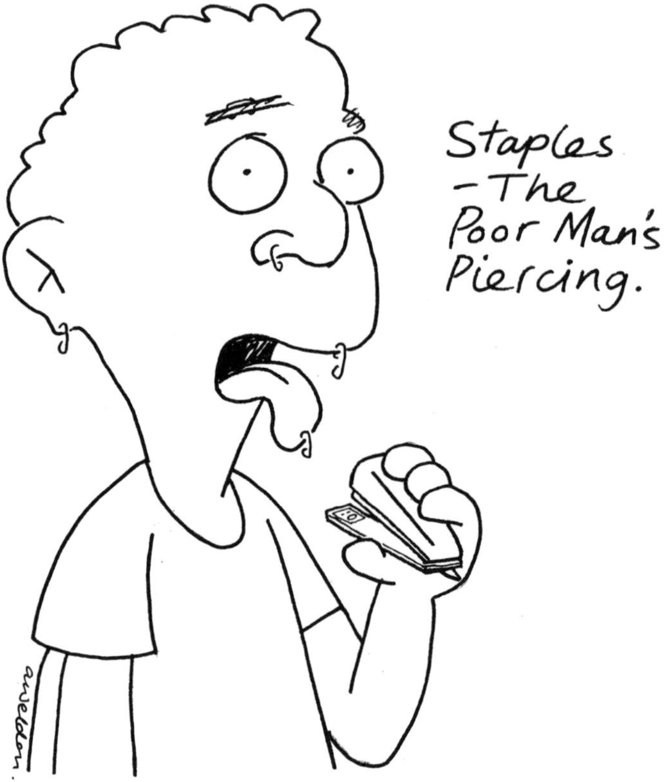
Staples
-The
Poor Man's
Piercing.
aweldon.

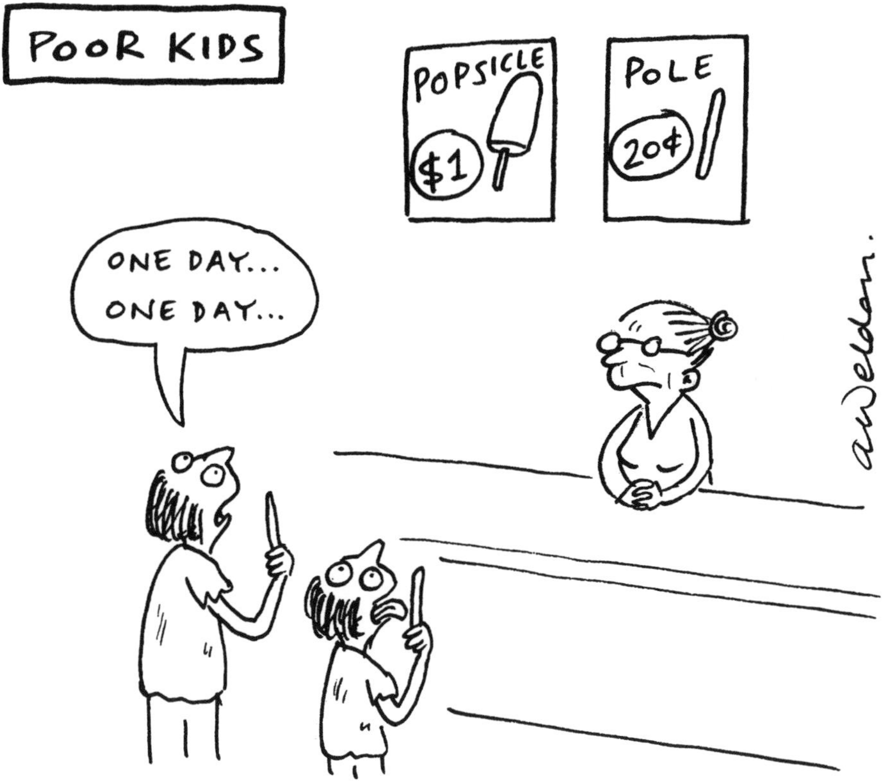
POOR KIDS
POPSICLE
$1
POLE
20¢
ONE DAY...
ONE DAY...
aweldon.

AUSTRALIAN DISAPPOINTMENT

#1 IN A SERIES

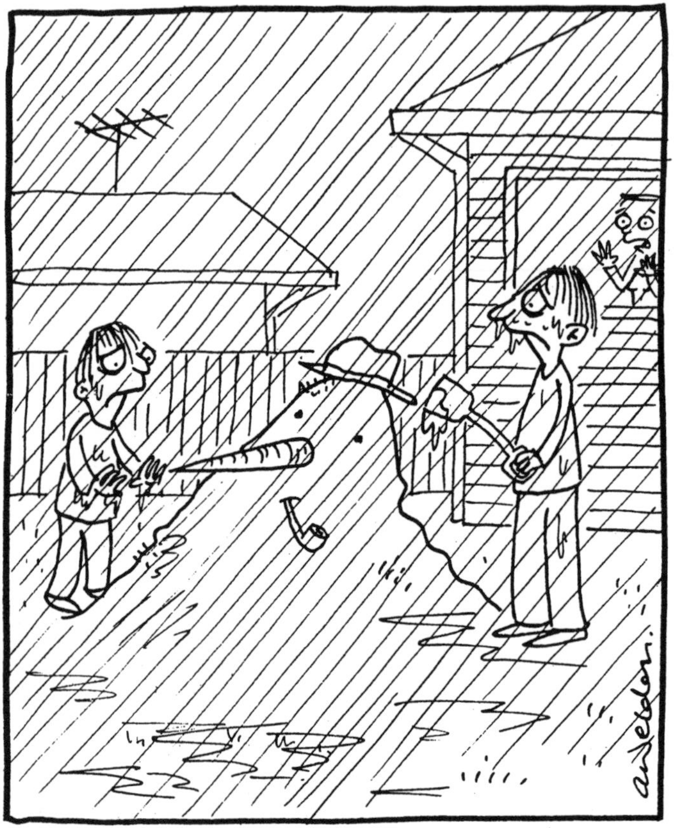
awelden.

MUD IS NO SUBSTITUTE FOR SNOW

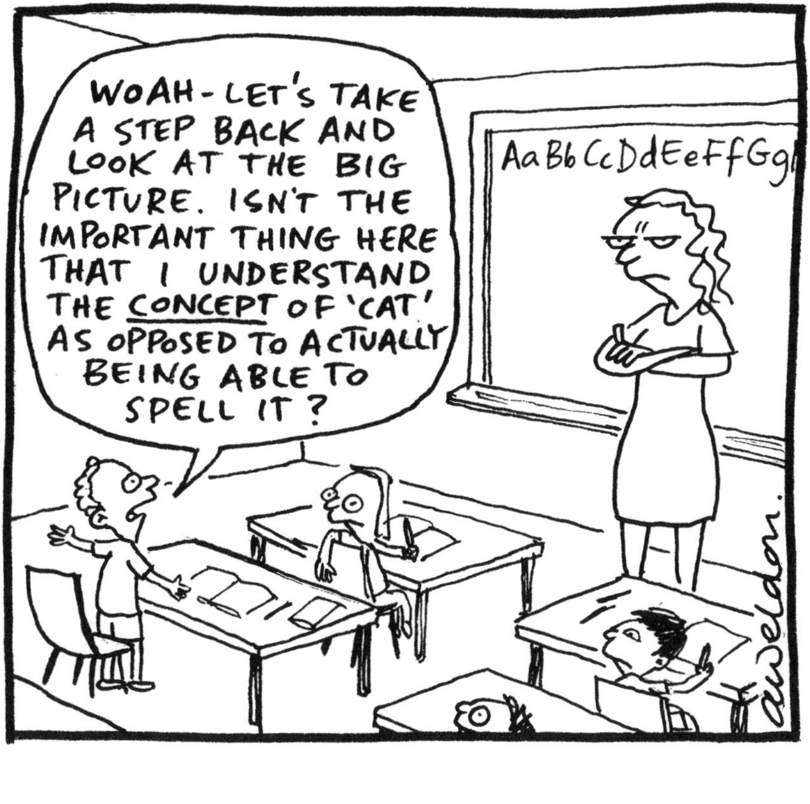
WOAH - LET'S TAKE A STEP BACK AND LOOK AT THE BIG PICTURE. ISN'T THE IMPORTANT THING HERE THAT I UNDERSTAND THE CONCEPT OF 'CAT' AS OPPOSED TO ACTUALLY BEING ABLE TO SPELL IT?
AaBbCcDdEeFfGg
aweldon.

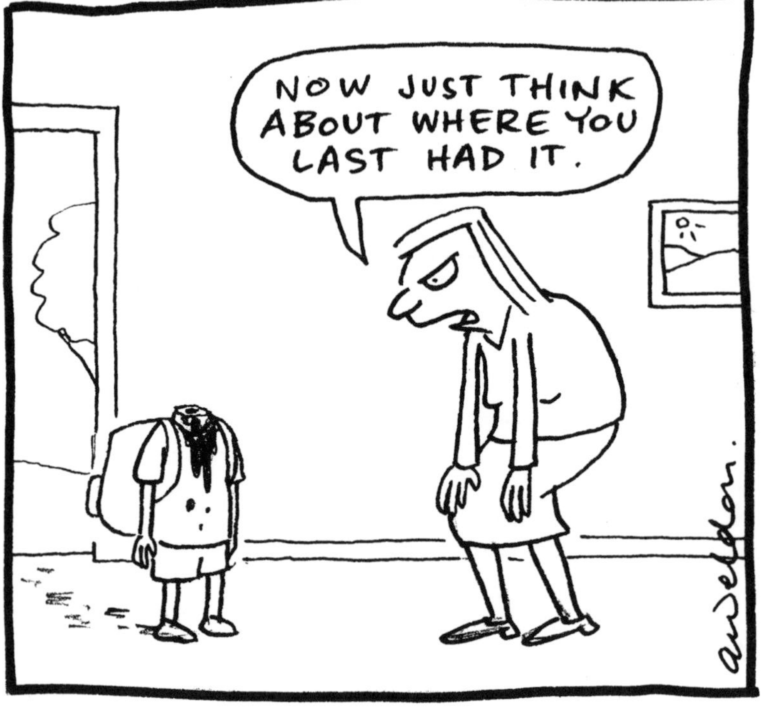
NOW JUST THINK ABOUT WHERE YOU LAST HAD IT.
anweldon.

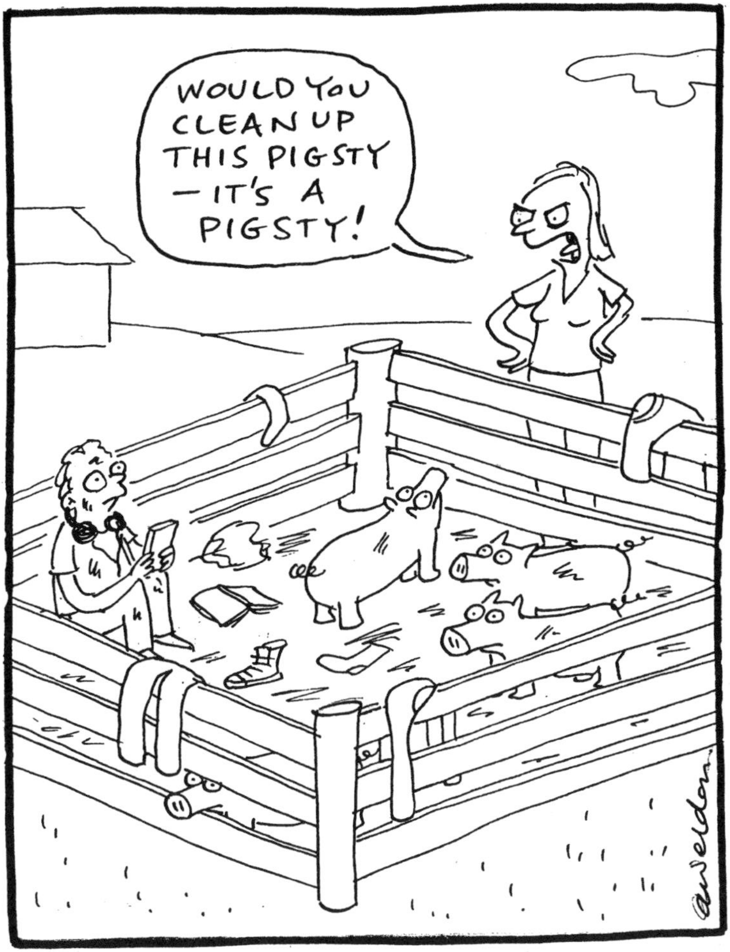
WOULD YOU CLEAN UP THIS PIGSTY —IT'S A PIGSTY!

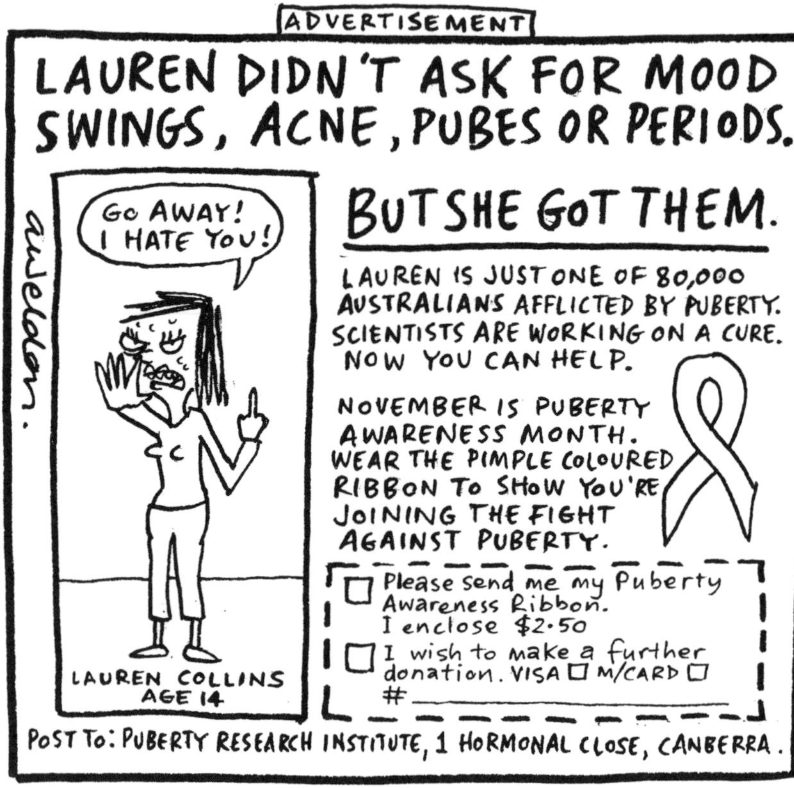
ADVERTISEMENT
LAUREN DIDN'T ASK FOR MOOD SWINGS, ACNE, PUBES OR PERIODS.
GO AWAY! I HATE YOU!
awheldon.
LAUREN COLLINS AGE 14
BUT SHE GOT THEM.
LAUREN IS JUST ONE OF 80,000 AUSTRALIANS AFFLICTED BY PUBERTY. SCIENTISTS ARE WORKING ON A CURE. NOW YOU CAN HELP.
NOVEMBER IS PUBERTY AWARENESS MONTH. WEAR THE PIMPLE COLOURED RIBBON TO SHOW YOU'RE JOINING THE FIGHT AGAINST PUBERTY.
Please send me my Puberty Awareness Ribbon. I enclose $2.50
I wish to make a further donation. VISA M/CARD
#
POST TO: PUBERTY RESEARCH INSTITUTE, 1 HORMONAL CLOSE, CANBERRA.

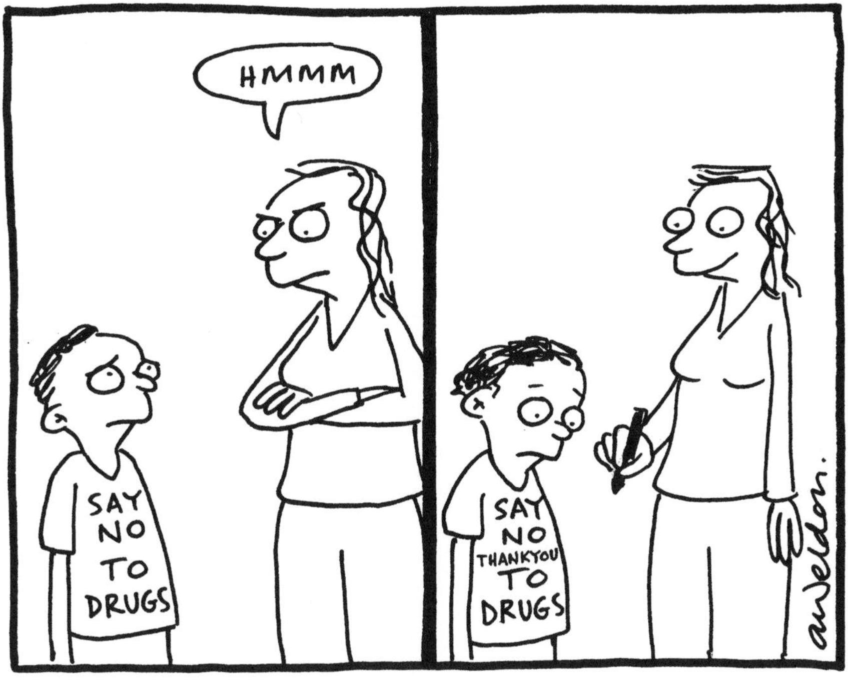
HMMM
SAY NO TO DRUGS
SAY NO THANKYOU TO DRUGS
aweldon.

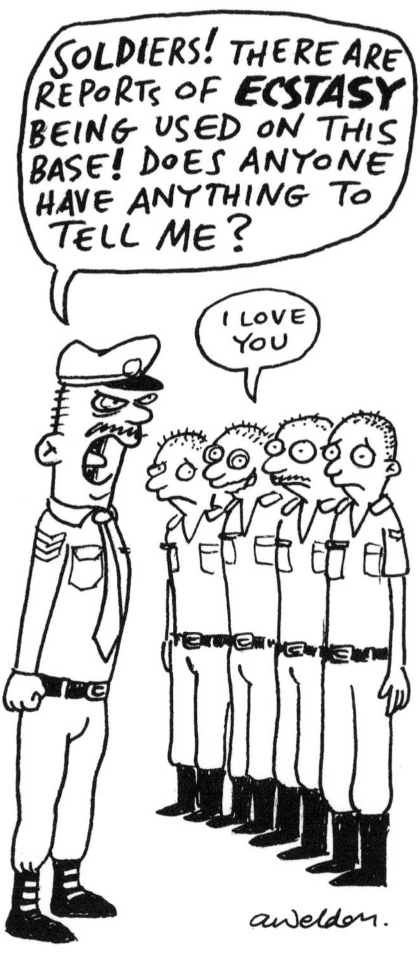
SOLDIERS! THERE ARE REPORTS OF ECSTASY BEING USED ON THIS BASE! DOES ANYONE HAVE ANYTHING TO TELL ME?
I LOVE YOU
aweldon.

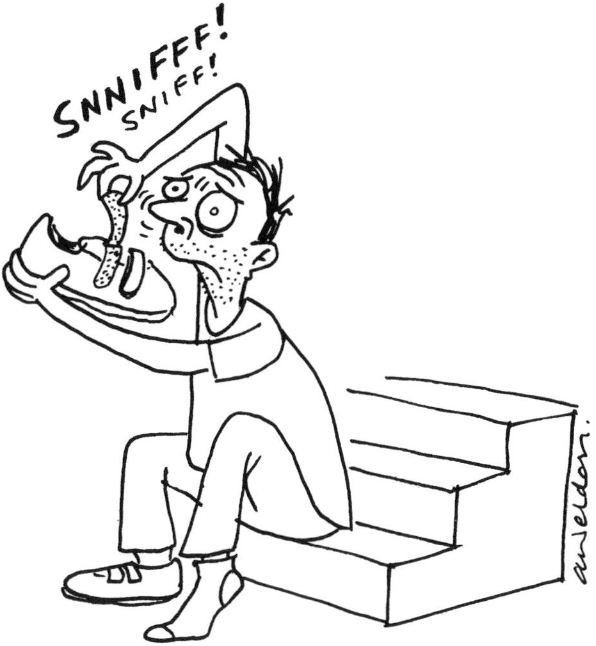
SNNIFFF!
SNIFF!
aweldon

STRUNG-OUT GLUE-SNIFFER DESPERATELY TRIES TO GET A HIGH OFF VELCRO

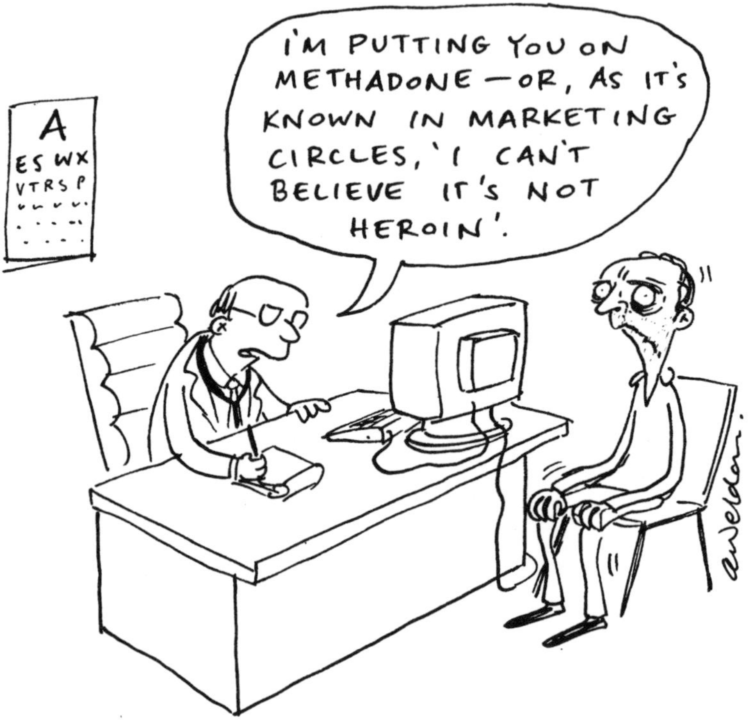
I'M PUTTING YOU ON METHADONE—OR, AS IT'S KNOWN IN MARKETING CIRCLES, 'I CAN'T BELIEVE IT'S NOT HEROIN'.
A
ES WX
VTRS P

ANT
RID
MMM –
SO SWEET
MMM
SWEEET
DAMN
JUNKIES
aweldon.

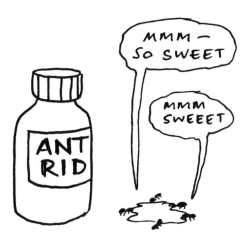

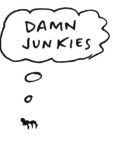

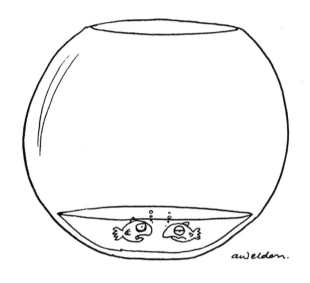

"I'M WORRIED ABOUT YOUR DRINKING".

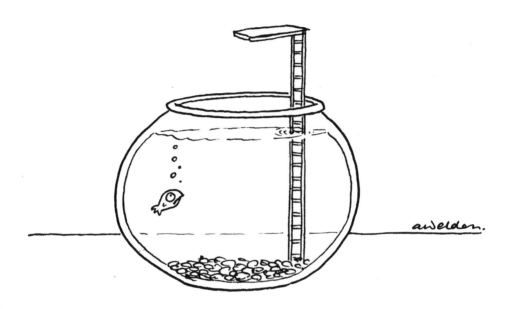

awelden.

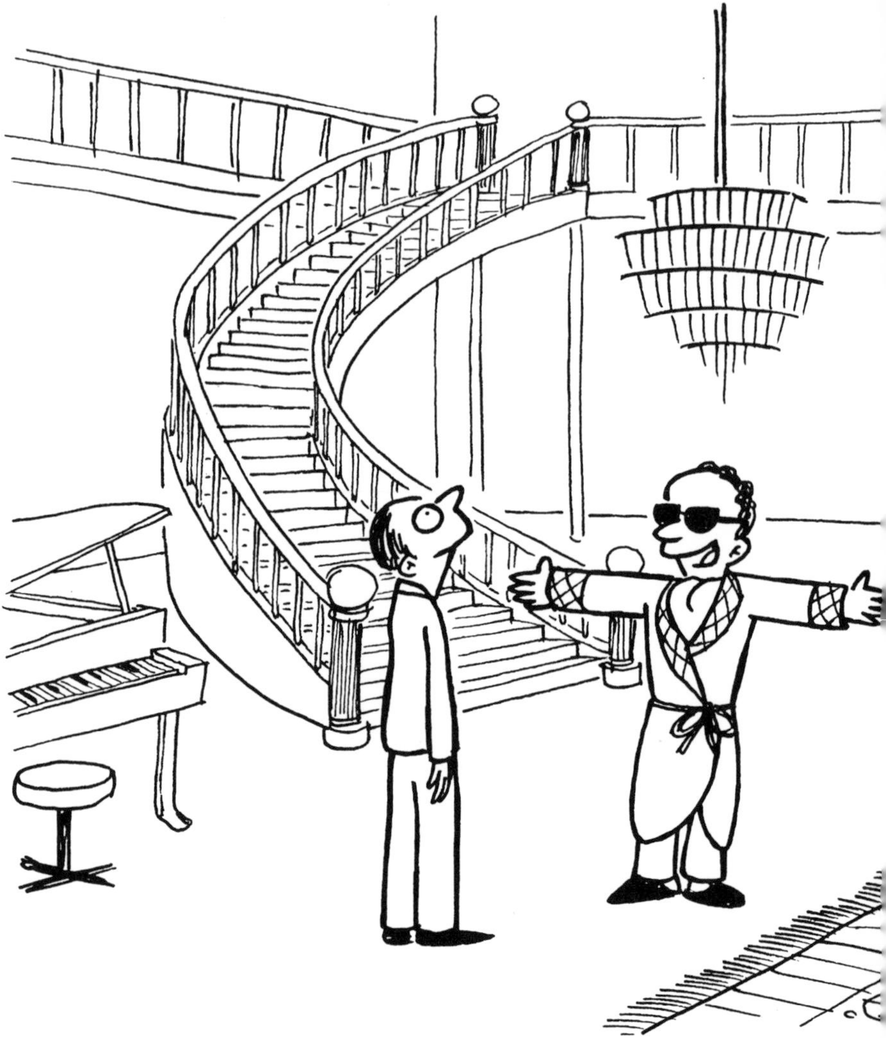

"WITH MY WINNINGS I BOUGHT THIS PLACE, BUT I DIDN'T FORGET MY OLD FRIEND FLIPPY."

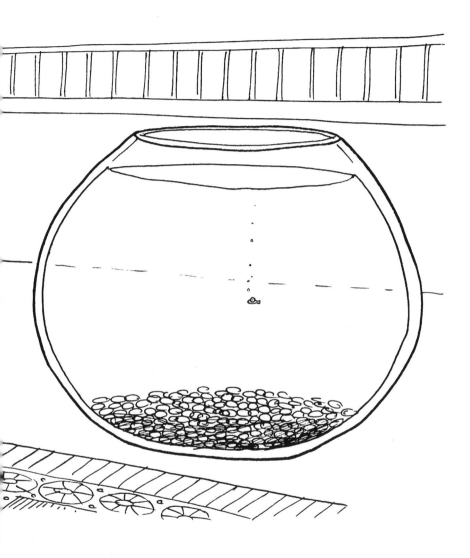

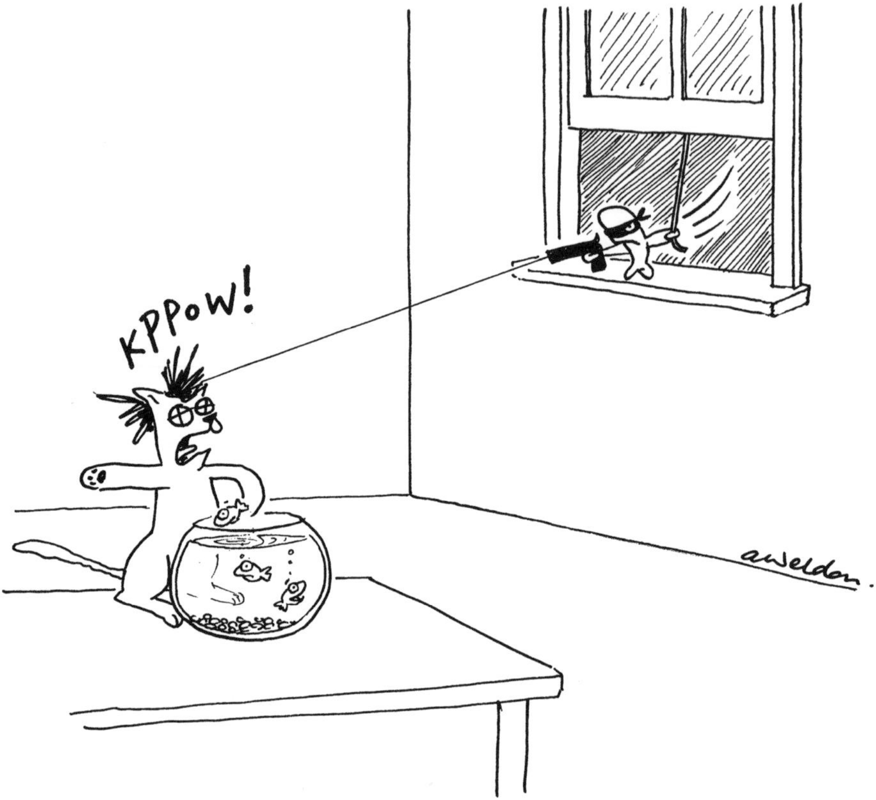
KPPOW!
aweldon.

"CAPTAIN FISH!"

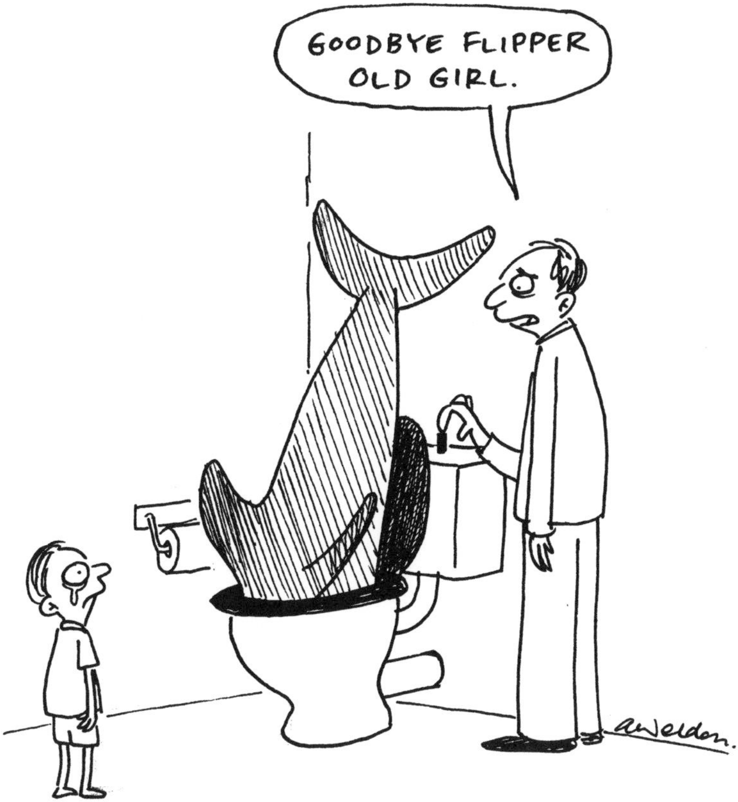
GOODBYE FLIPPER OLD GIRL.
aWeldon.

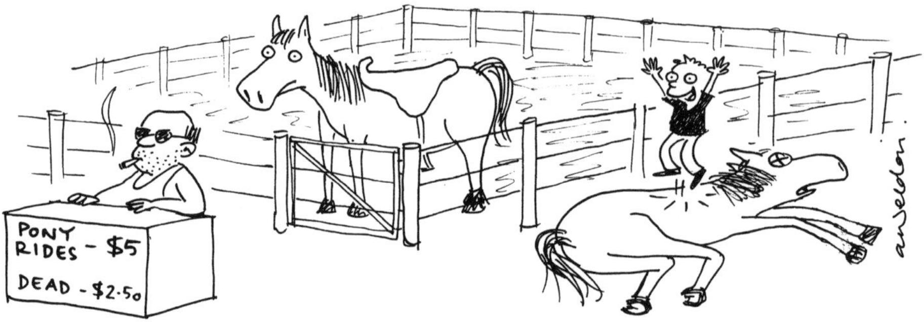
PONY RIDES - $5
DEAD - $2.50

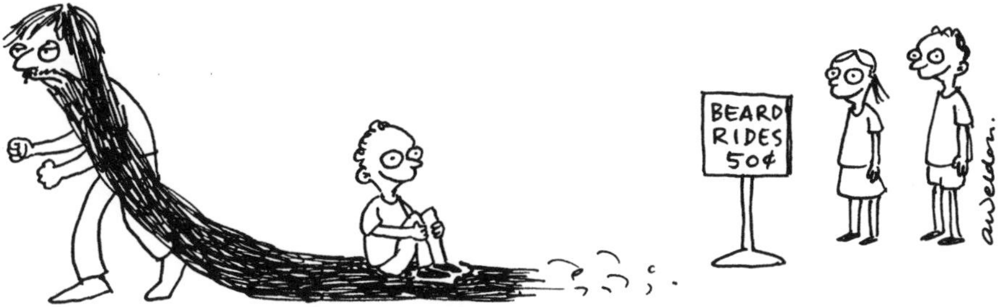
BEARD
RIDES
50¢

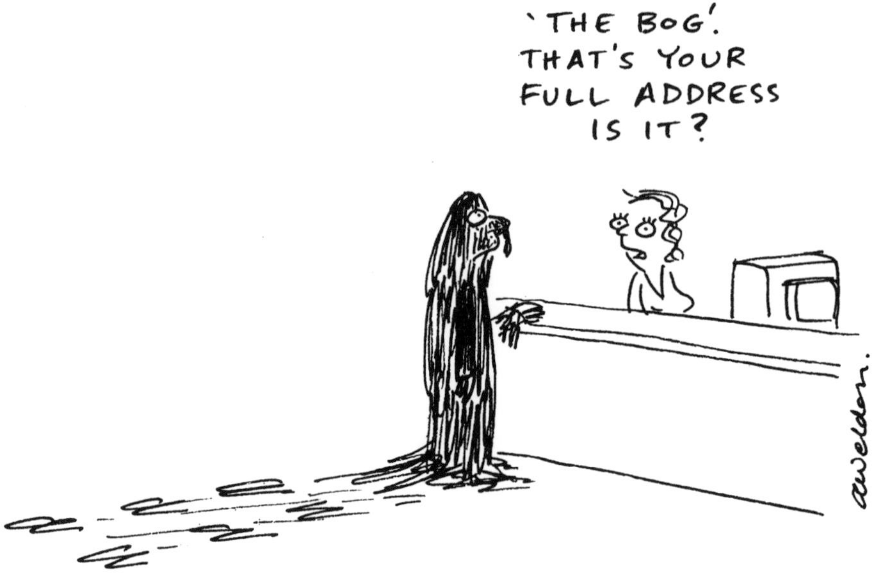
'THE BOG'. THAT'S YOUR FULL ADDRESS IS IT?

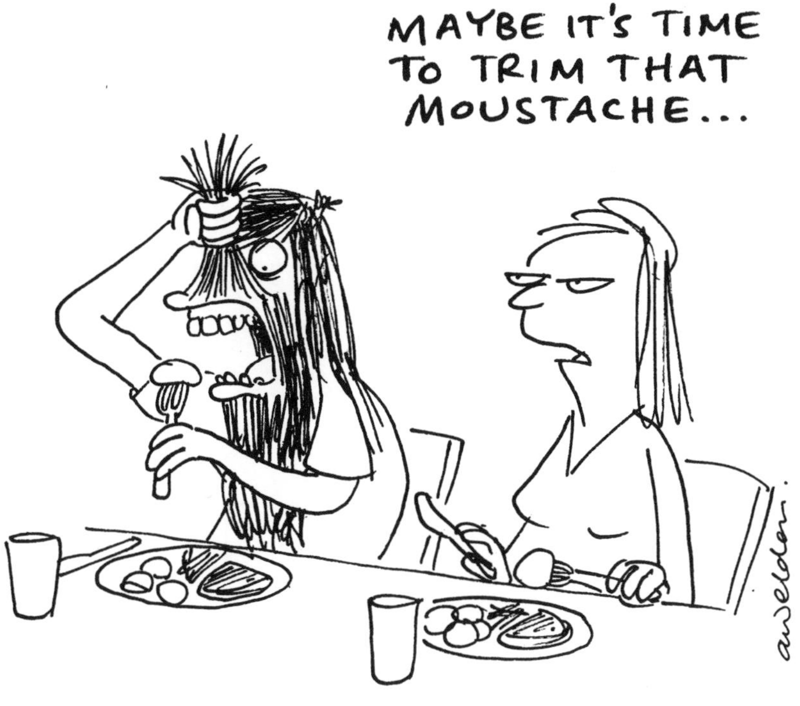
MAYBE IT'S TIME
TO TRIM THAT
MOUSTACHE...
aweldon.

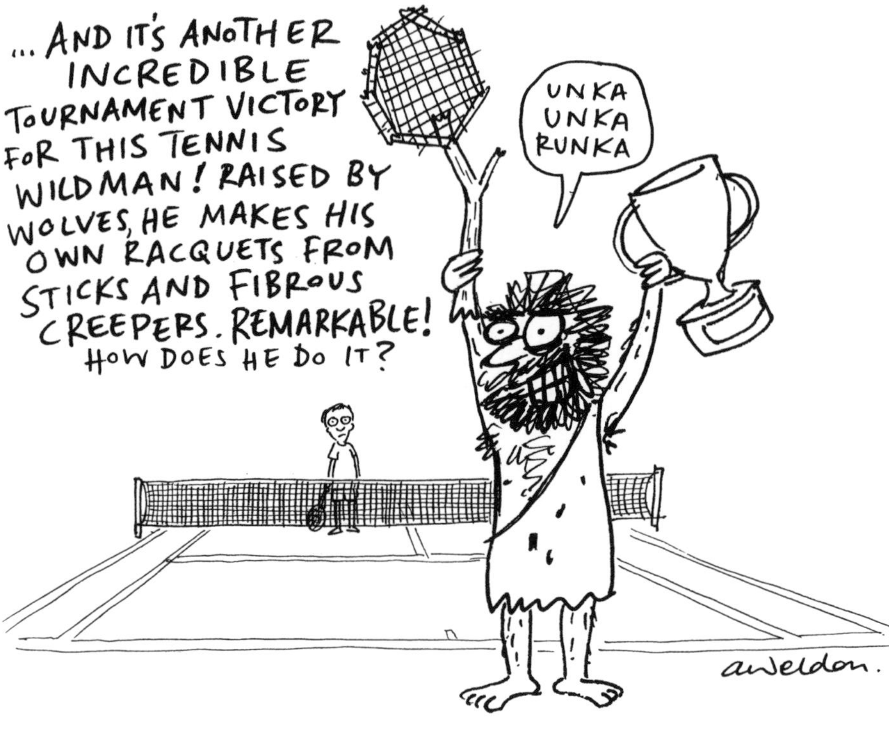
...AND IT'S ANOTHER INCREDIBLE TOURNAMENT VICTORY FOR THIS TENNIS WILDMAN! RAISED BY WOLVES, HE MAKES HIS OWN RACQUETS FROM STICKS AND FIBROUS CREEPERS. REMARKABLE! HOW DOES HE DO IT?
UNKA UNKA RUNKA
aweldon.

EXTREME
YO-YO
aweldon.

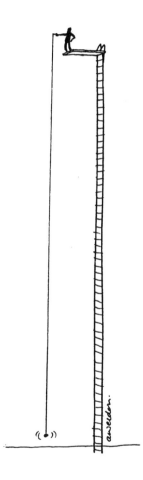

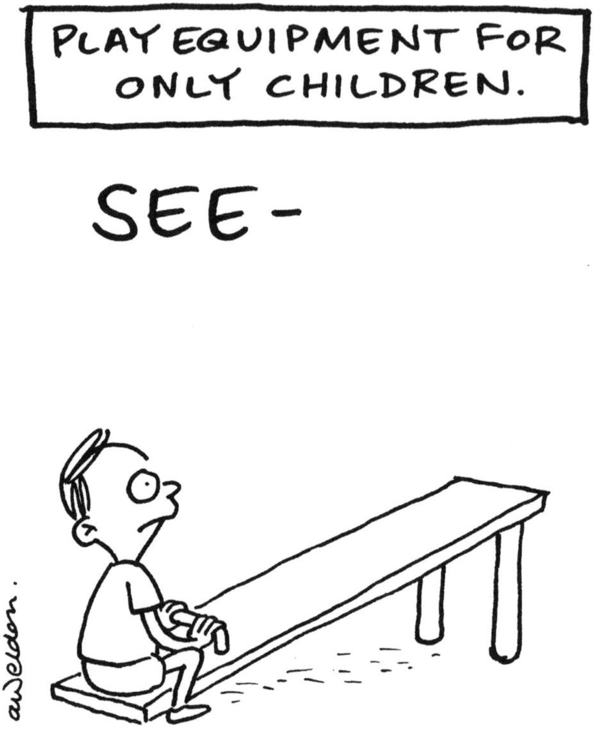
PLAY EQUIPMENT FOR ONLY CHILDREN.
SEE-
aweldon.

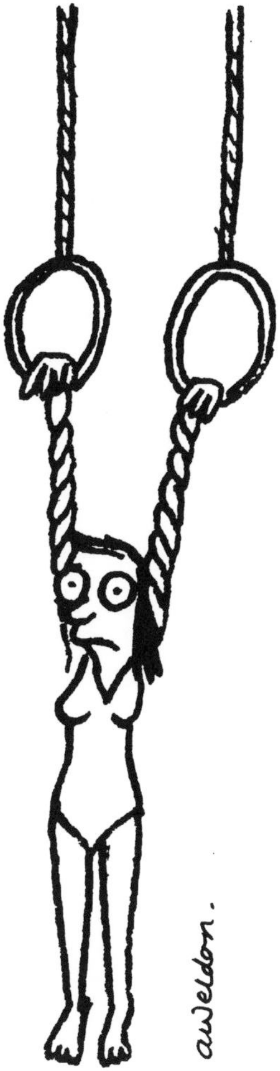
aweldon.

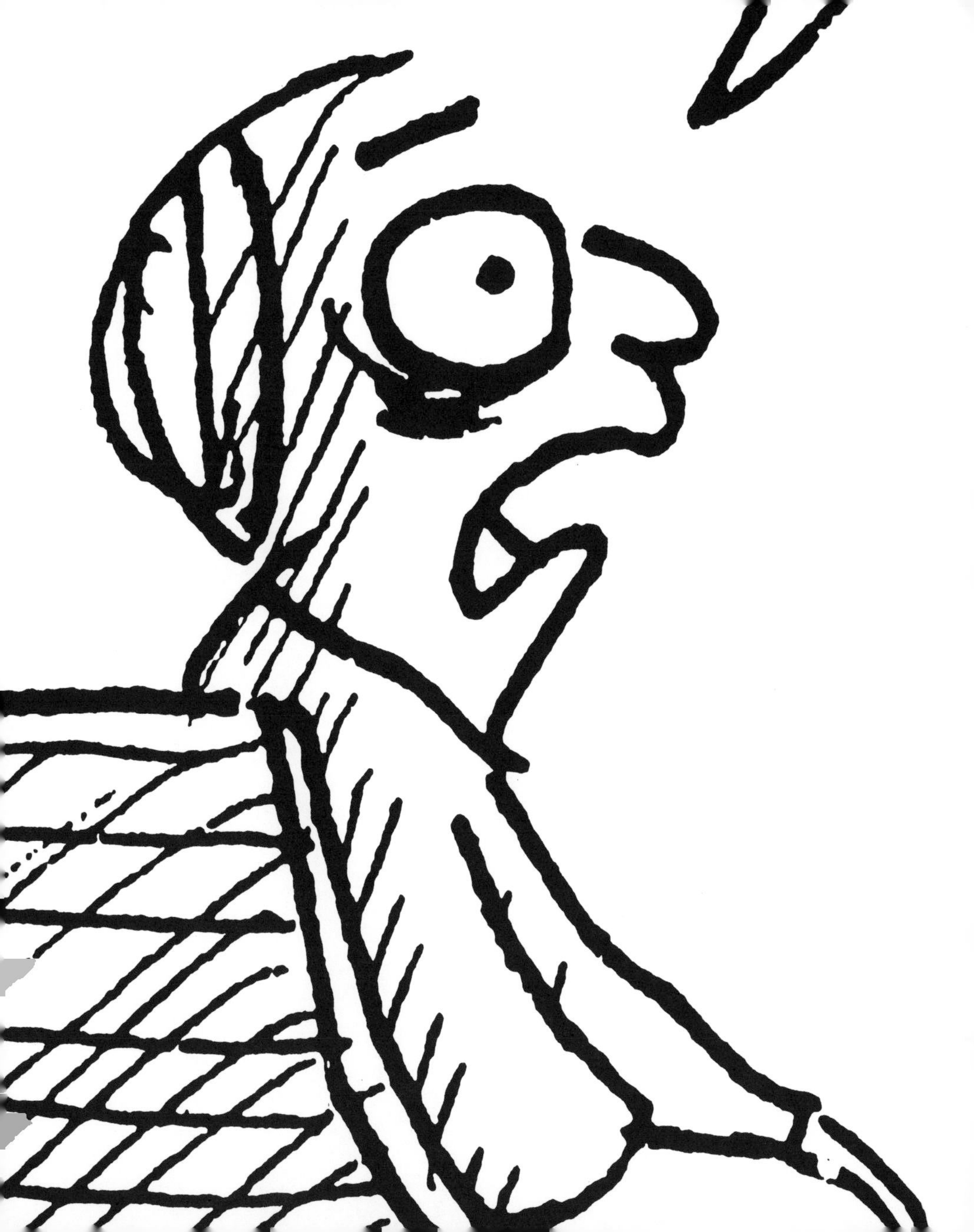

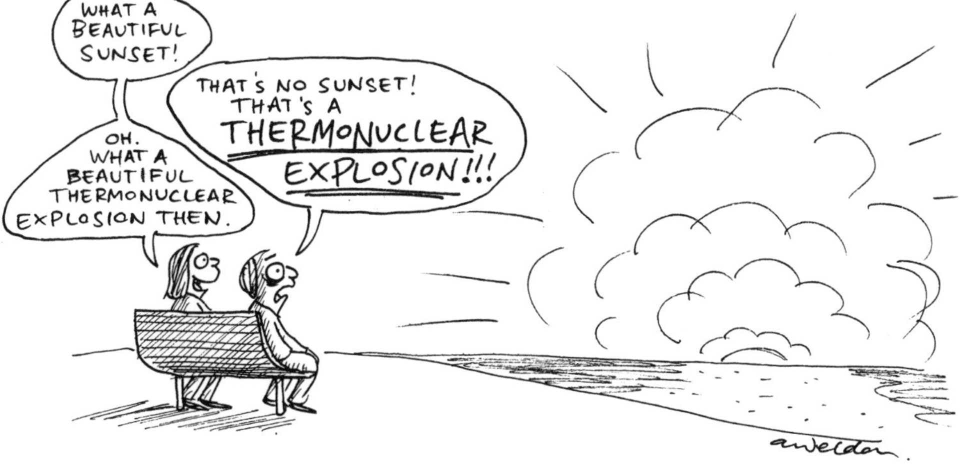
WHAT A BEAUTIFUL SUNSET!
THAT'S NO SUNSET! THAT'S A THERMONUCLEAR EXPLOSION!!!
OH. WHAT A BEAUTIFUL THERMONUCLEAR EXPLOSION THEN.
aweldon.

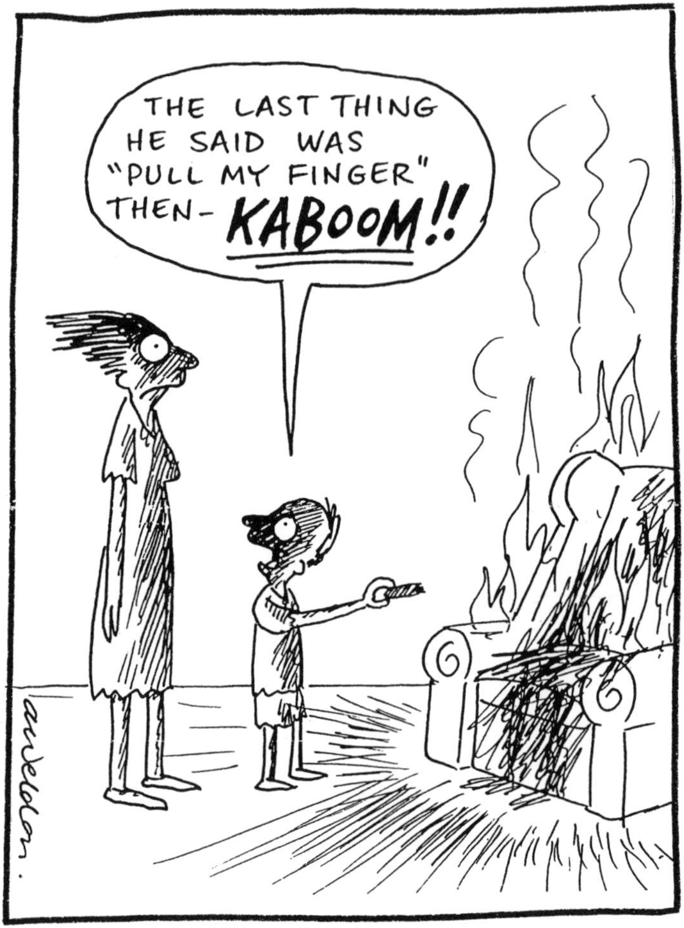
THE LAST THING HE SAID WAS "PULL MY FINGER" THEN- KABOOM!!
ardeldon.

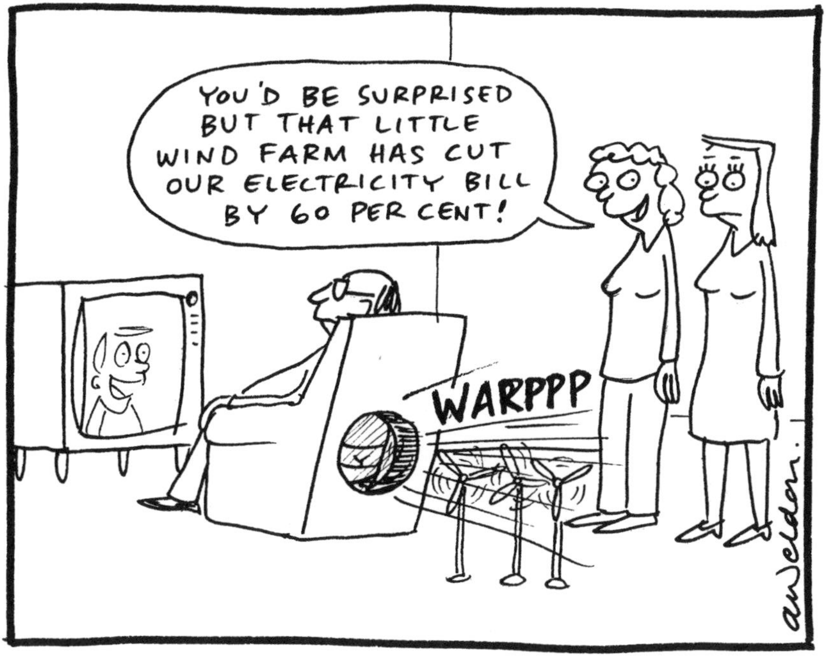
YOU'D BE SURPRISED BUT THAT LITTLE WIND FARM HAS CUT OUR ELECTRICITY BILL BY 60 PER CENT!
WARPPP
aWeldon.

DAD, DAD, AND TWO KIDS —WE'RE WHAT YOU MIGHT CALL A NUQUEER FAMILY UNIT.

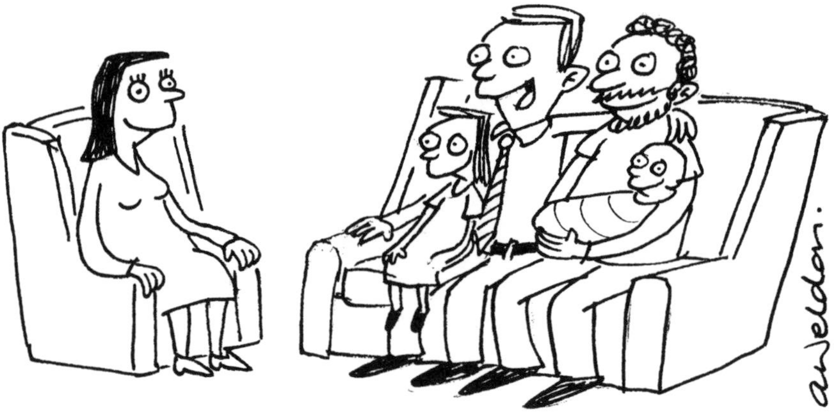
aweldon.

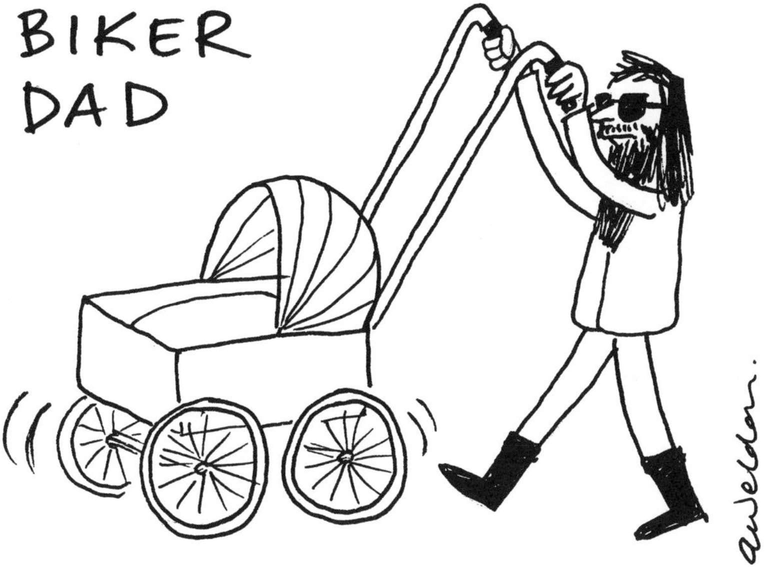
BIKER DAD
aweldon.

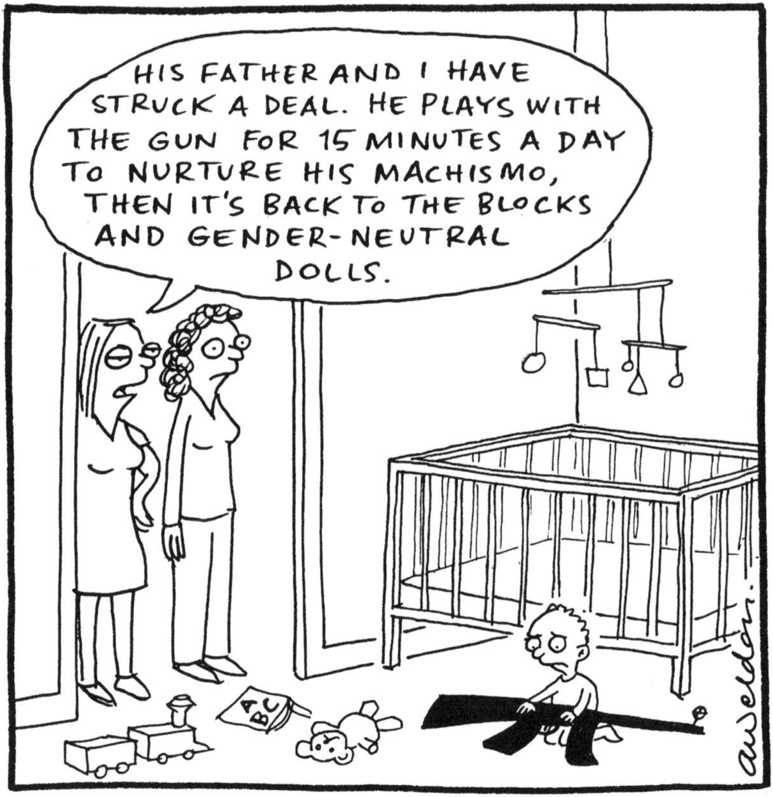
HIS FATHER AND I HAVE STRUCK A DEAL. HE PLAYS WITH THE GUN FOR 15 MINUTES A DAY TO NURTURE HIS MACHISMO, THEN IT'S BACK TO THE BLOCKS AND GENDER-NEUTRAL DOLLS.
ABC
a weldon.

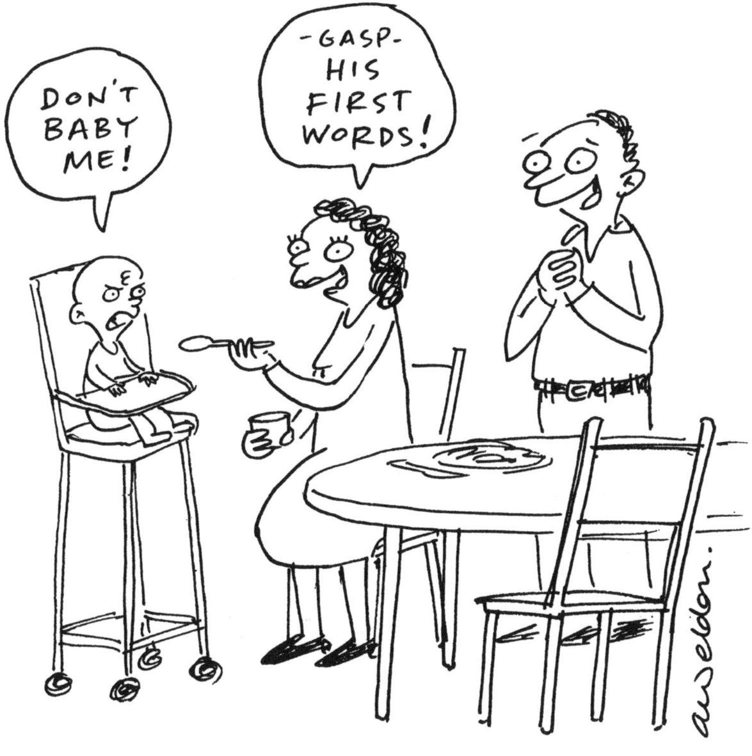
DON'T BABY ME!
-GASP- HIS FIRST WORDS!
a weldon.

THE PRECOCIOUS CHILD

USES FOR AN UNSETTLED BABY

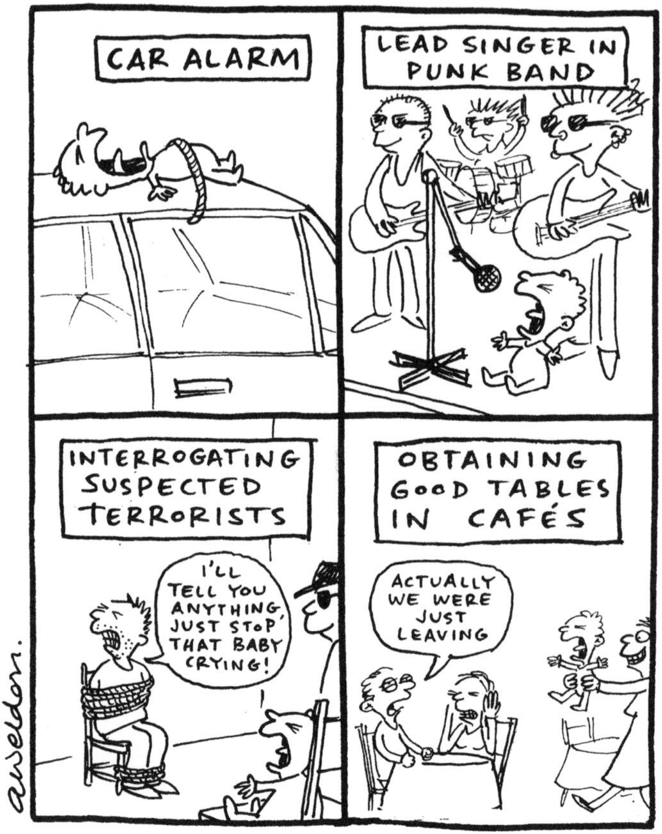

CAR ALARM
LEAD SINGER IN PUNK BAND
INTERROGATING SUSPECTED TERRORISTS
I'LL TELL YOU ANYTHING, JUST STOP THAT BABY CRYING!
OBTAINING GOOD TABLES IN CAFÉS
ACTUALLY WE WERE JUST LEAVING
aweldon.

ADVANCES IN GENETIC ENGINEERING.

THE SNOOZE-BUTTON BABY.

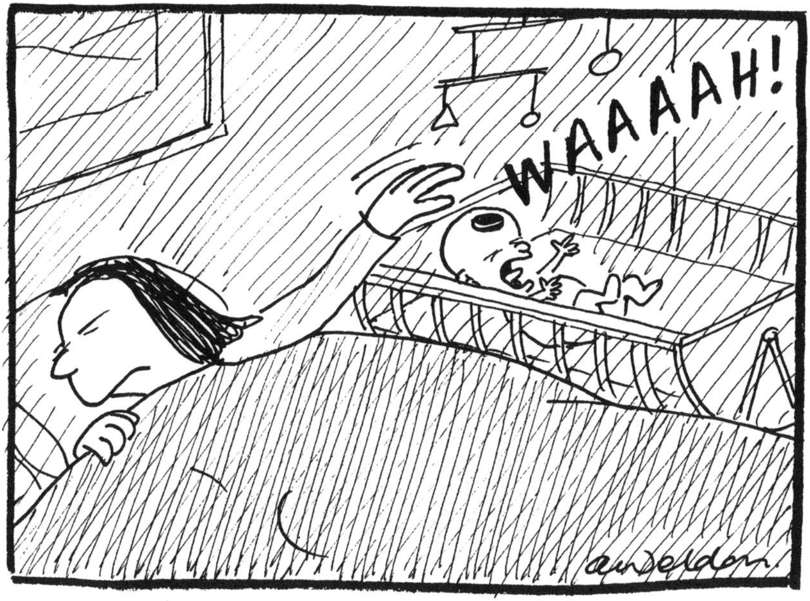
WAAAAAH!
awelden

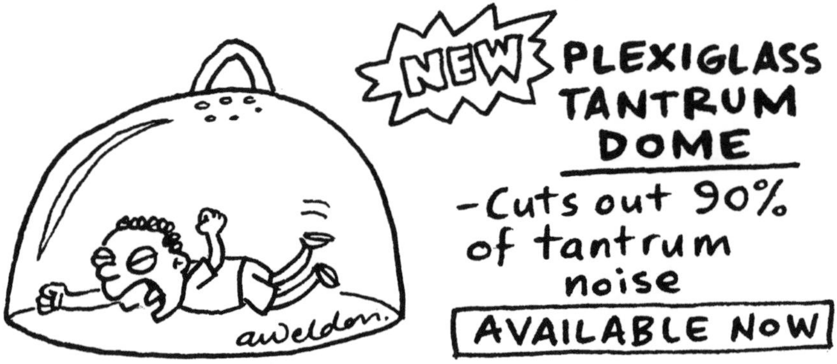
NEW
PLEXIGLASS TANTRUM DOME
-Cuts out 90% of tantrum noise
AVAILABLE NOW
aweldon.

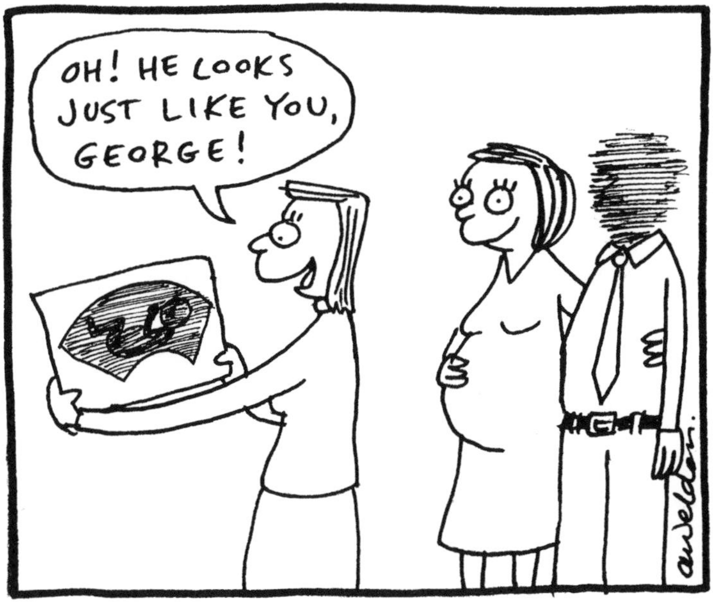
OH! HE LOOKS JUST LIKE YOU, GEORGE!
anweldon.

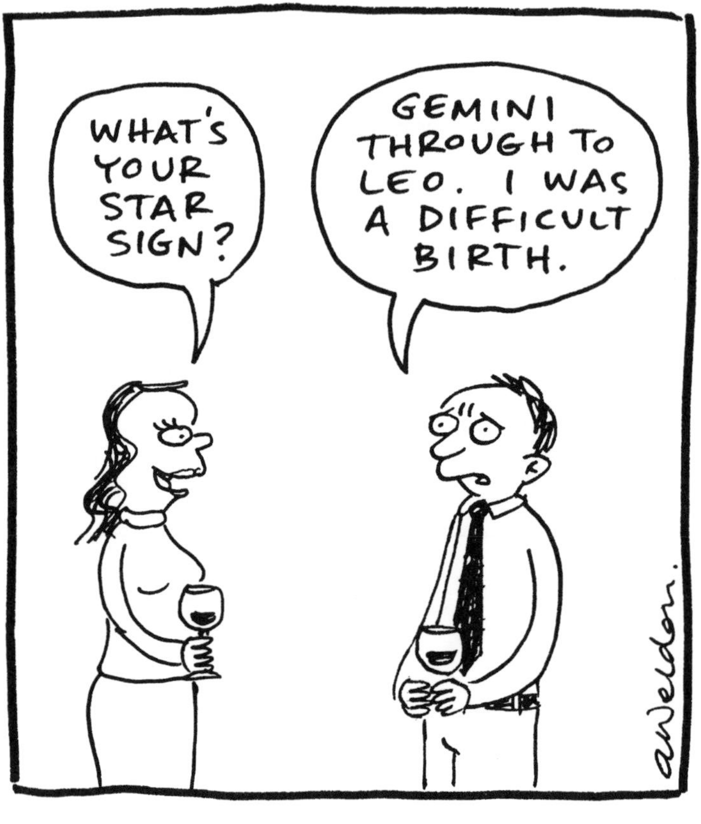
WHAT'S YOUR STAR SIGN?
GEMINI THROUGH TO LEO. I WAS A DIFFICULT BIRTH.
aweldon.

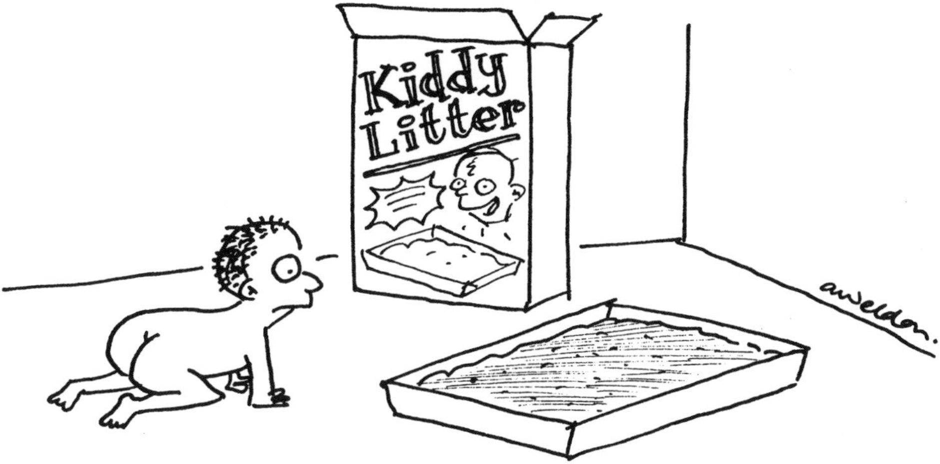
Kiddy Litter
aweldon.

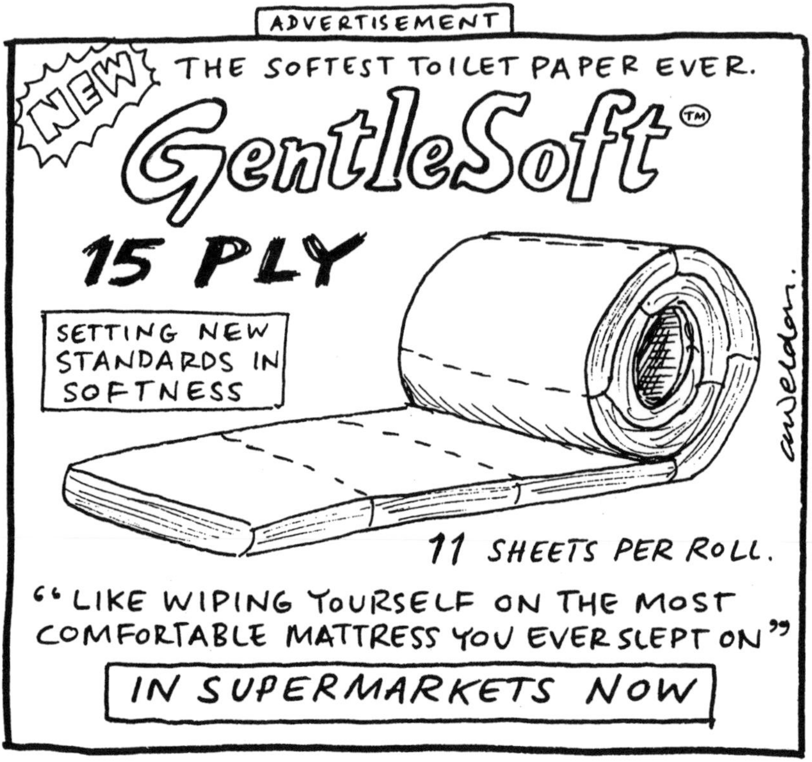
ADVERTISEMENT
NEW
THE SOFTEST TOILET PAPER EVER.
GentleSoft™
15 PLY
SETTING NEW STANDARDS IN SOFTNESS
11 SHEETS PER ROLL.
"LIKE WIPING YOURSELF ON THE MOST COMFORTABLE MATTRESS YOU EVER SLEPT ON"
IN SUPERMARKETS NOW

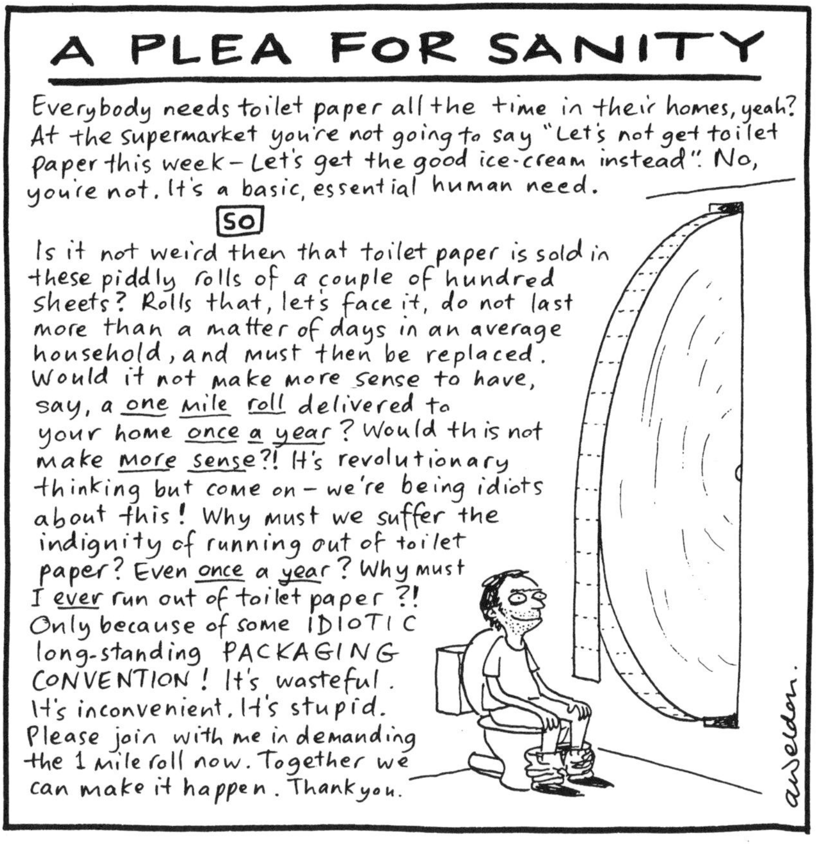
A PLEA FOR SANITY
Everybody needs toilet paper all the time in their homes, yeah? At the supermarket you're not going to say "Let's not get toilet paper this week - Let's get the good ice-cream instead". No, you're not. It's a basic, essential human need.
SO
Is it not weird then that toilet paper is sold in these piddly rolls of a couple of hundred sheets? Rolls that, let's face it, do not last more than a matter of days in an average household, and must then be replaced. Would it not make more sense to have, say, a one mile roll delivered to your home once a year? Would this not make more sense?! It's revolutionary thinking but come on - we're being idiots about this! Why must we suffer the indignity of running out of toilet paper? Even once a year? Why must I ever run out of toilet paper ?! Only because of some IDIOTIC long-standing PACKAGING CONVENTION! It's wasteful. It's inconvenient. It's stupid. Please join with me in demanding the 1 mile roll now. Together we can make it happen. Thank you.
aweldon.

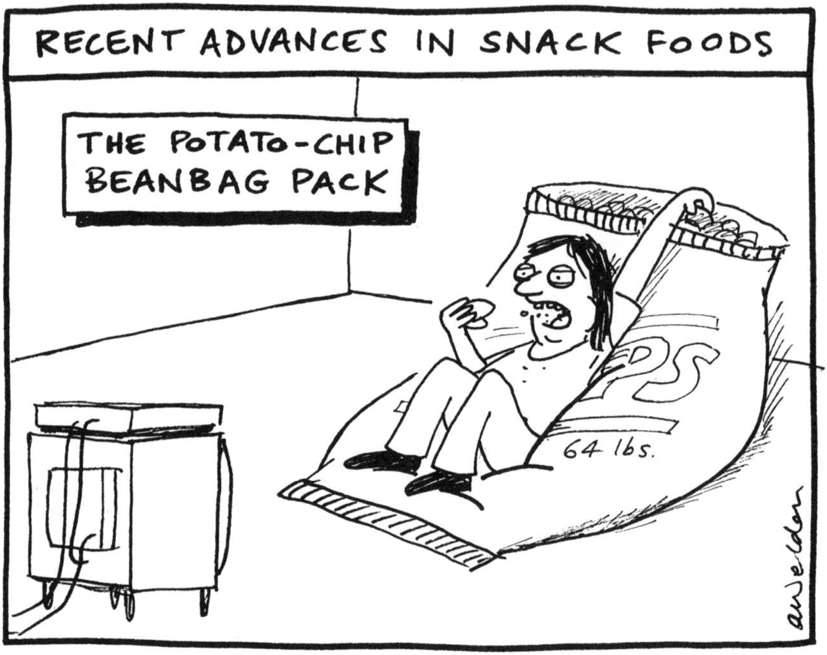
RECENT ADVANCES IN SNACK FOODS
THE POTATO-CHIP BEANBAG PACK
64 lbs.
aweldon

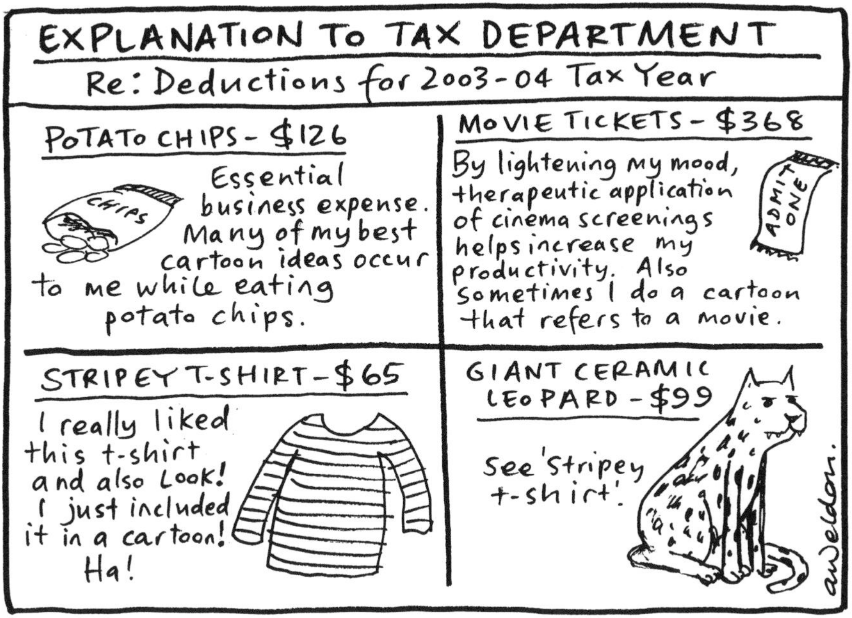

EXPLANATION TO TAX DEPARTMENT

Re: Deductions for 2003-04 Tax Year

POTATO CHIPS - $126

Essential business expense. Many of my best cartoon ideas occur to me while eating potato chips.

MOVIE TICKETS - $368

By lightening my mood, therapeutic application of cinema screenings helps increase my productivity. Also sometimes I do a cartoon that refers to a movie.

STRIPEY T-SHIRT - $65

I really liked this t-shirt and also Look! I just included it in a cartoon! Ha!

GIANT CERAMIC LEOPARD - $99

See 'Stripey t-shirt'.

aweldon.

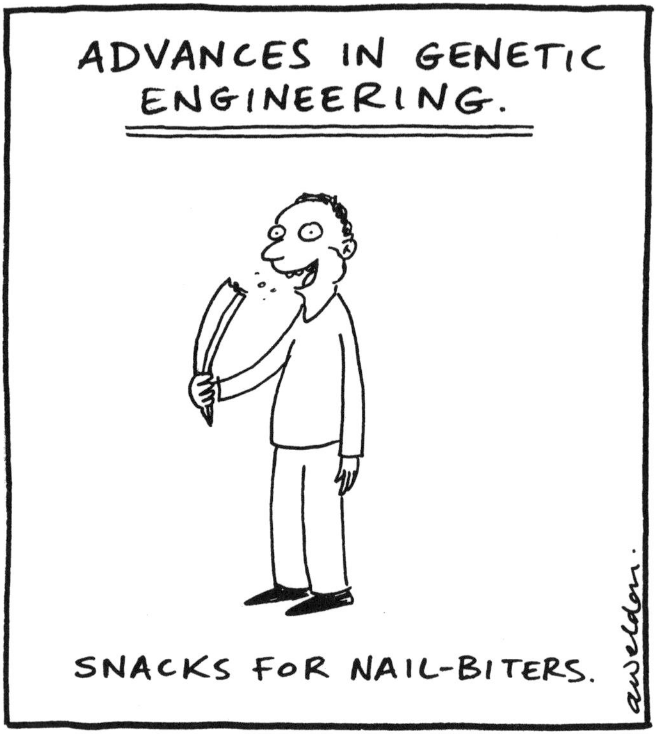
ADVANCES IN GENETIC ENGINEERING.
SNACKS FOR NAIL-BITERS.
aweldon.

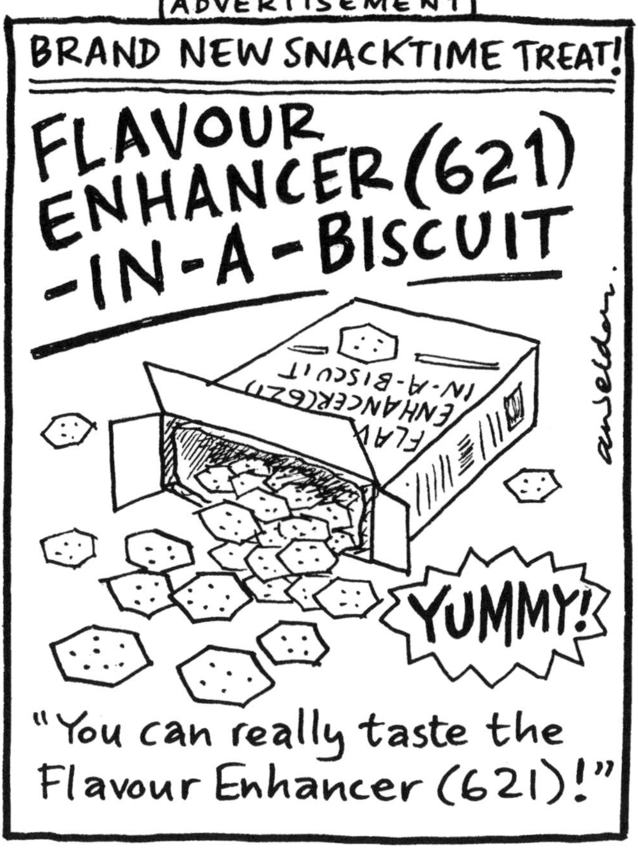
ADVERTISEMENT
BRAND NEW SNACKTIME TREAT!
FLAVOUR ENHANCER (621) -IN-A-BISCUIT
FLAV ENHANCER(621) IN-A-BISCUIT
YUMMY!
"You can really taste the Flavour Enhancer (621)!"
anseldon.

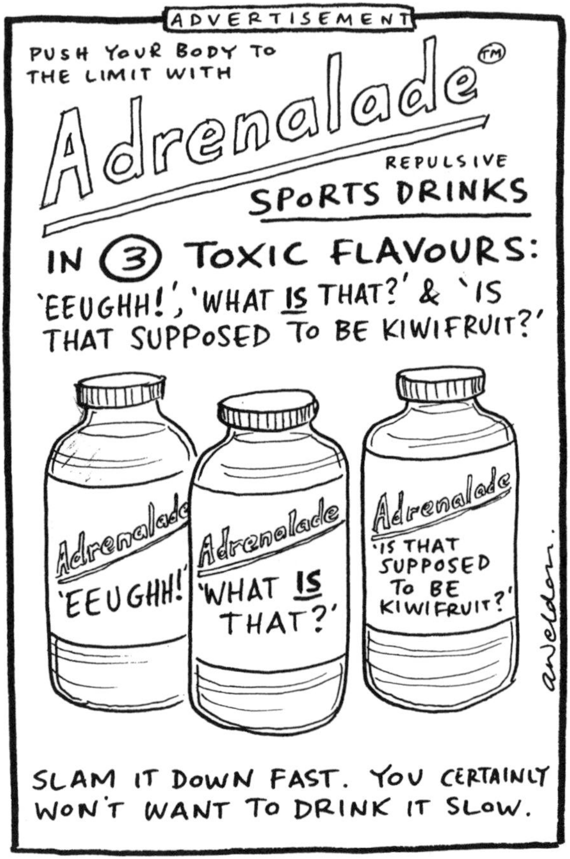
ADVERTISEMENT
PUSH YOUR BODY TO THE LIMIT WITH
Adrenalade™
REPULSIVE SPORTS DRINKS
IN ③ TOXIC FLAVOURS:
'EEUGHH!', 'WHAT IS THAT?' & 'IS THAT SUPPOSED TO BE KIWIFRUIT?'
Adrenalade 'EEUGHH!'
Adrenalade 'WHAT IS THAT?'
Adrenalade 'IS THAT SUPPOSED TO BE KIWIFRUIT?'
aweldon.
SLAM IT DOWN FAST. YOU CERTAINLY WON'T WANT TO DRINK IT SLOW.

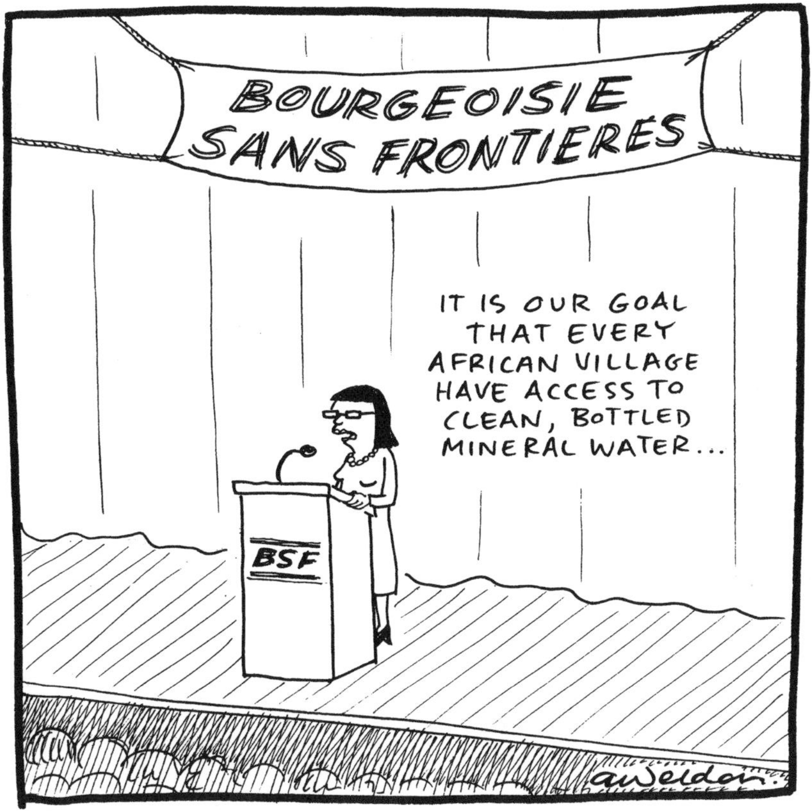
BOURGEOISIE SANS FRONTIERES
IT IS OUR GOAL THAT EVERY AFRICAN VILLAGE HAVE ACCESS TO CLEAN, BOTTLED MINERAL WATER...
BSF
aWeldon

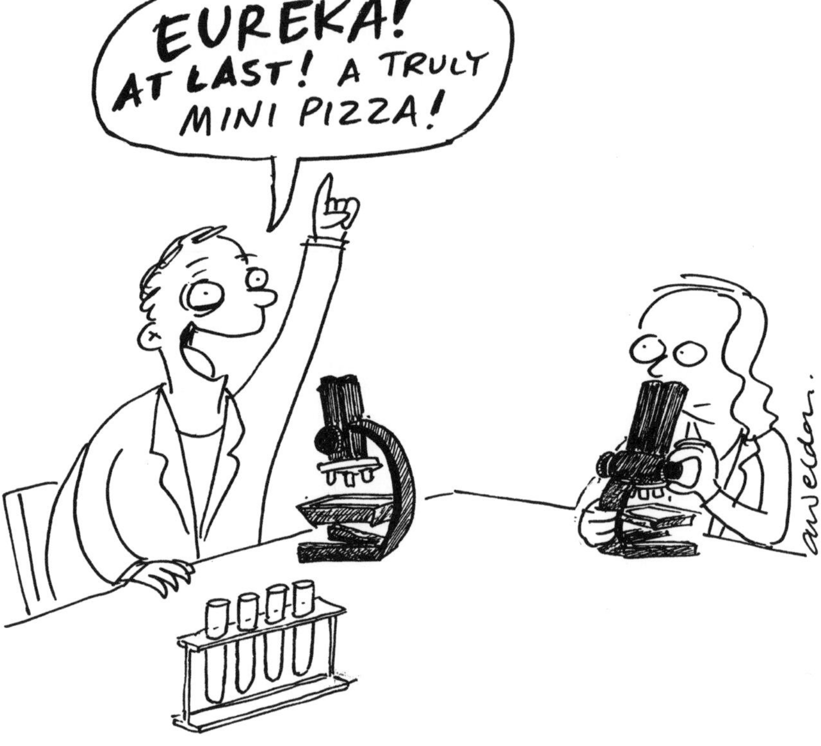
EUREKA!
AT LAST! A TRULY
MINI PIZZA!

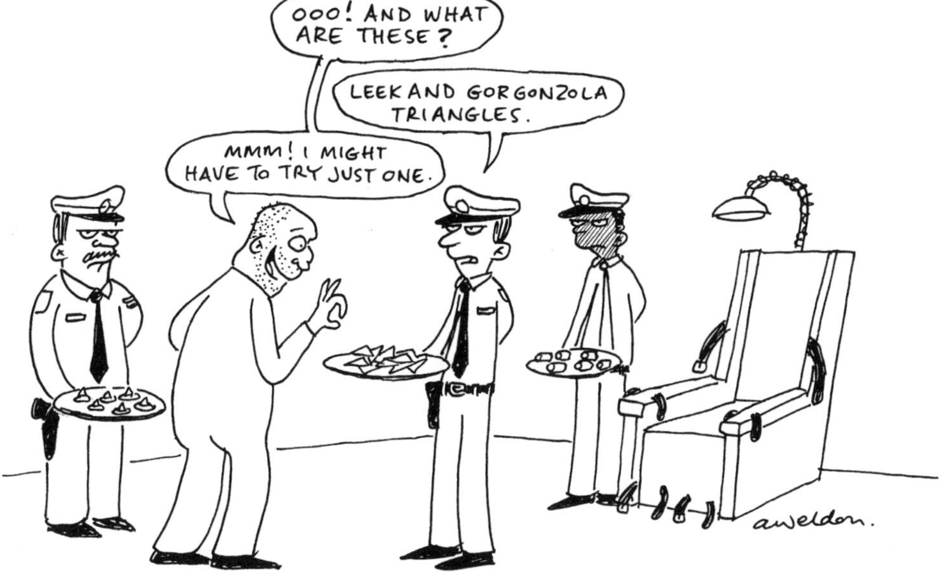
OOO! AND WHAT ARE THESE?
LEEK AND GORGONZOLA TRIANGLES.
MMM! I MIGHT HAVE TO TRY JUST ONE.
aweldon.

DEATH ROW INMATE LEROY SCHNEIDER CHOSE 'FINGER FOOD' AS HIS LAST MEAL.

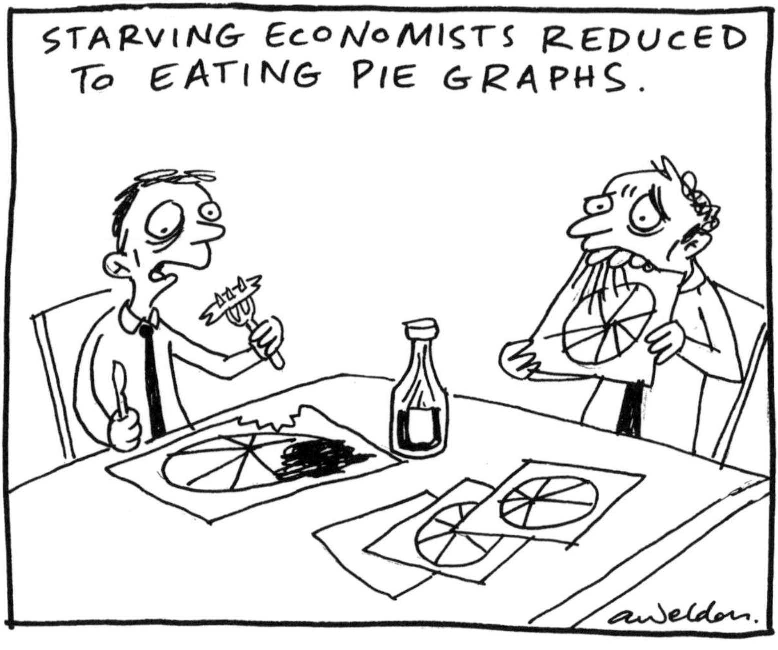
STARVING ECONOMISTS REDUCED TO EATING PIE GRAPHS.
a Weldon.

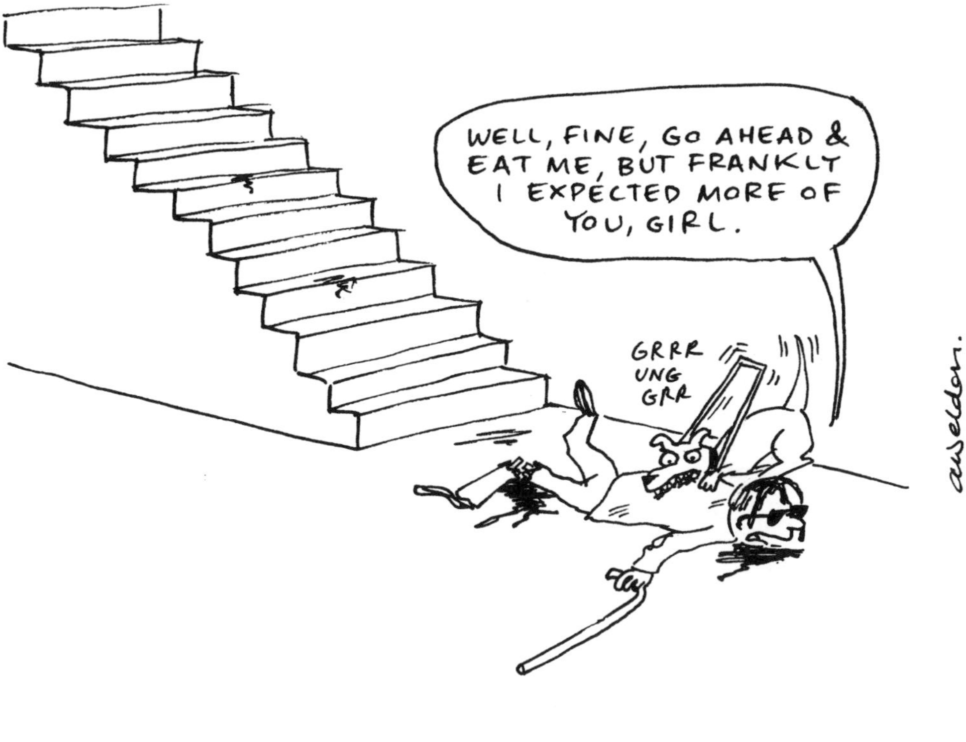

WELL, FINE, GO AHEAD & EAT ME, BUT FRANKLY I EXPECTED MORE OF YOU, GIRL.
GRRR UNG GRR

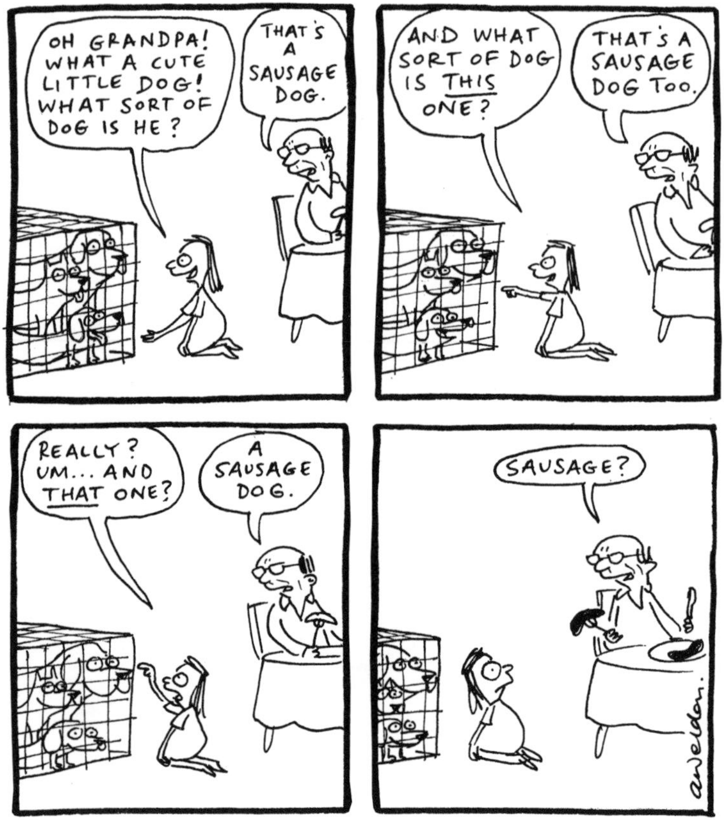
OH GRANDPA! WHAT A CUTE LITTLE DOG! WHAT SORT OF DOG IS HE?
THAT'S A SAUSAGE DOG.
AND WHAT SORT OF DOG IS THIS ONE?
THAT'S A SAUSAGE DOG TOO.
REALLY? UM... AND THAT ONE?
A SAUSAGE DOG.
SAUSAGE?
aweldon.

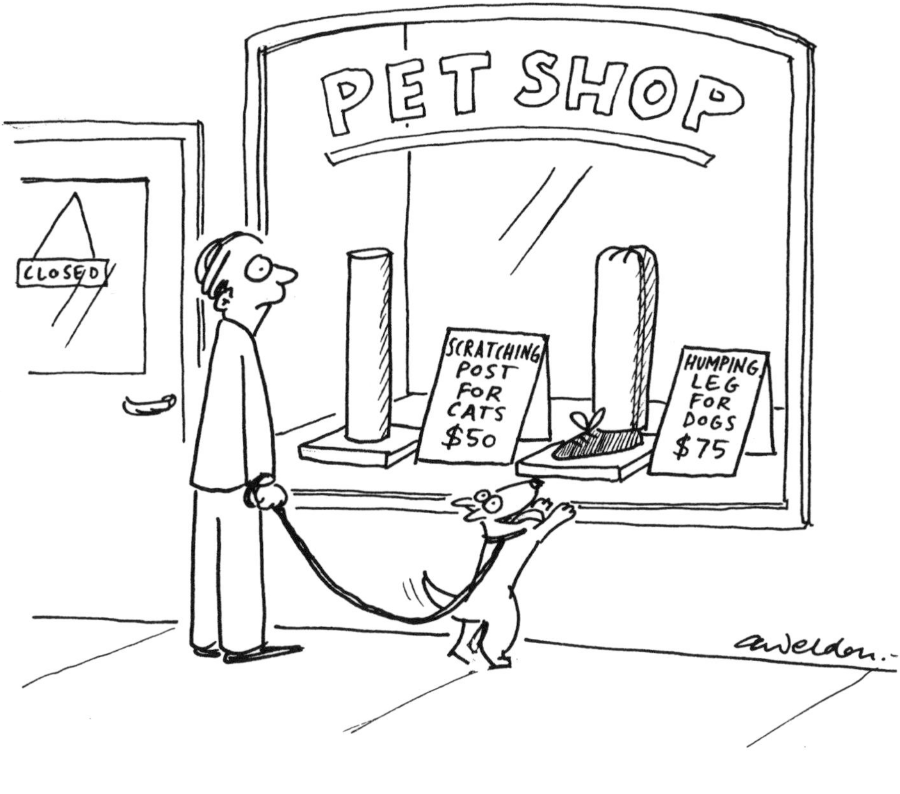
PET SHOP
CLOSED
SCRATCHING POST FOR CATS $50
HUMPING LEG FOR DOGS $75
aweldon.

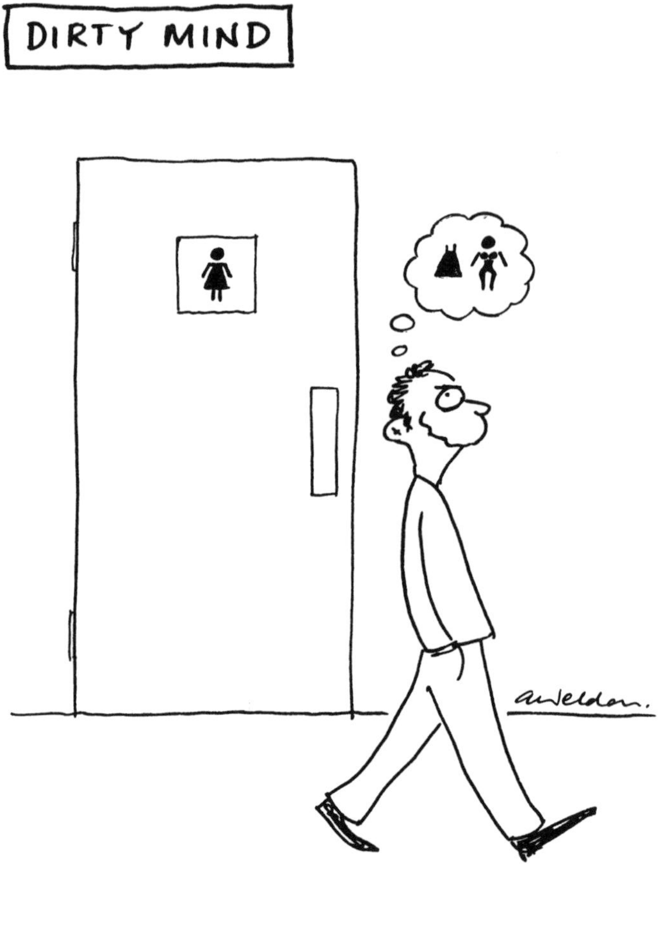
DIRTY MIND
aWeldon.

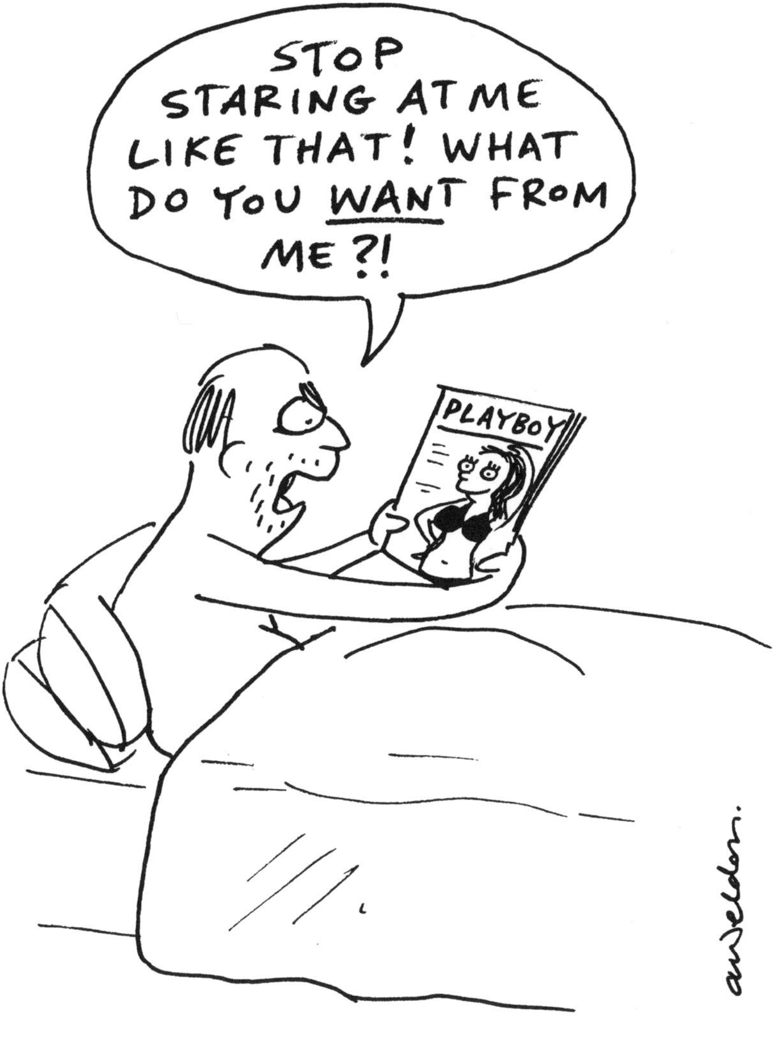
STOP STARING AT ME LIKE THAT! WHAT DO YOU WANT FROM ME?!
PLAYBOY
aweldon.

INCOMPATIBLE PERVERSIONS:

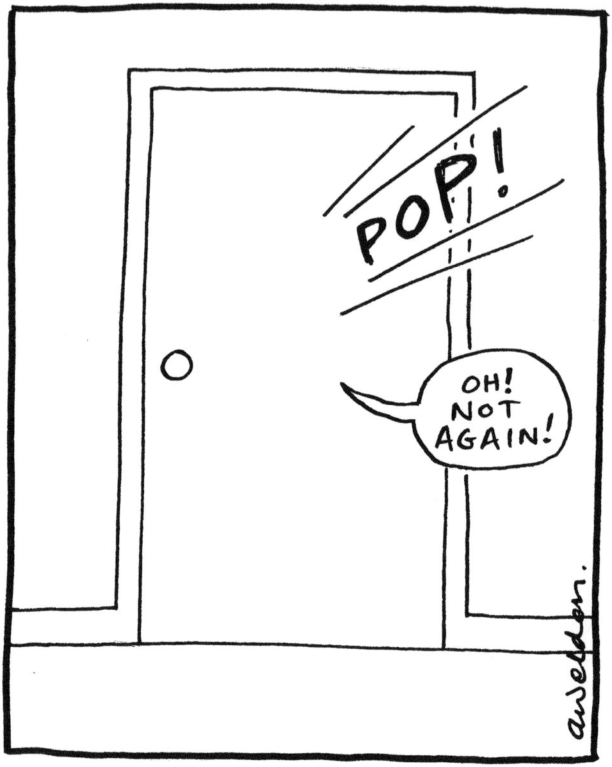
POP!
OH! NOT AGAIN!
aweldon.

INFLATABLE SEX DOLLS / S&M.

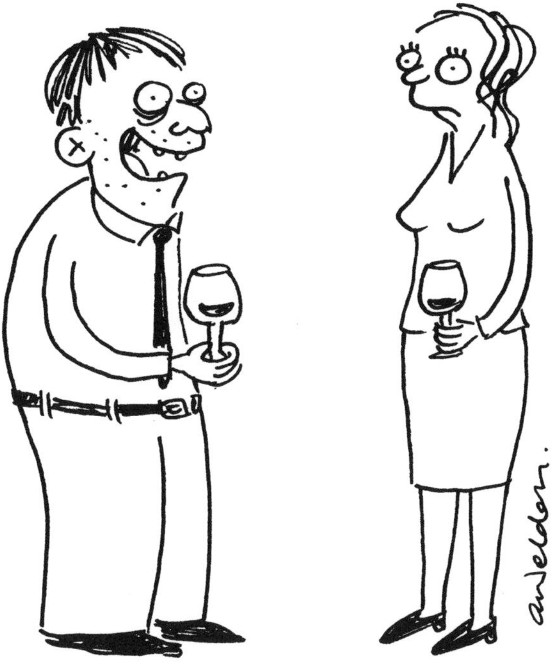
aweldon.

"I'M AN EAR, NOSE AND THROAT FETISHIST."

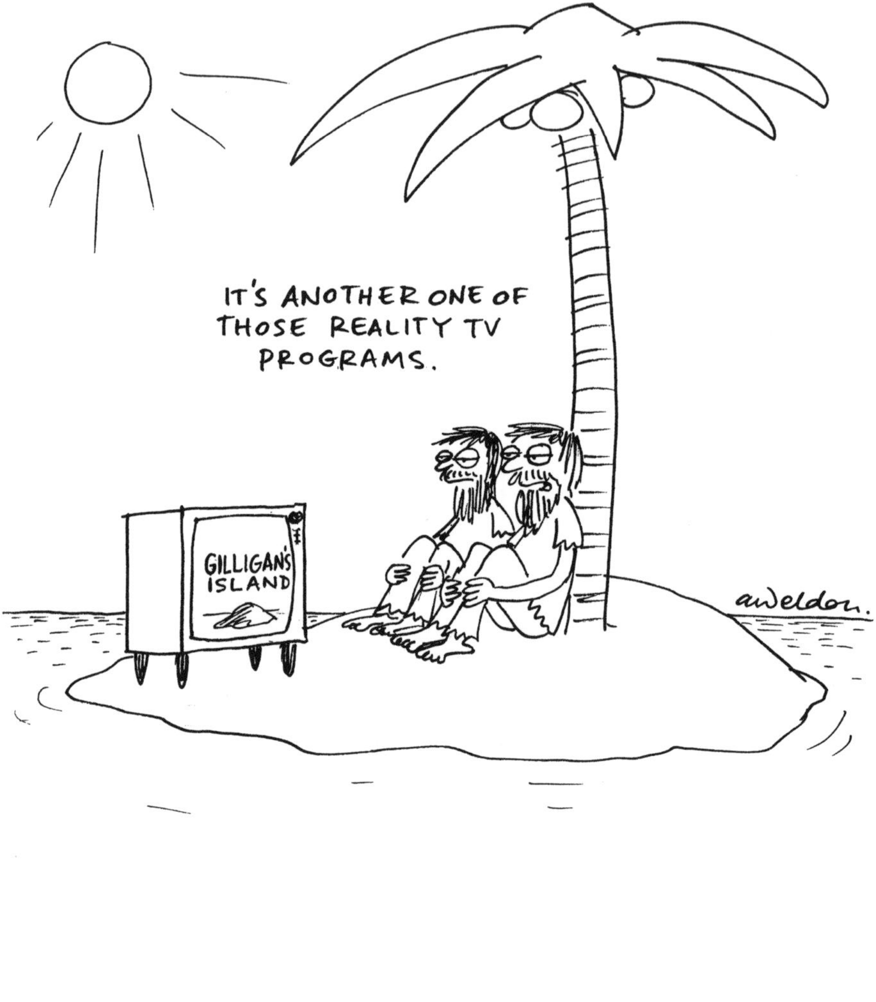
IT'S ANOTHER ONE OF THOSE REALITY TV PROGRAMS.
GILLIGAN'S ISLAND
aweldon.

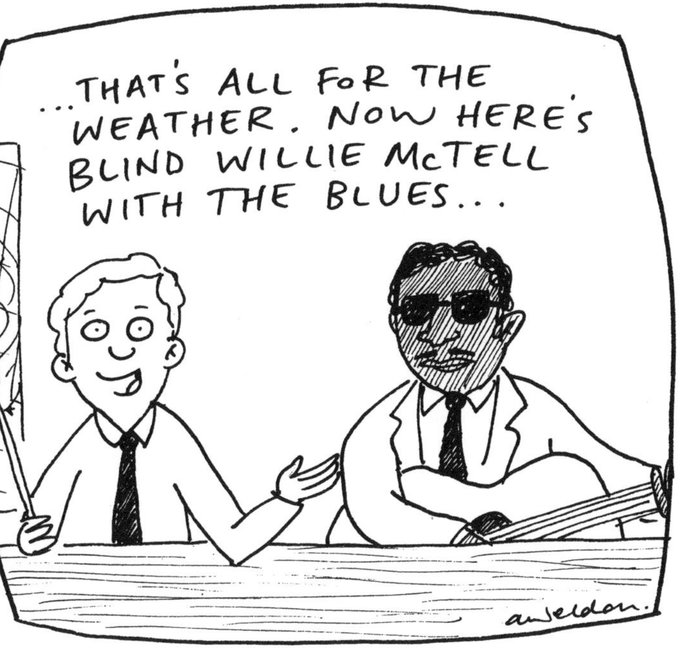
...THAT'S ALL FOR THE WEATHER. NOW HERE'S BLIND WILLIE McTELL WITH THE BLUES...
a weldon.

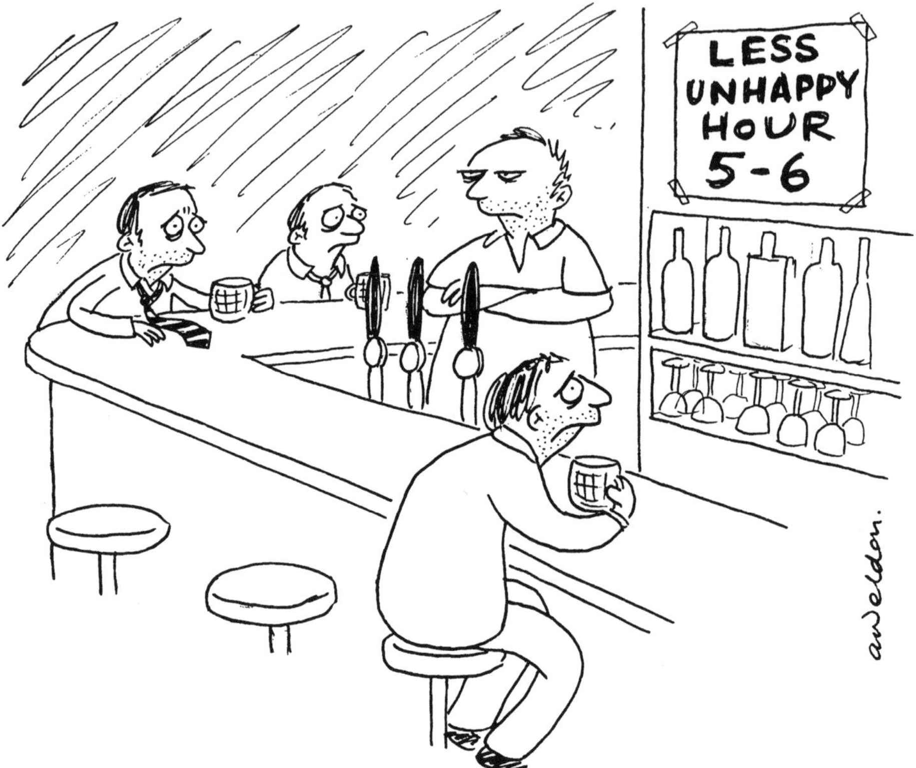
LESS
UNHAPPY
HOUR
5-6
aweldon.

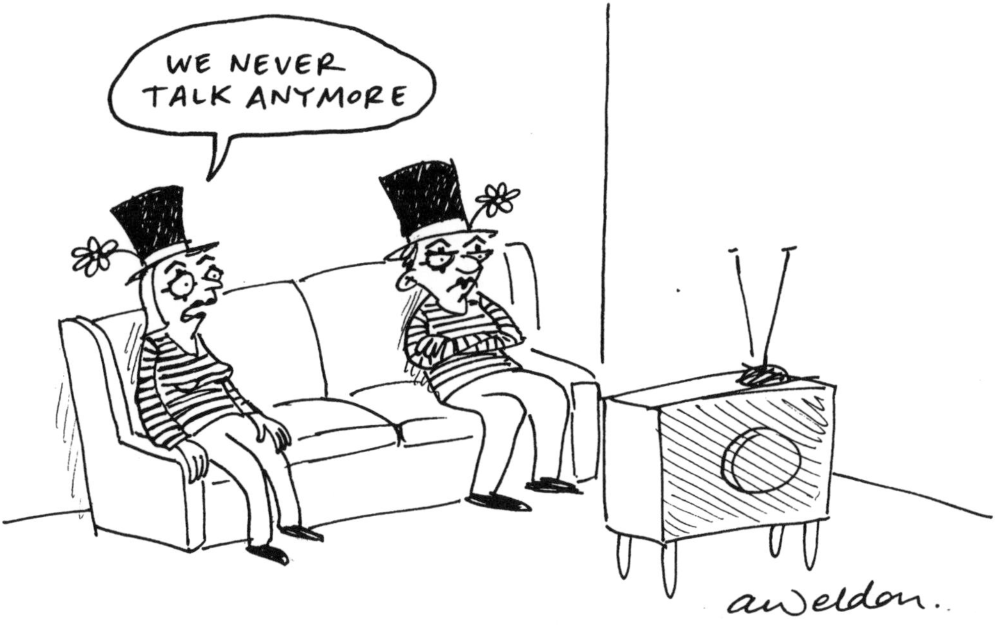
WE NEVER TALK ANYMORE
aweldon..

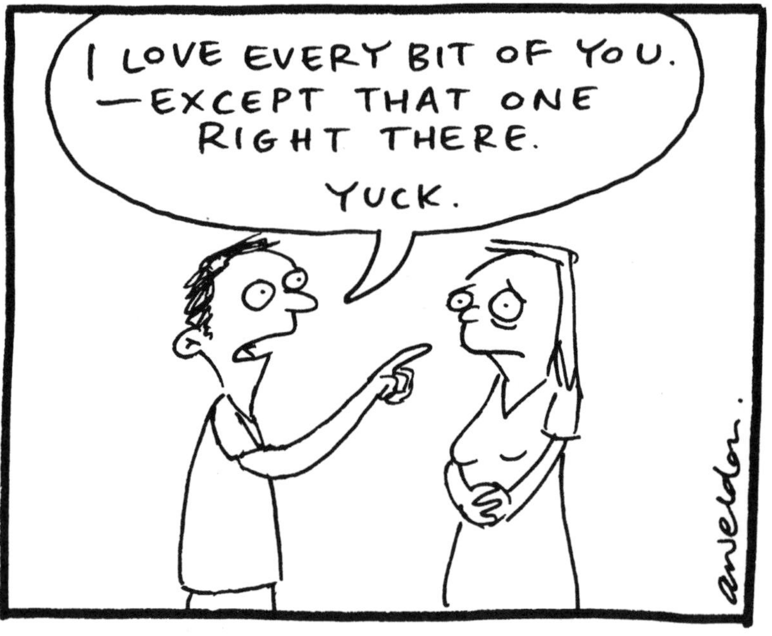
I LOVE EVERY BIT OF YOU.
—EXCEPT THAT ONE RIGHT THERE.
YUCK.
anweldon.

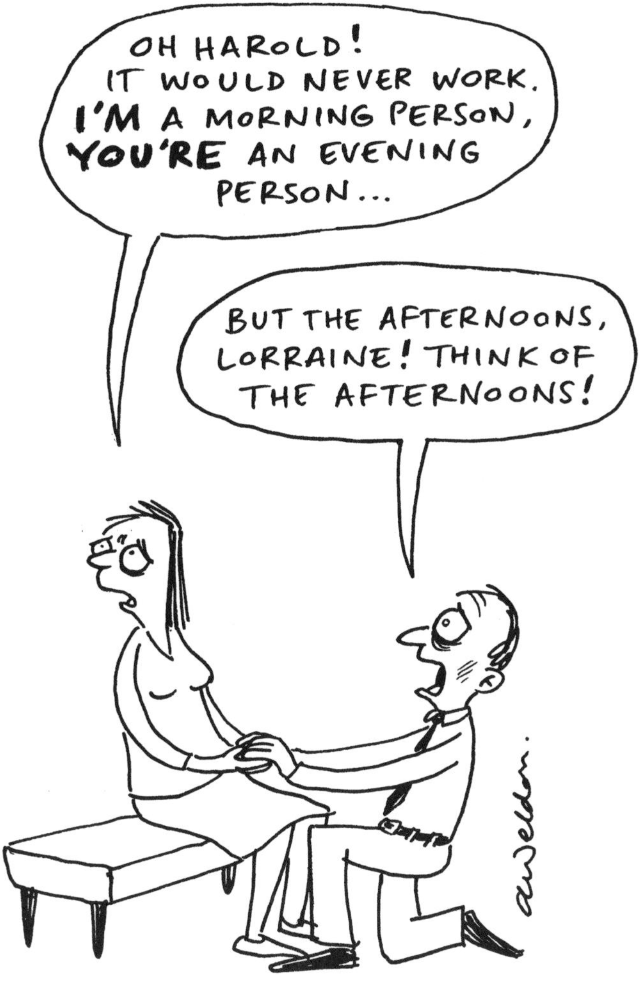
OH HAROLD! IT WOULD NEVER WORK. I'M A MORNING PERSON, YOU'RE AN EVENING PERSON...
BUT THE AFTERNOONS, LORRAINE! THINK OF THE AFTERNOONS!

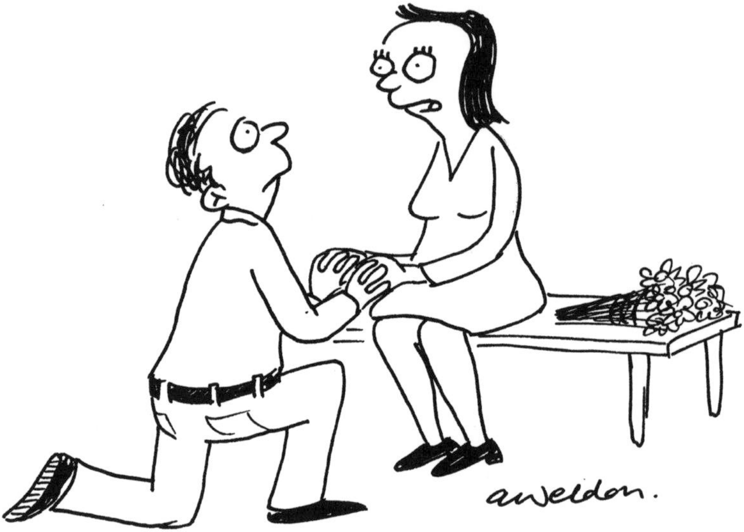
aweldon.

"I WOULD DO THE WEDDING, I'M JUST NOT SURE ABOUT THE MARRIAGE."

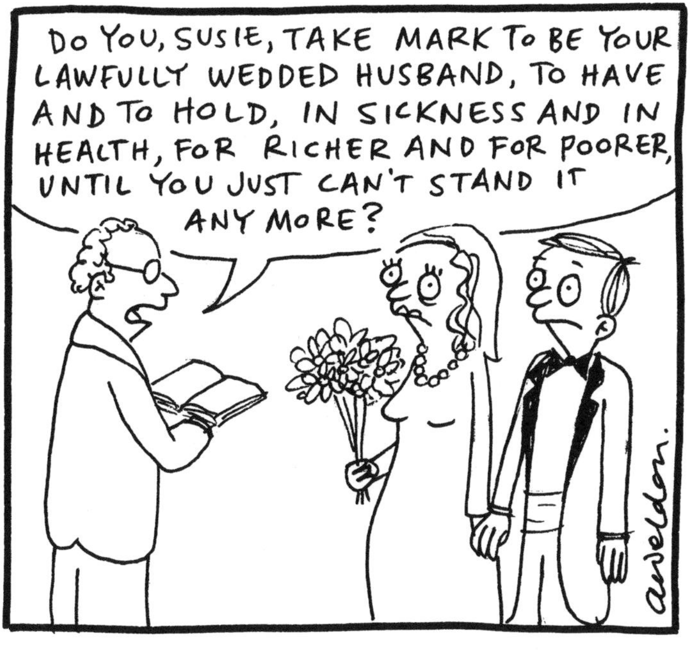
DO YOU, SUSIE, TAKE MARK TO BE YOUR LAWFULLY WEDDED HUSBAND, TO HAVE AND TO HOLD, IN SICKNESS AND IN HEALTH, FOR RICHER AND FOR POORER, UNTIL YOU JUST CAN'T STAND IT ANY MORE?
aweldon.

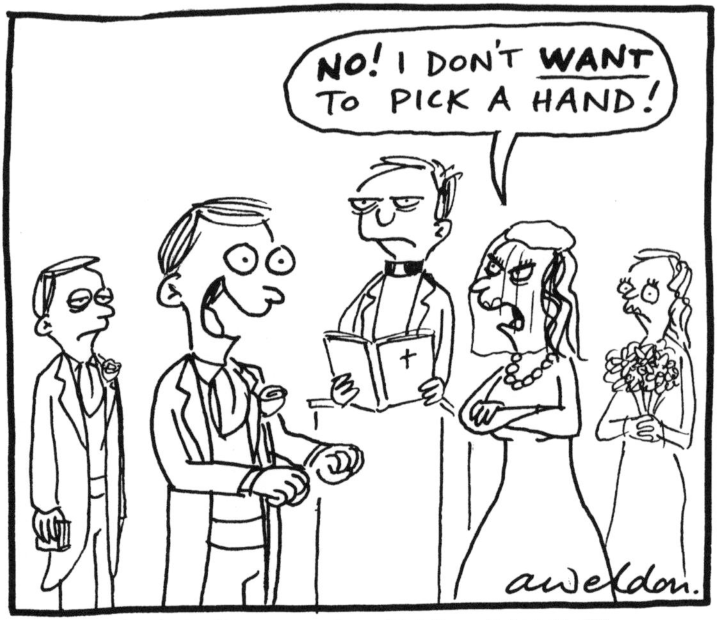
NO! I DON'T WANT TO PICK A HAND!
aweldon.

OFF TO A BAD START.

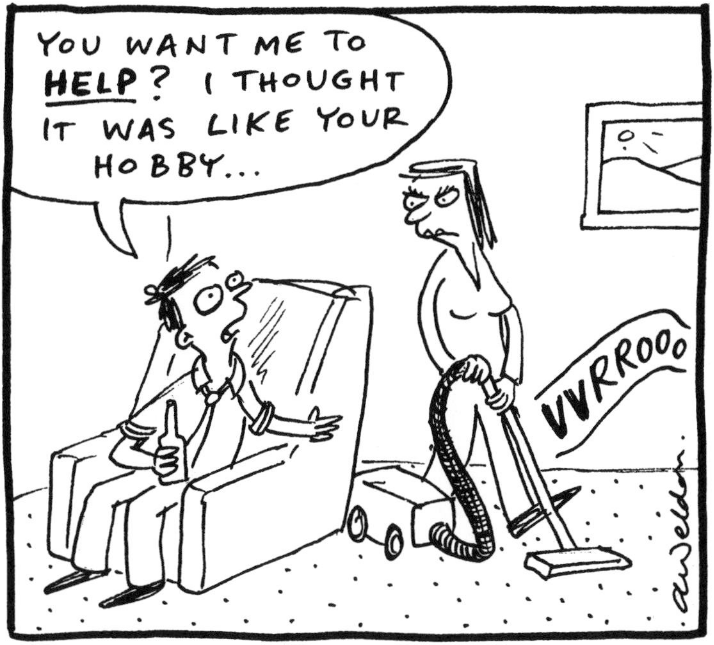
YOU WANT ME TO **HELP**? I THOUGHT IT WAS LIKE YOUR HOBBY...
VVRROOo
a weldon

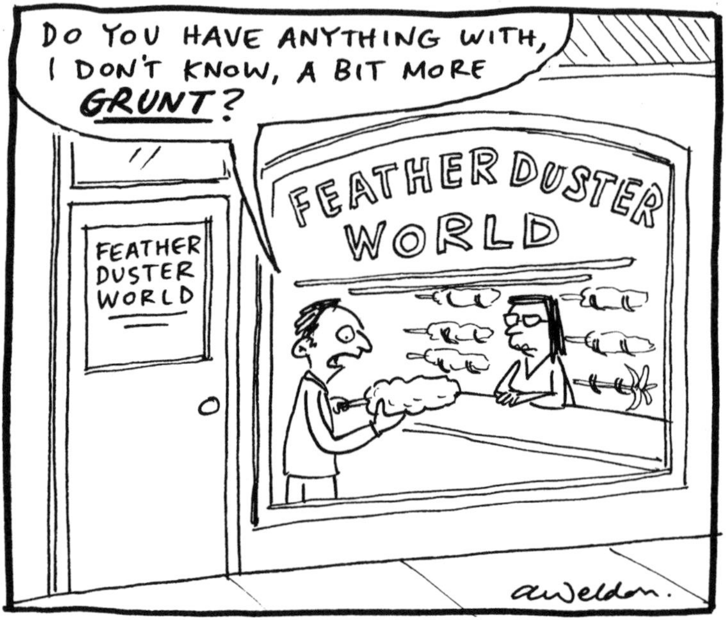
DO YOU HAVE ANYTHING WITH, I DON'T KNOW, A BIT MORE GRUNT?
FEATHER DUSTER WORLD
FEATHER DUSTER WORLD
a weldon.

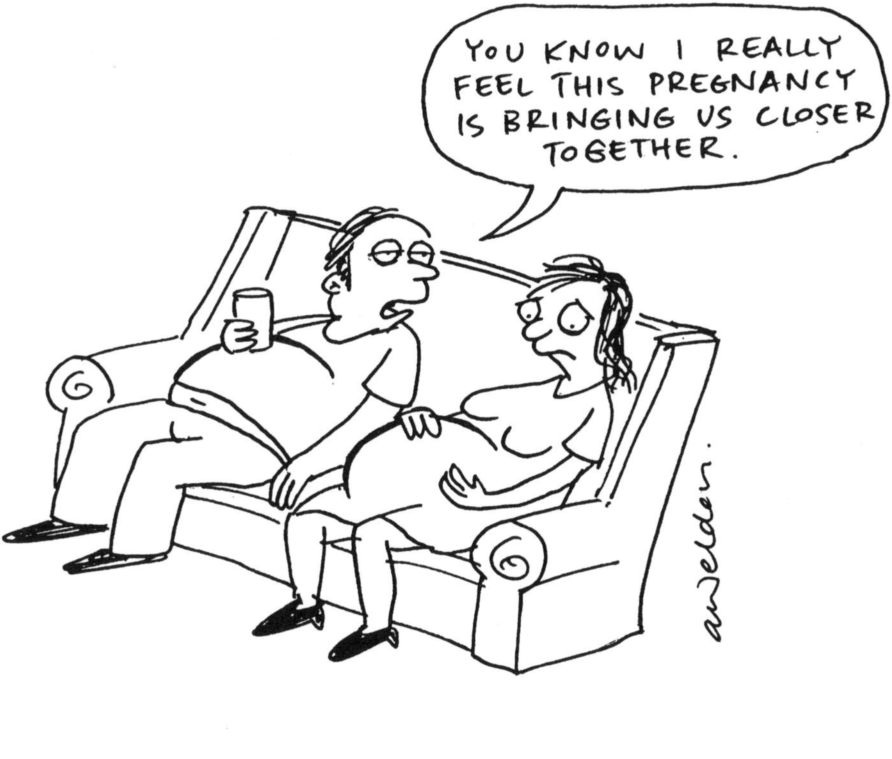
YOU KNOW I REALLY FEEL THIS PREGNANCY IS BRINGING US CLOSER TOGETHER.
awelden.

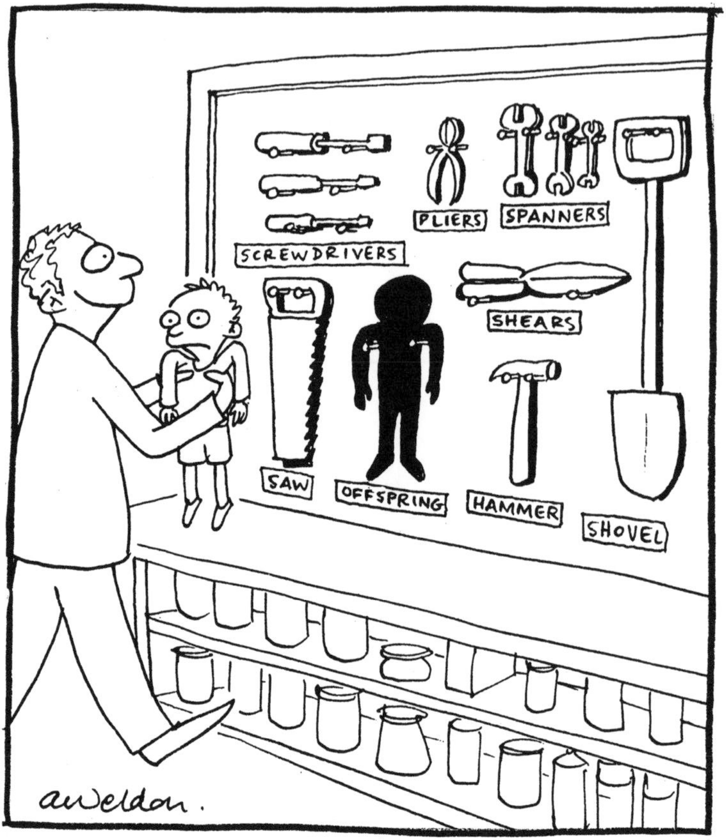
SCREWDRIVERS
PLIERS
SPANNERS
SAW
OFFSPRING
SHEARS
HAMMER
SHOVEL
aweldon.

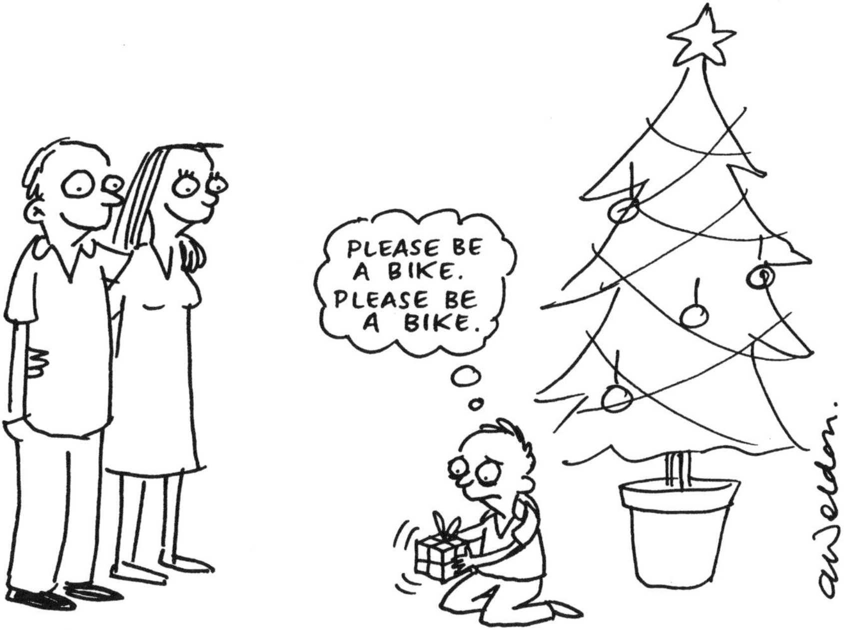
PLEASE BE A BIKE. PLEASE BE A BIKE.
aweldon.

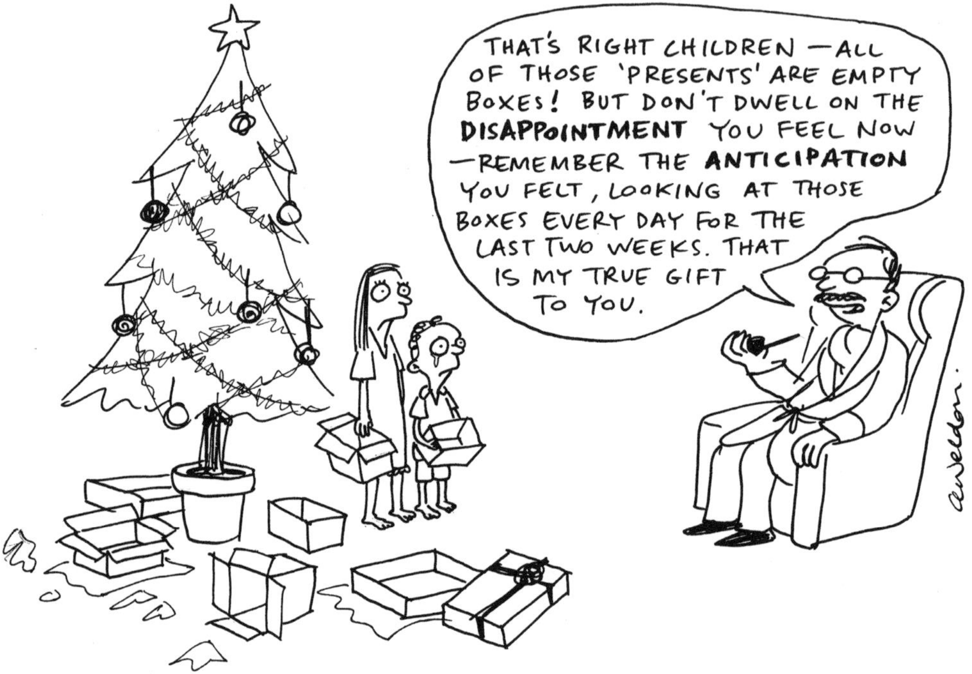
THAT'S RIGHT CHILDREN —ALL OF THOSE 'PRESENTS' ARE EMPTY BOXES! BUT DON'T DWELL ON THE DISAPPOINTMENT YOU FEEL NOW —REMEMBER THE ANTICIPATION YOU FELT, LOOKING AT THOSE BOXES EVERY DAY FOR THE LAST TWO WEEKS. THAT IS MY TRUE GIFT TO YOU.
aweldon.

A CHRISTMAS PUZZLE

Ⓠ CAN YOU HELP SANTA FIND HIS WAY THROUGH THE SNOW-MAZE TO BRING PRESENTS TO THE LITTLE CHILDREN?

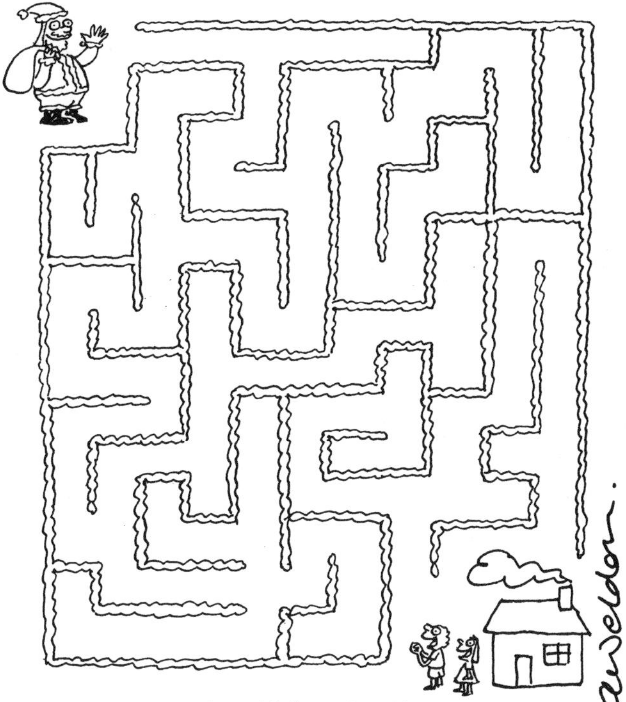

a weldon

Ⓐ NO YOU CAN'T, CAN YOU? WELL THAT'S JUST **GREAT**. NO PRESENTS FOR THE LITTLE CHILDREN THIS YEAR! I HOPE YOU'RE HAPPY.

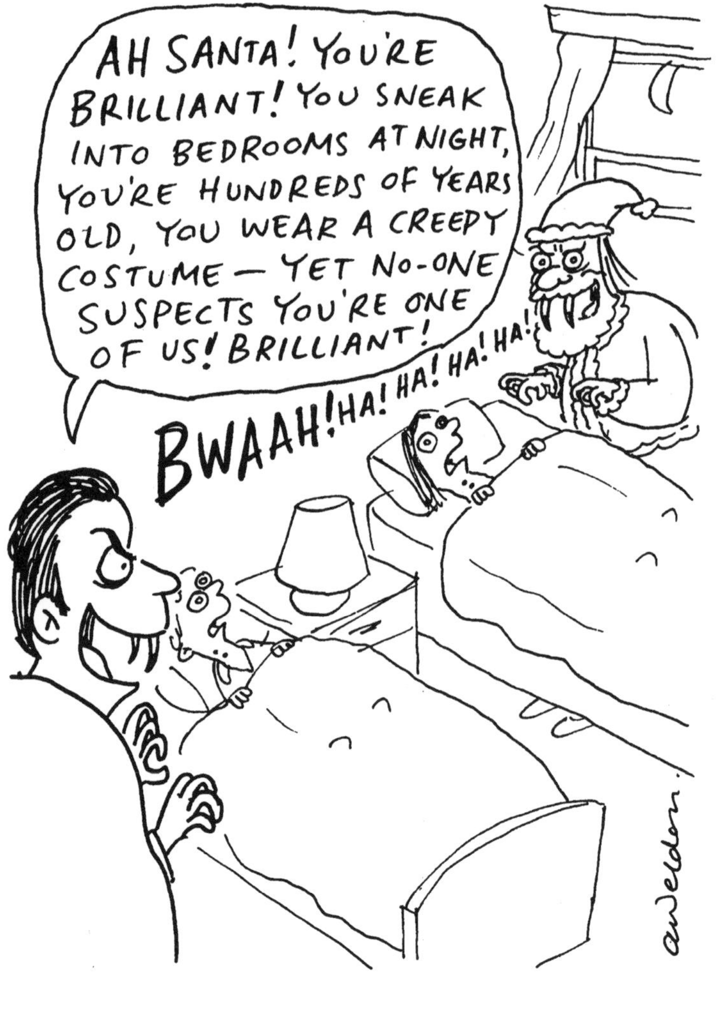
AH SANTA! YOU'RE BRILLIANT! YOU SNEAK INTO BEDROOMS AT NIGHT, YOU'RE HUNDREDS OF YEARS OLD, YOU WEAR A CREEPY COSTUME — YET NO-ONE SUSPECTS YOU'RE ONE OF US! BRILLIANT!
BWAAH! HA! HA! HA! HA!
aweldon

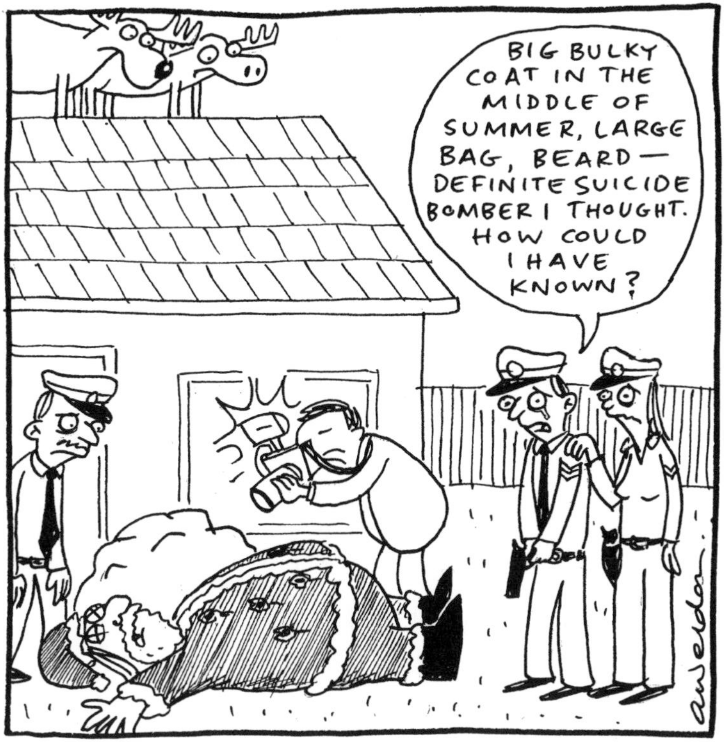
BIG BULKY COAT IN THE MIDDLE OF SUMMER, LARGE BAG, BEARD — DEFINITE SUICIDE BOMBER I THOUGHT. HOW COULD I HAVE KNOWN?
aweldon

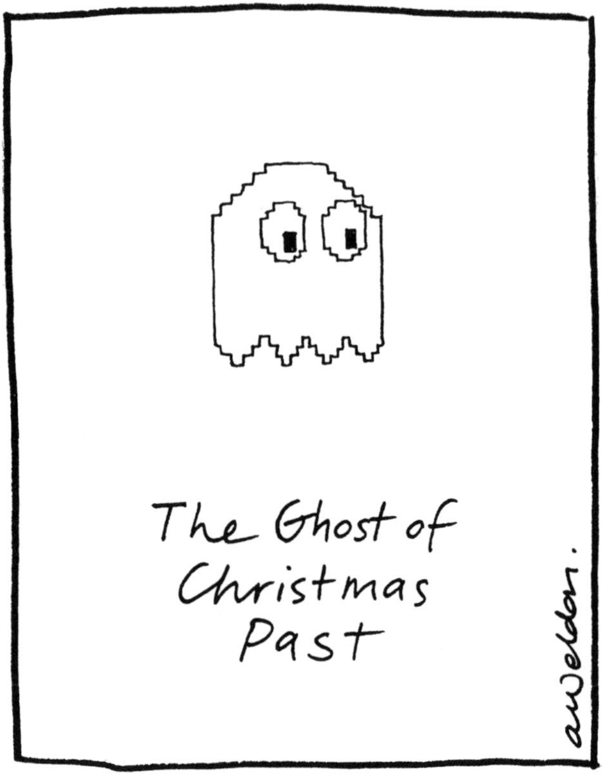
The Ghost of
Christmas
Past
aweldon.

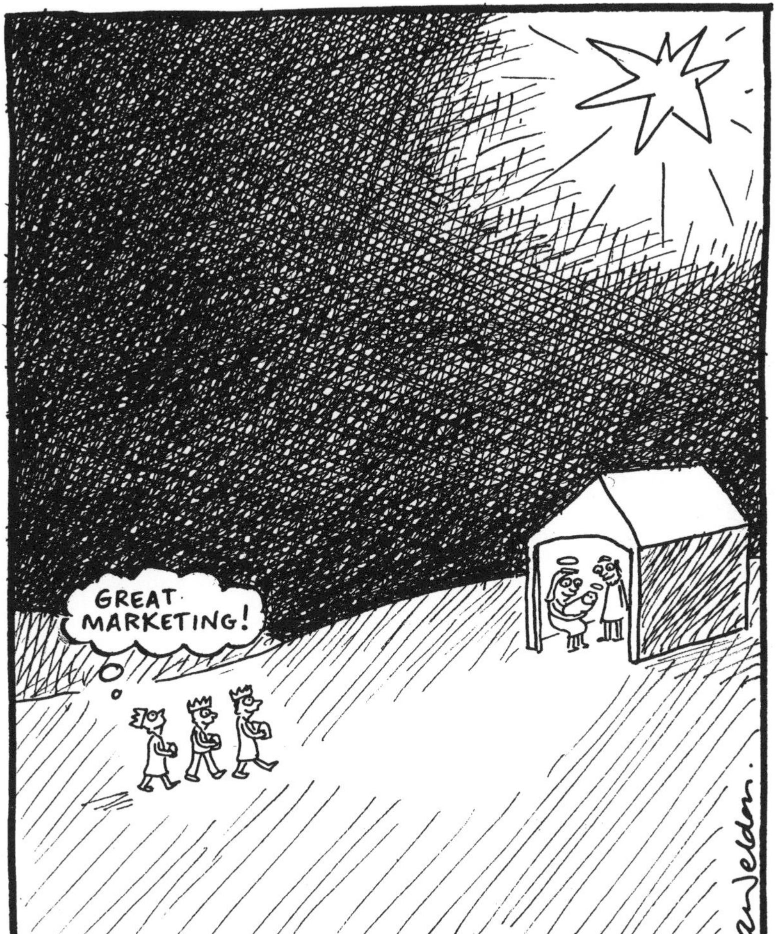
GREAT MARKETING!

THE VIRGIN

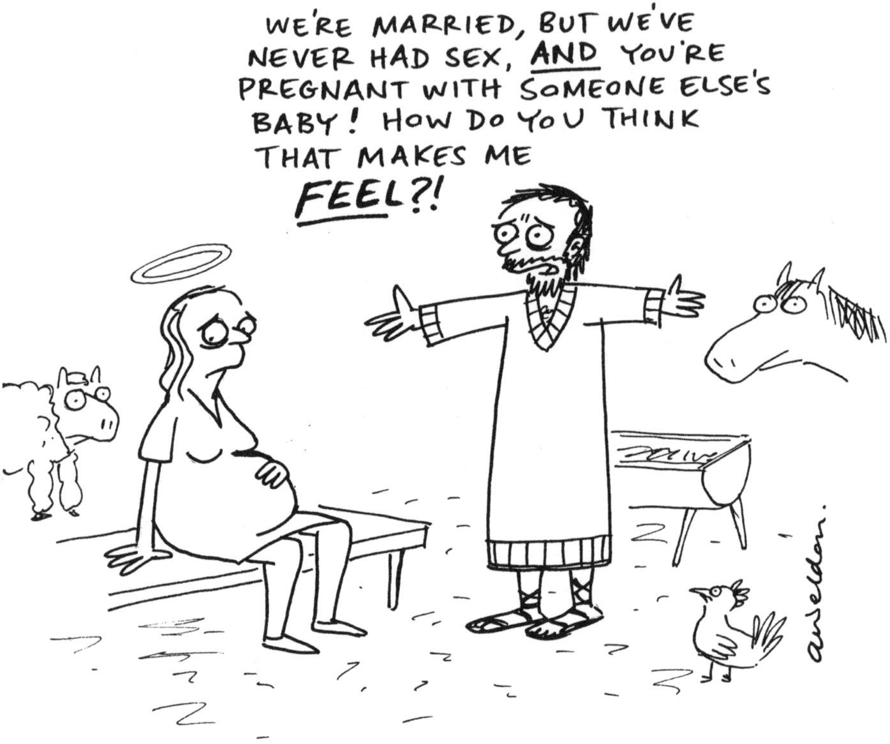
WE'RE MARRIED, BUT WE'VE NEVER HAD SEX, AND YOU'RE PREGNANT WITH SOMEONE ELSE'S BABY! HOW DO YOU THINK THAT MAKES ME FEEL?!

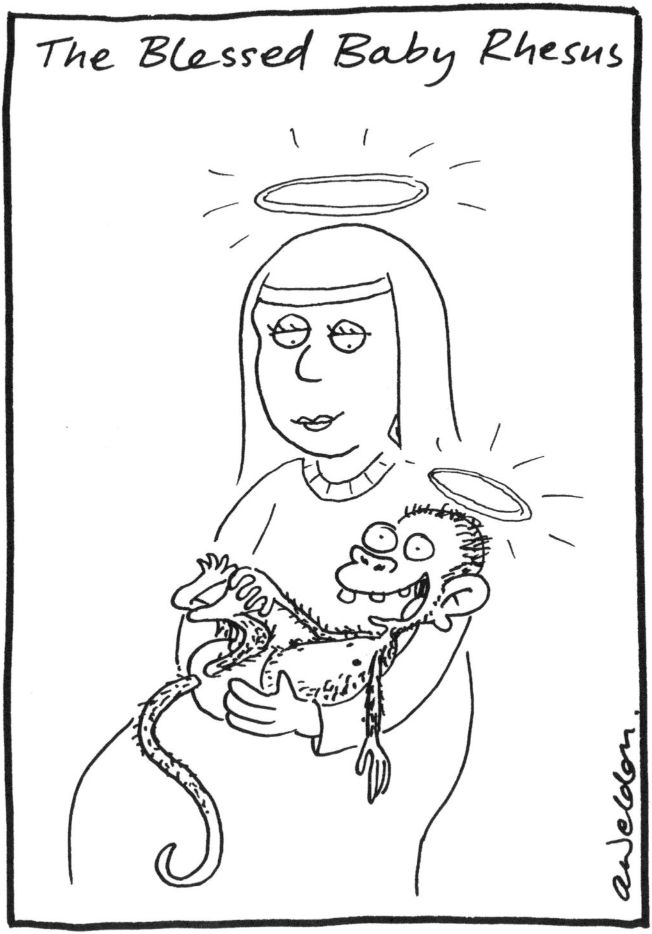
The Blessed Baby Rhesus
a weldon.

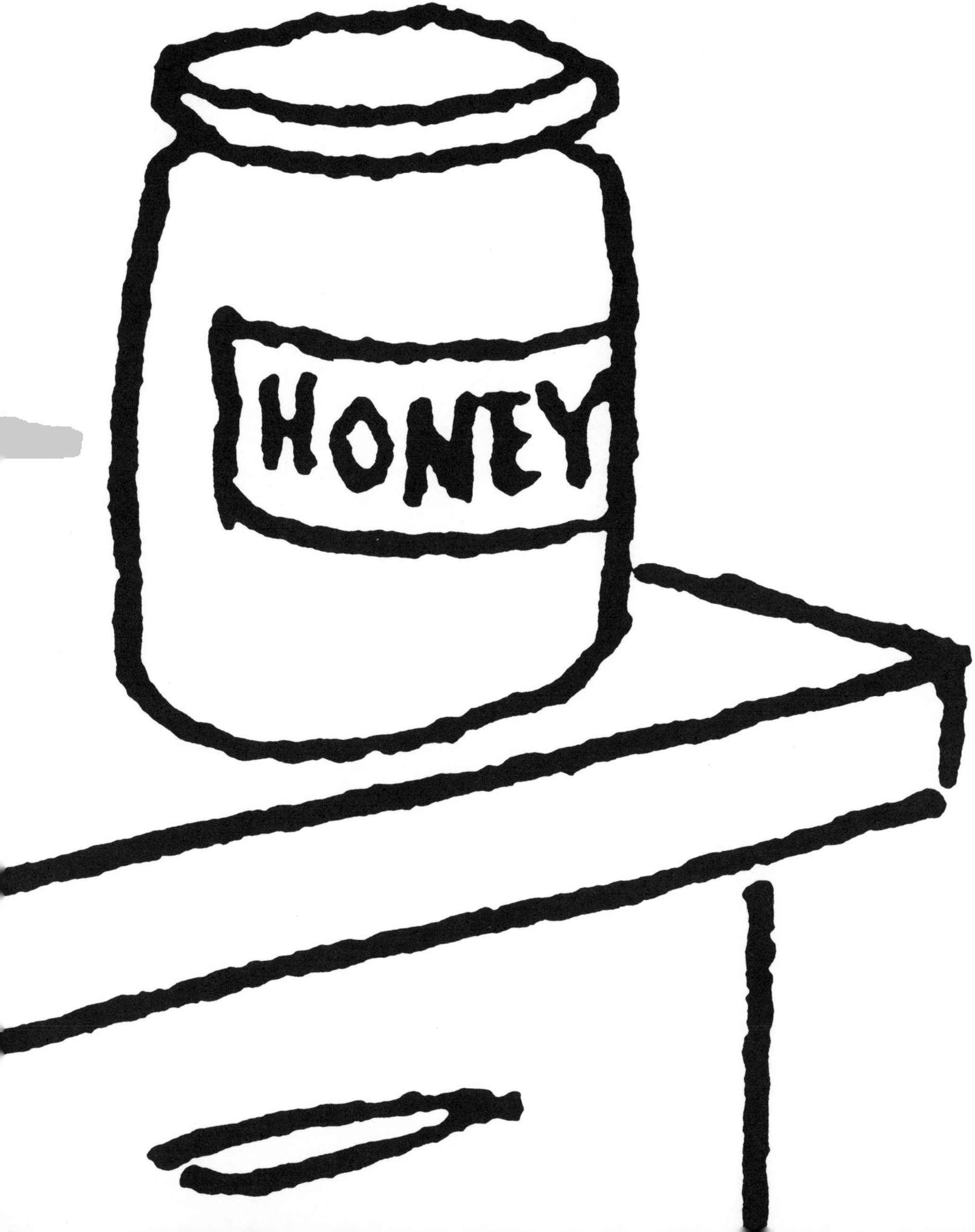
HONEY

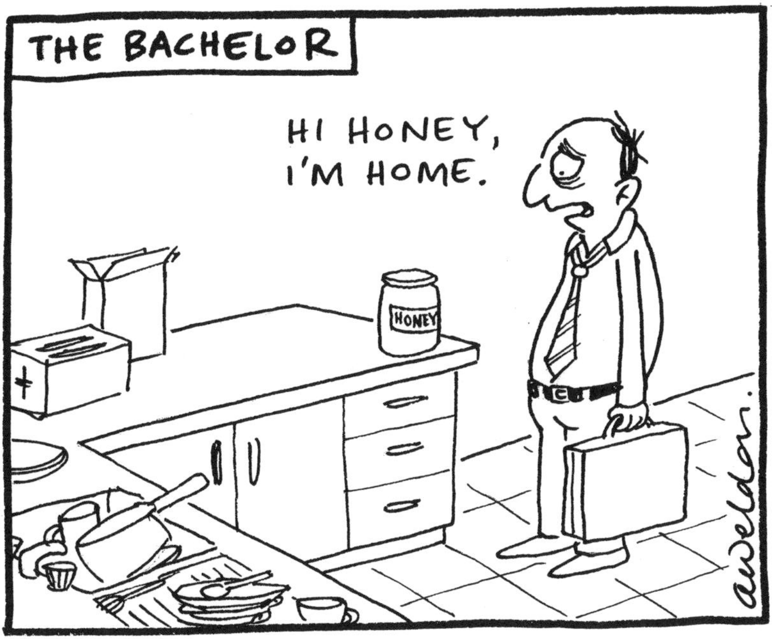
THE BACHELOR
HI HONEY,
I'M HOME.
HONEY
aweldon.

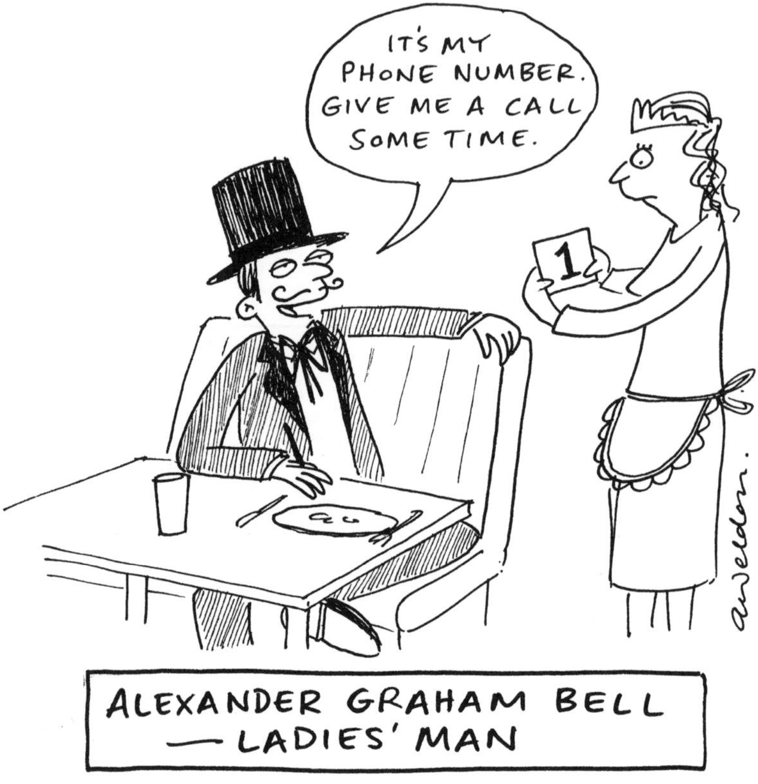
IT'S MY PHONE NUMBER. GIVE ME A CALL SOME TIME.
1
aweldon.

ALEXANDER GRAHAM BELL — LADIES' MAN

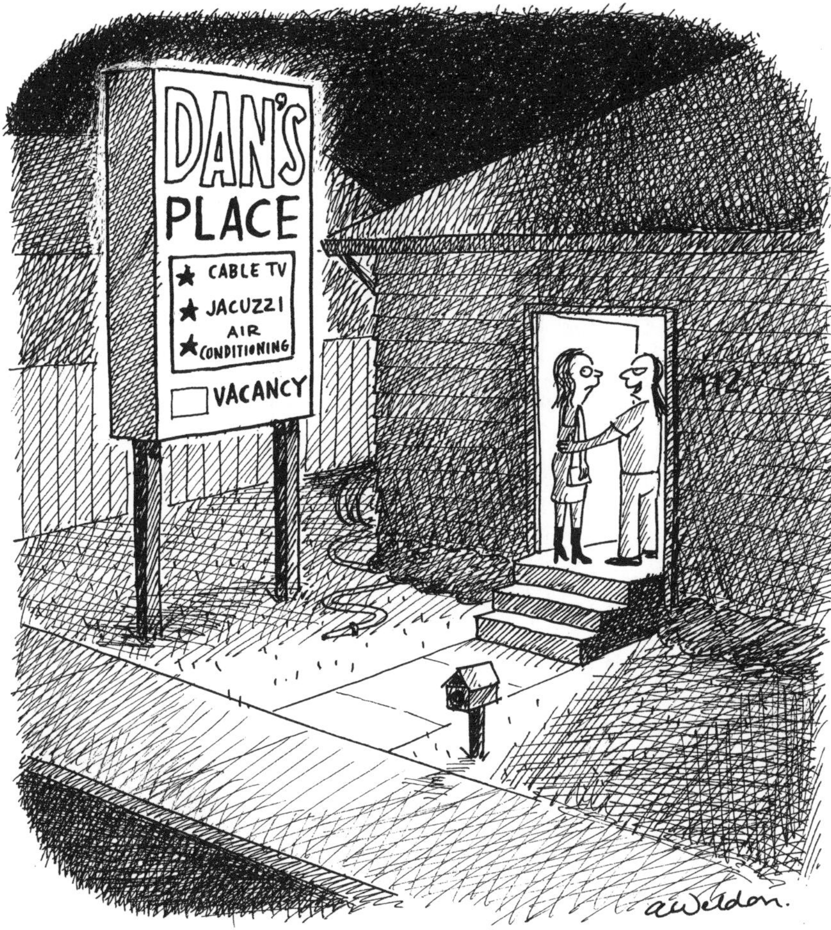
DAN'S
PLACE
CABLE TV
JACUZZI
AIR
CONDITIONING
VACANCY
112
a Weldon.

"YOU MAKE YOURSELF COMFORTABLE — I'VE JUST GOT TO CHANGE THE SIGN."

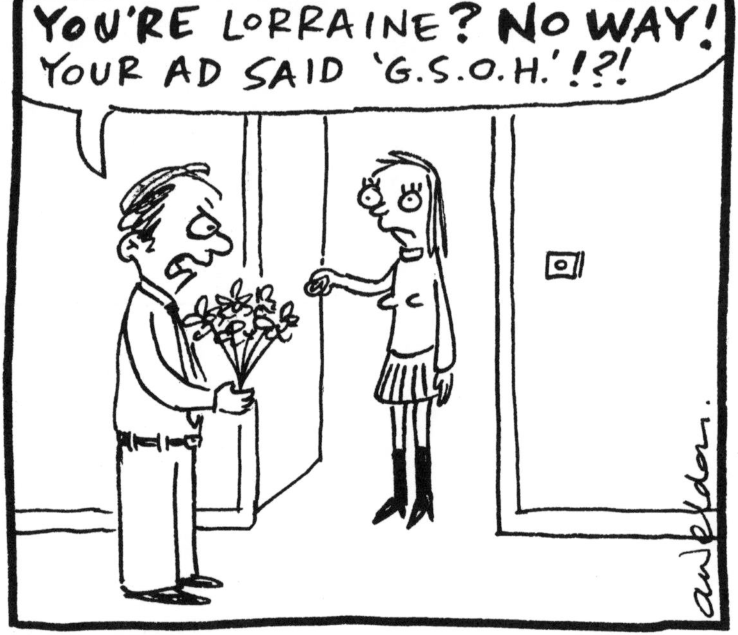
YOU'RE LORRAINE? NO WAY! YOUR AD SAID 'G.S.O.H.'!?!

IT TOOK DARREN FOUR DATES TO WORK OUT THAT 'G.S.O.H.' DID NOT STAND FOR 'GOOD SET OF HOOTERS.'

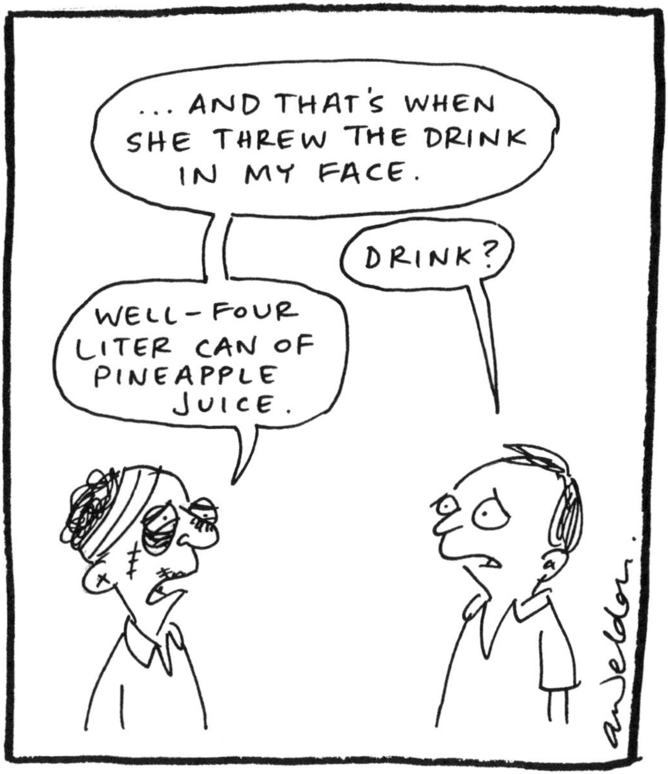
... AND THAT'S WHEN SHE THREW THE DRINK IN MY FACE.
DRINK?
WELL - FOUR LITER CAN OF PINEAPPLE JUICE.
aweldon.

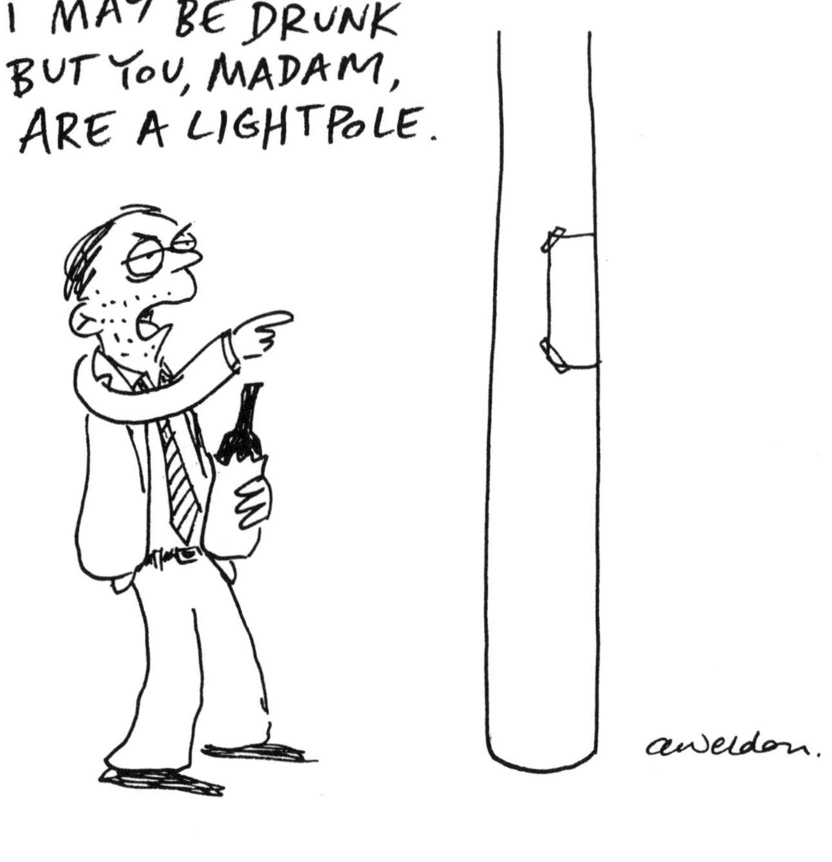
I MAY BE DRUNK
BUT YOU, MADAM,
ARE A LIGHTPOLE.
aweldon.

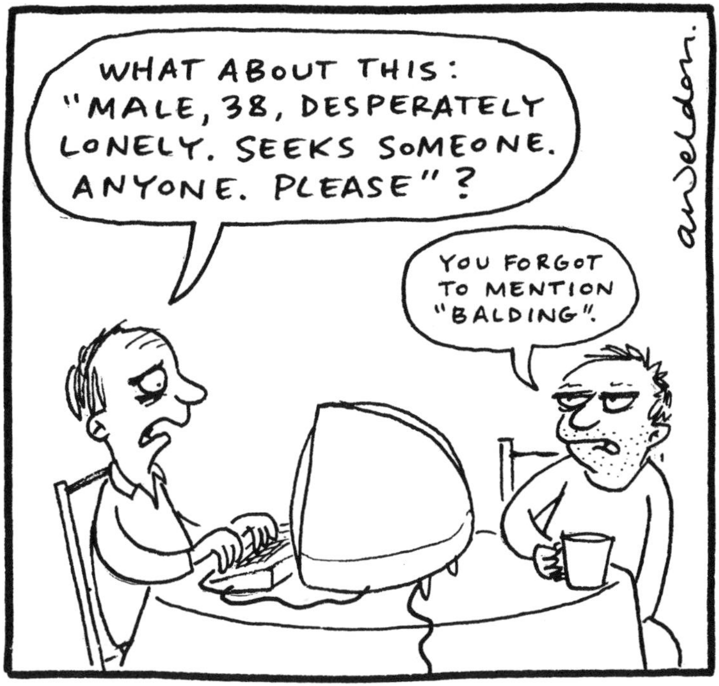
WHAT ABOUT THIS: "MALE, 38, DESPERATELY LONELY. SEEKS SOMEONE. ANYONE. PLEASE"?
YOU FORGOT TO MENTION "BALDING".
anweldon.

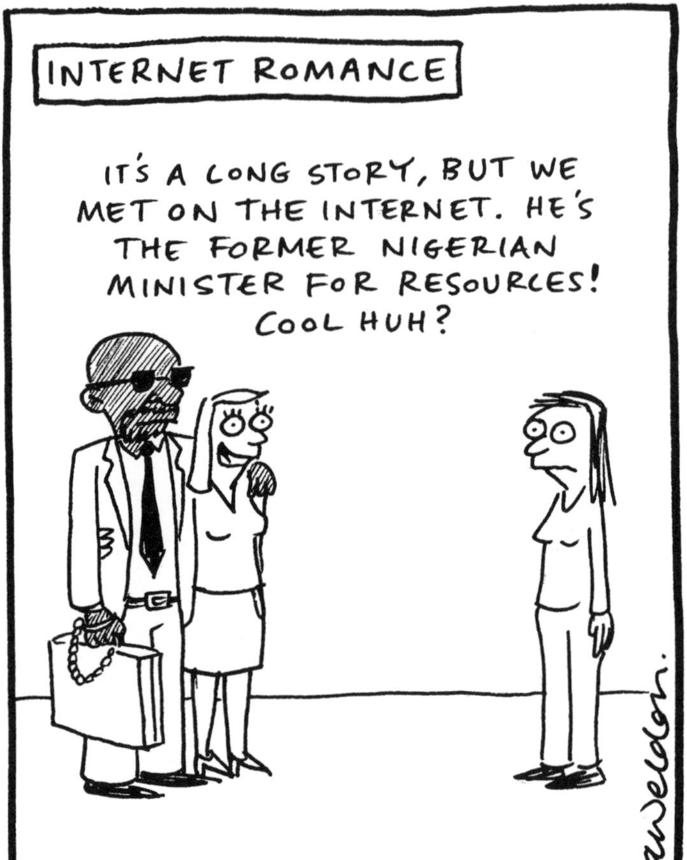
INTERNET ROMANCE
IT'S A LONG STORY, BUT WE MET ON THE INTERNET. HE'S THE FORMER NIGERIAN MINISTER FOR RESOURCES! COOL HUH?

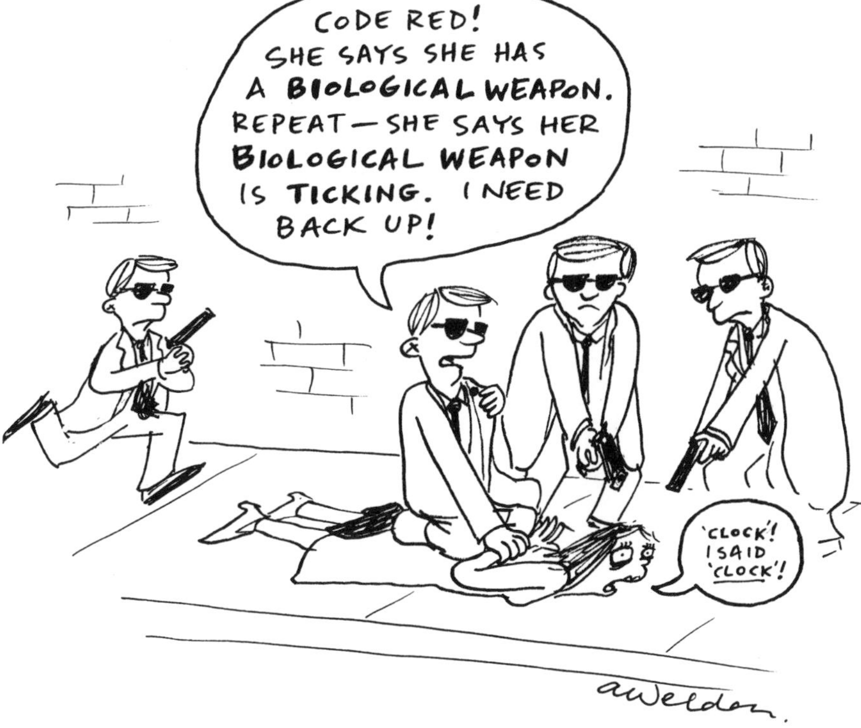
CODE RED! SHE SAYS SHE HAS A BIOLOGICAL WEAPON. REPEAT—SHE SAYS HER BIOLOGICAL WEAPON IS TICKING. I NEED BACK UP!
'CLOCK'! I SAID 'CLOCK'!
aWeldon.

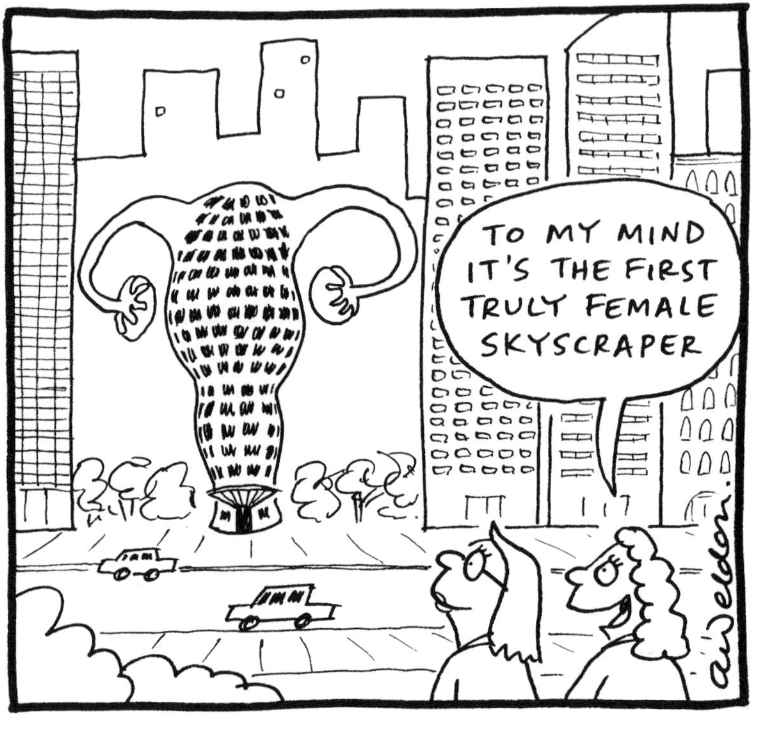
TO MY MIND IT'S THE FIRST TRULY FEMALE SKYSCRAPER
a weldon.

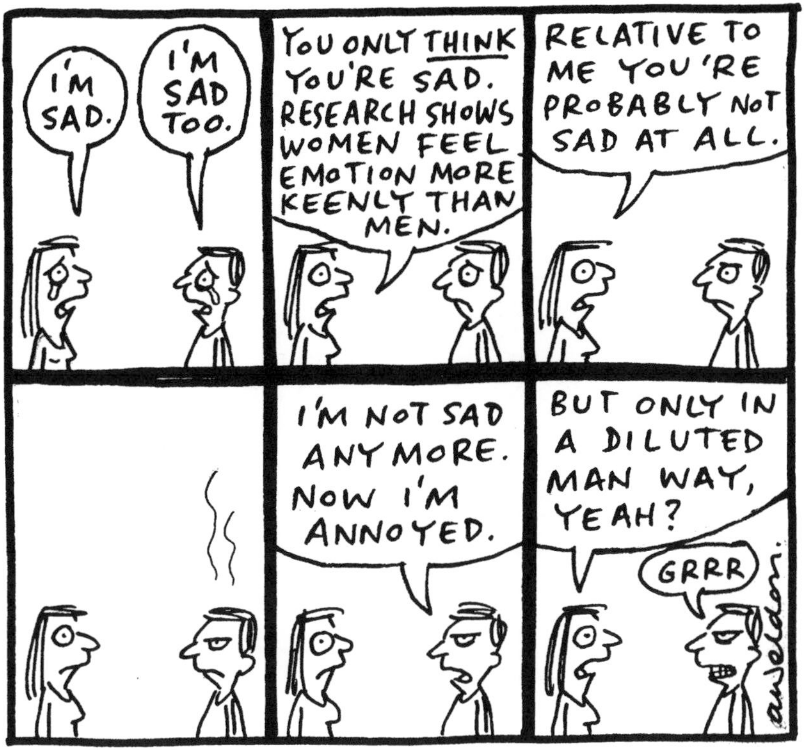
I'M SAD.
I'M SAD TOO.
YOU ONLY THINK YOU'RE SAD. RESEARCH SHOWS WOMEN FEEL EMOTION MORE KEENLY THAN MEN.
RELATIVE TO ME YOU'RE PROBABLY NOT SAD AT ALL.
I'M NOT SAD ANYMORE. NOW I'M ANNOYED.
BUT ONLY IN A DILUTED MAN WAY, YEAH?
GRRR
aweldon.

YEAH LOOK, I CAN'T TALK NOW
— I'VE GOT MY LEG CAUGHT
IN THE SHREDDER.

"I DON'T CARE HOW 'ERGONOMIC' IT IS!"

I'M GLAD YOU COULD ALL MAKE IT TO THE MEETING HERE THIS MORNING – IT GIVES MY SECRETARY A CHANCE TO RIFLE THROUGH YOUR DESKS.

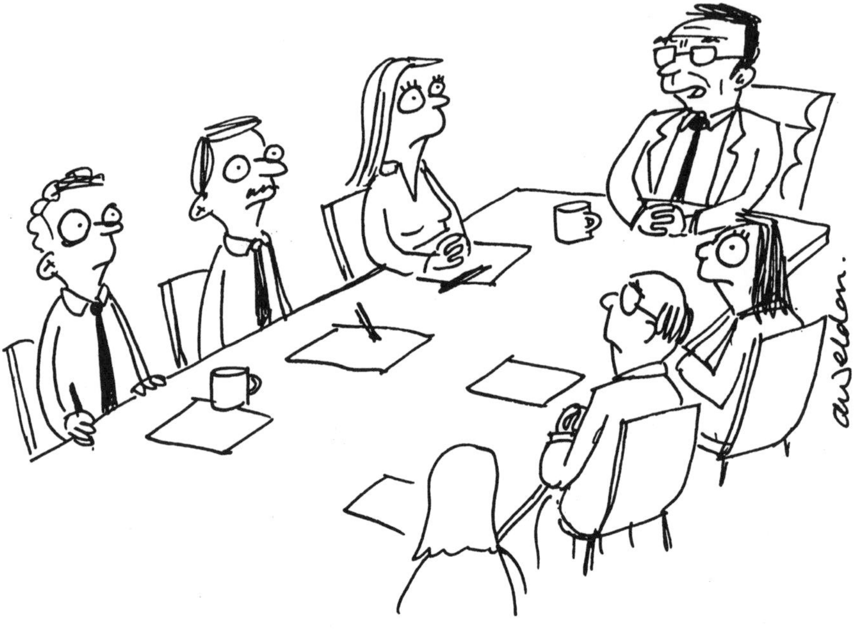

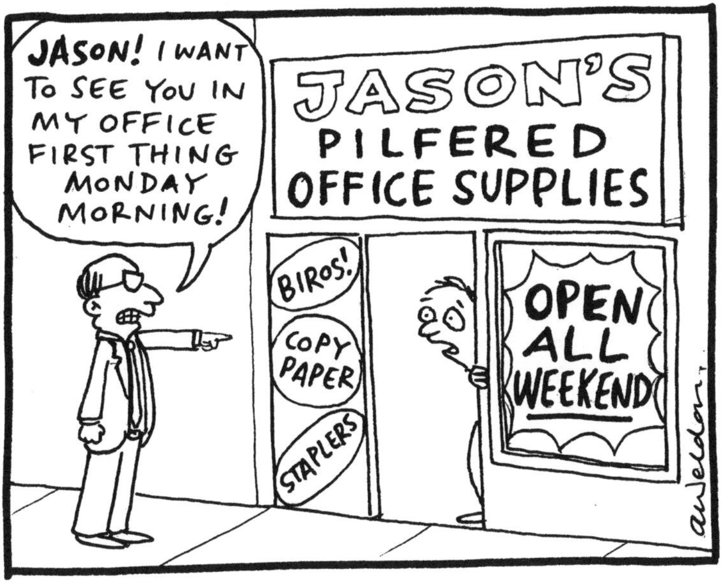
JASON! I WANT TO SEE YOU IN MY OFFICE FIRST THING MONDAY MORNING!
JASON'S
PILFERED
OFFICE SUPPLIES
BIROS!
COPY PAPER
STAPLERS
OPEN ALL WEEKEND
aweldon

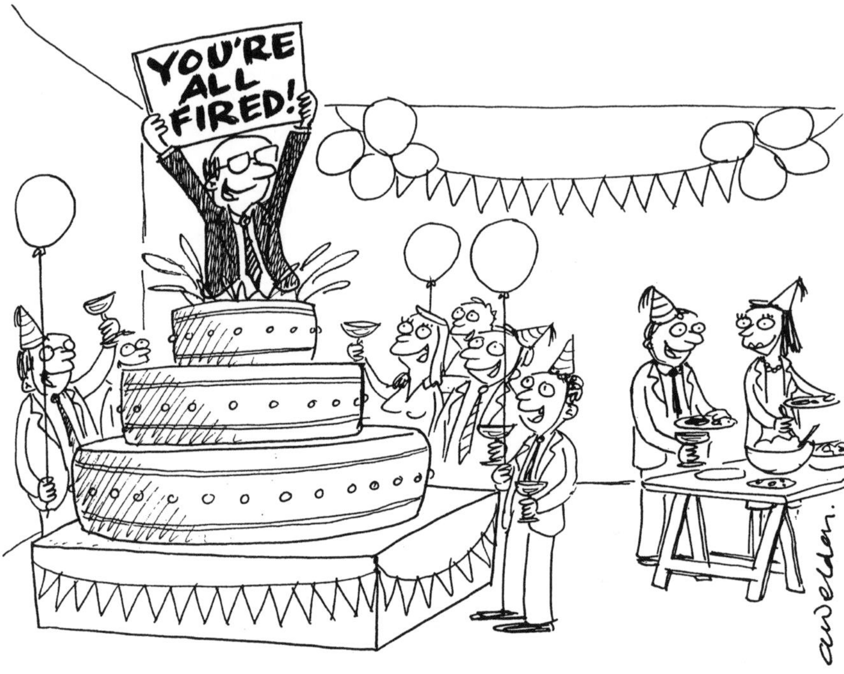
YOU'RE ALL FIRED!
awelden.

"THEY DO A GREAT RETRENCHMENT HERE."

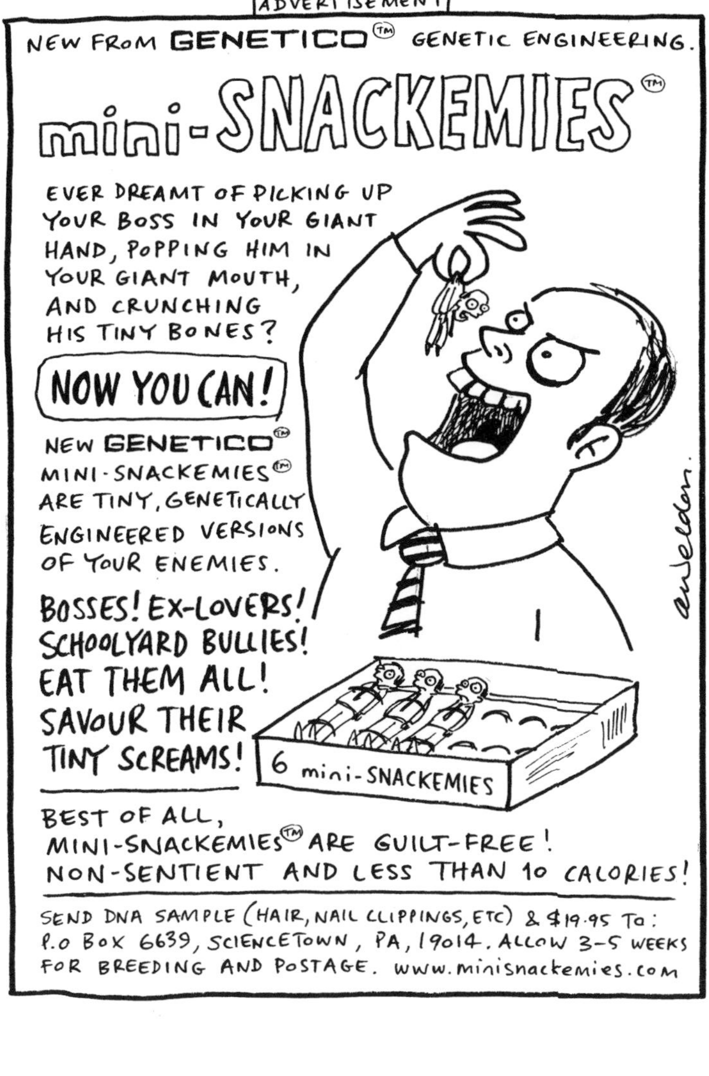
ADVERTISEMENT
NEW FROM GENETICO(TM) GENETIC ENGINEERING.
mini-SNACKEMIES(TM)
EVER DREAMT OF PICKING UP YOUR BOSS IN YOUR GIANT HAND, POPPING HIM IN YOUR GIANT MOUTH, AND CRUNCHING HIS TINY BONES?
NOW YOU CAN!
NEW GENETICO(TM) MINI-SNACKEMIES(TM) ARE TINY, GENETICALLY ENGINEERED VERSIONS OF YOUR ENEMIES.
BOSSES! EX-LOVERS! SCHOOLYARD BULLIES! EAT THEM ALL! SAVOUR THEIR TINY SCREAMS!
6 mini-SNACKEMIES
BEST OF ALL, MINI-SNACKEMIES(TM) ARE GUILT-FREE! NON-SENTIENT AND LESS THAN 10 CALORIES!
SEND DNA SAMPLE (HAIR, NAIL CLIPPINGS, ETC) & $19.95 TO: P.O BOX 6639, SCIENCETOWN, PA, 19014. ALLOW 3-5 WEEKS FOR BREEDING AND POSTAGE. www.minisnackemies.com
aweldon.

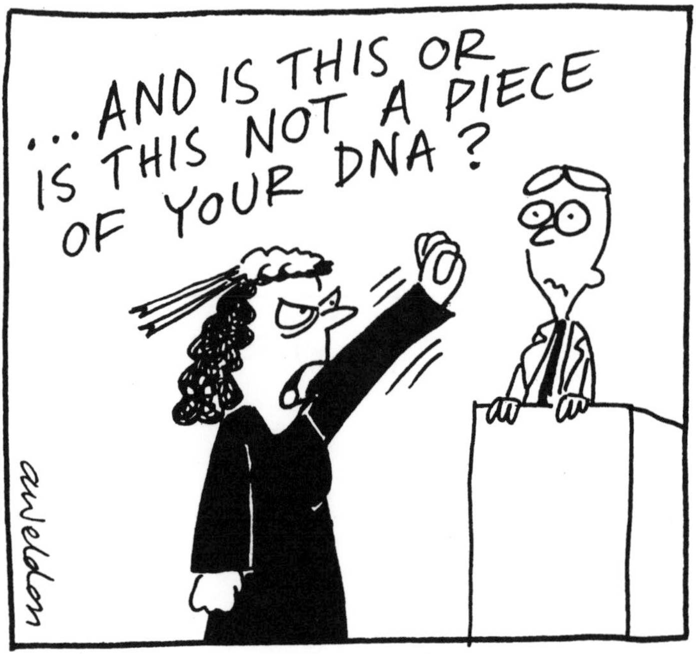
... AND IS THIS OR IS THIS NOT A PIECE OF YOUR DNA?
aweldon

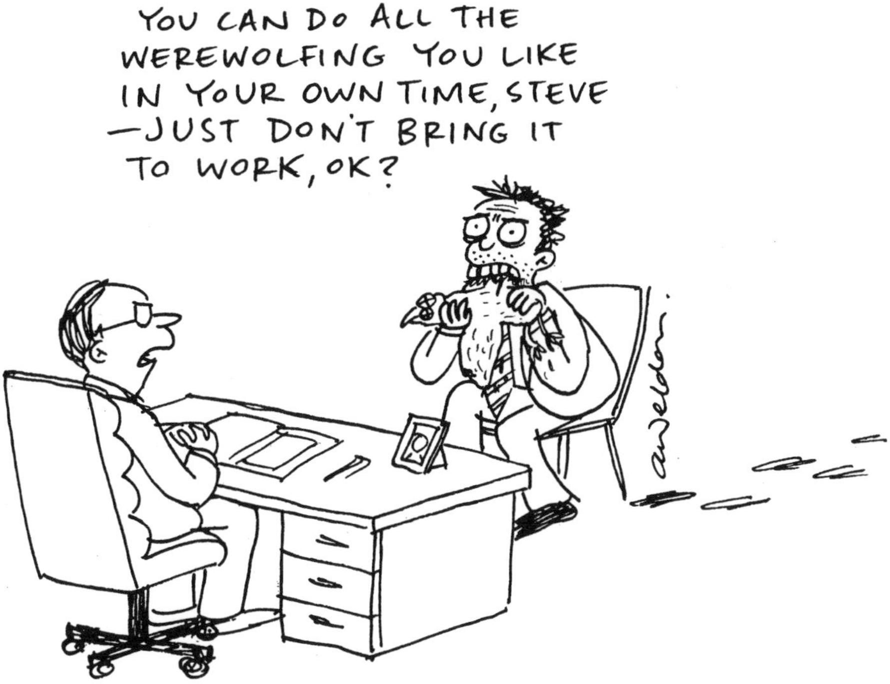
YOU CAN DO ALL THE WEREWOLFING YOU LIKE IN YOUR OWN TIME, STEVE —JUST DON'T BRING IT TO WORK, OK?

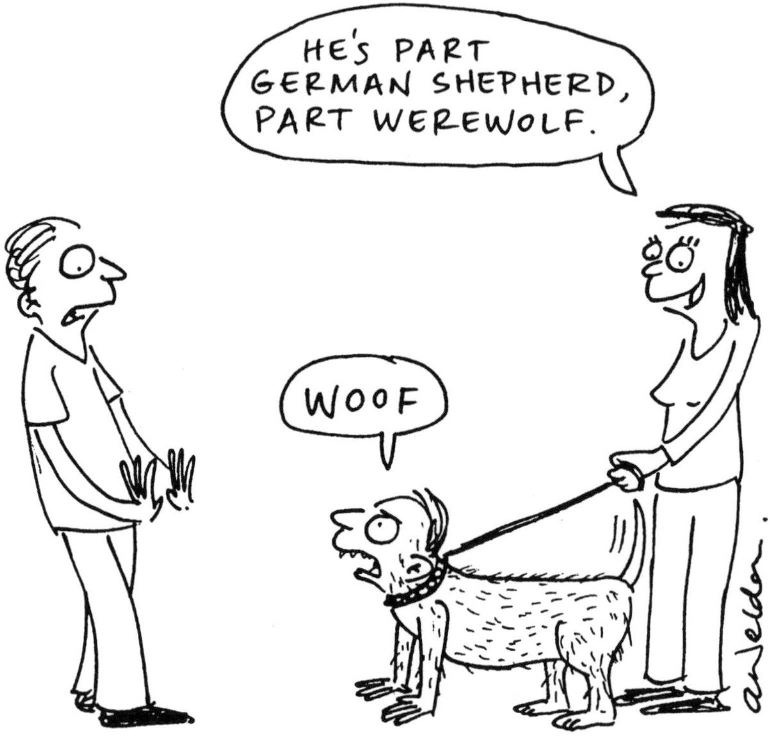
HE'S PART GERMAN SHEPHERD, PART WEREWOLF.
WOOF

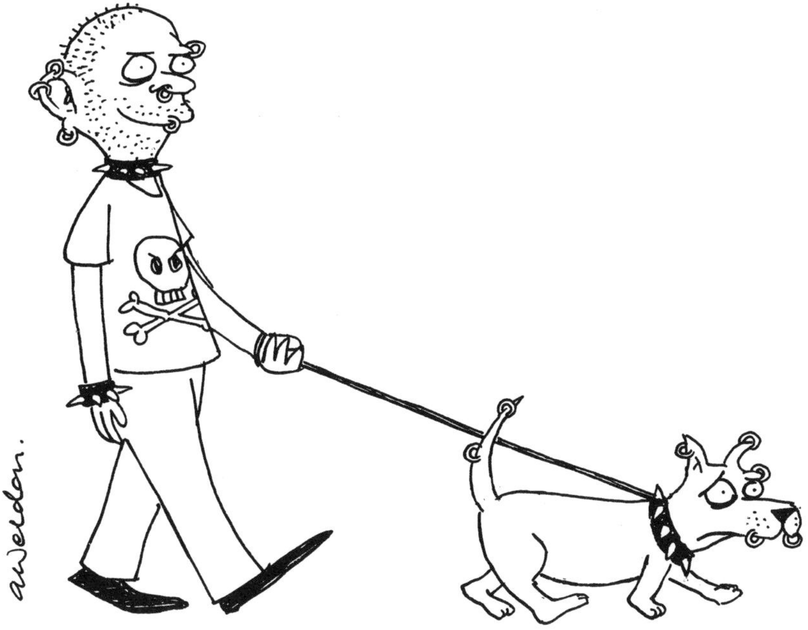
aweldon.

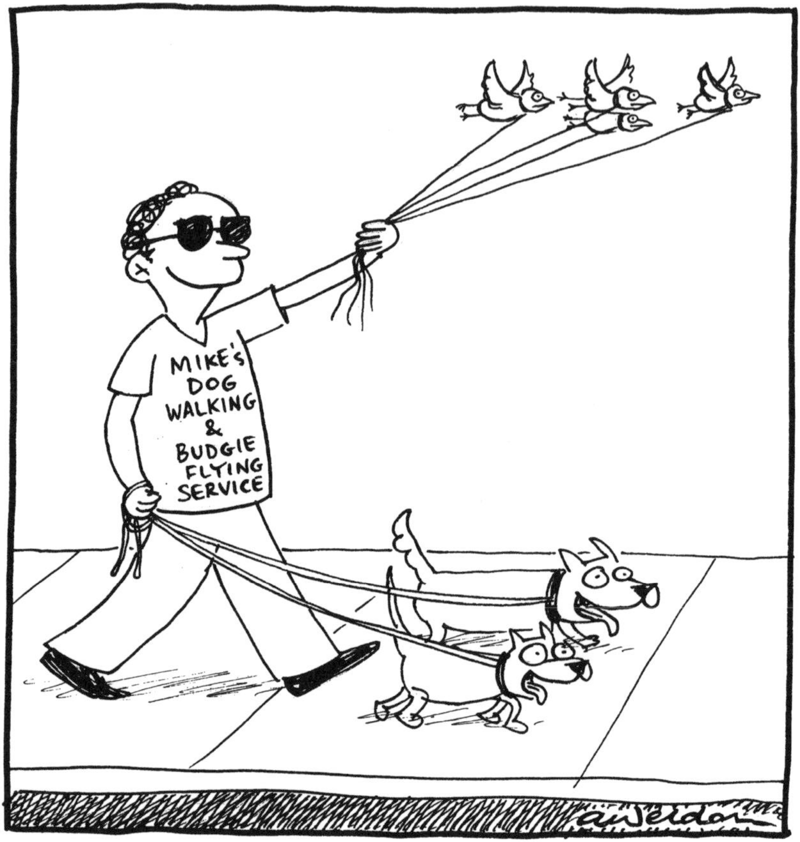
MIKE'S
DOG
WALKING
&
BUDGIE
FLYING
SERVICE

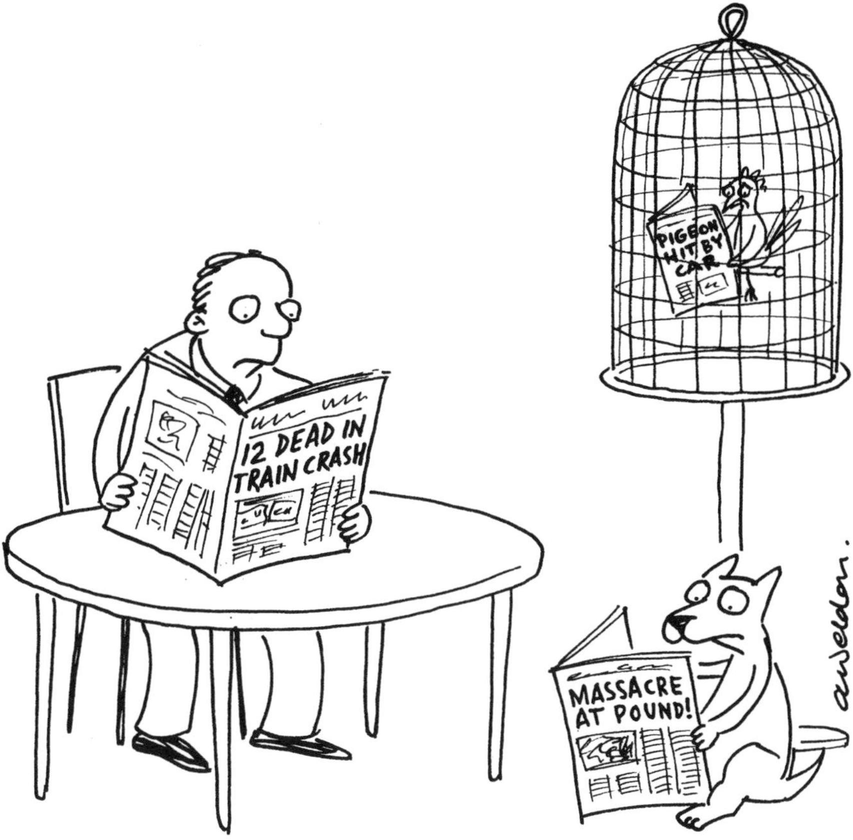
12 DEAD IN TRAIN CRASH
PIGEON HIT BY CAR
MASSACRE AT POUND!
aweldon.

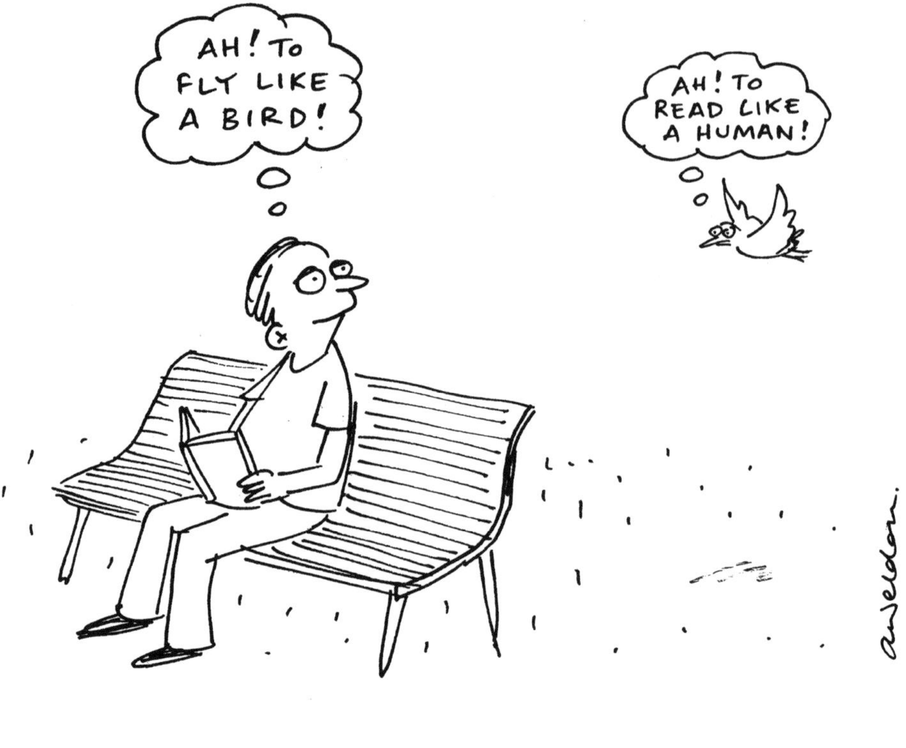
AH! TO FLY LIKE A BIRD!
AH! TO READ LIKE A HUMAN!
aweldon

BIRDVEND - The World's First Vending Machine For Birds.

INSERT SHINY THING HERE

BIRDVEND

⌂ SEED

⤬ TWIGS

CUTTLE-FISH

∿ WORM

BEETLE

GRUB

PECK SELECTED BUTTON

COLLECT ITEM HERE

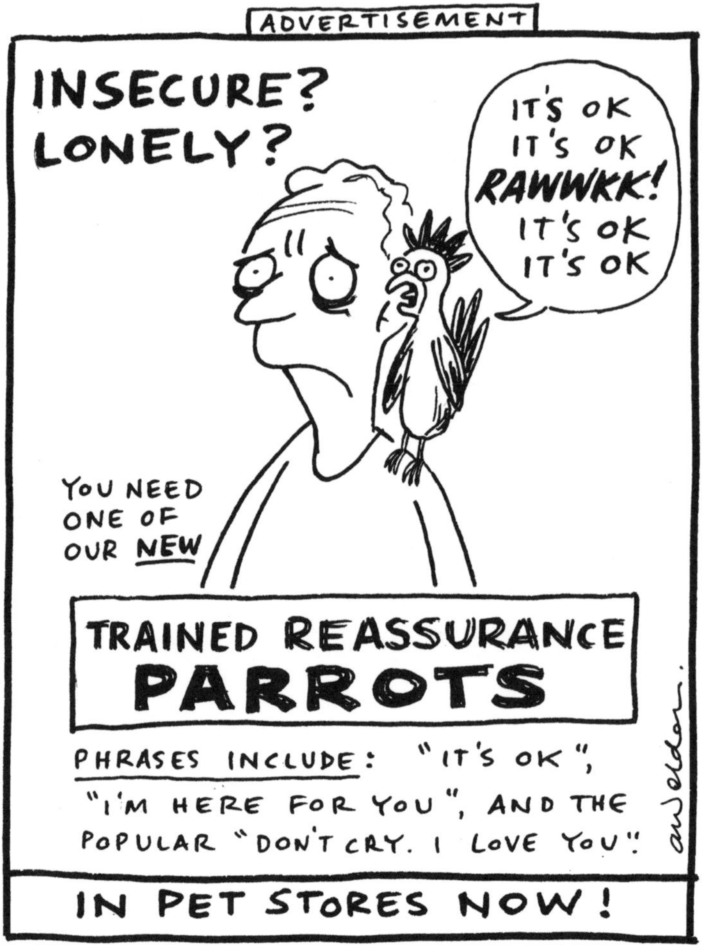
ADVERTISEMENT
INSECURE? LONELY?
IT'S OK IT'S OK RAWWKK! IT'S OK IT'S OK
YOU NEED ONE OF OUR NEW
TRAINED REASSURANCE PARROTS
PHRASES INCLUDE: "IT'S OK", "I'M HERE FOR YOU", AND THE POPULAR "DON'T CRY. I LOVE YOU".
IN PET STORES NOW!
aweldon.

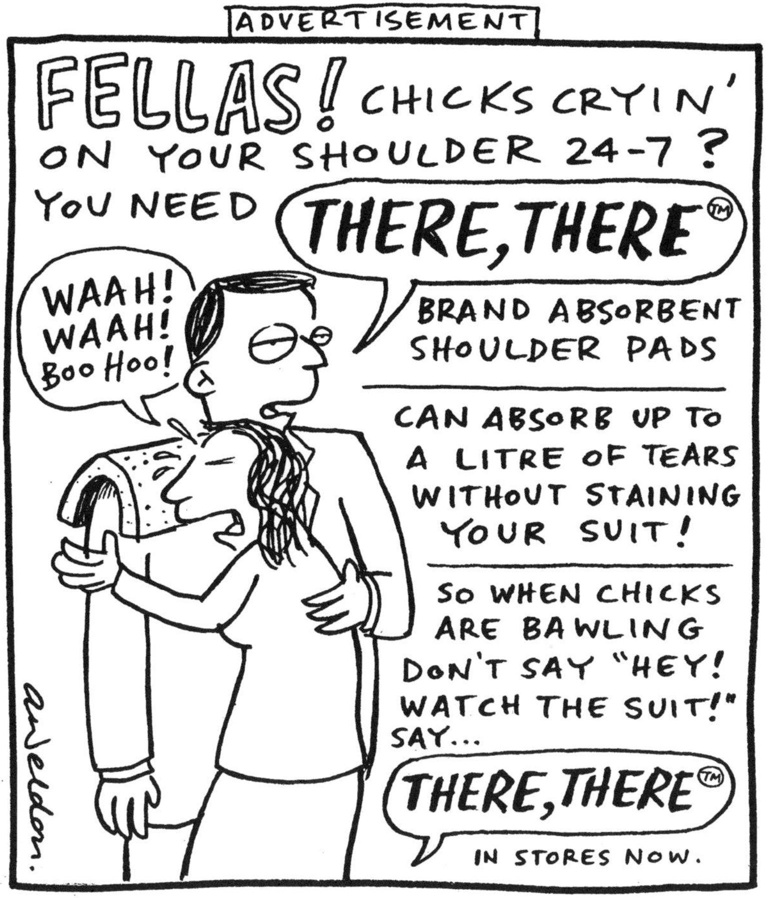
ADVERTISEMENT
FELLAS! CHICKS CRYIN' ON YOUR SHOULDER 24-7?
YOU NEED
THERE, THERE™
WAAH! WAAH! BOO HOO!
BRAND ABSORBENT SHOULDER PADS
CAN ABSORB UP TO A LITRE OF TEARS WITHOUT STAINING YOUR SUIT!
SO WHEN CHICKS ARE BAWLING DON'T SAY "HEY! WATCH THE SUIT!" SAY...
THERE, THERE™
IN STORES NOW.
aWeldon.

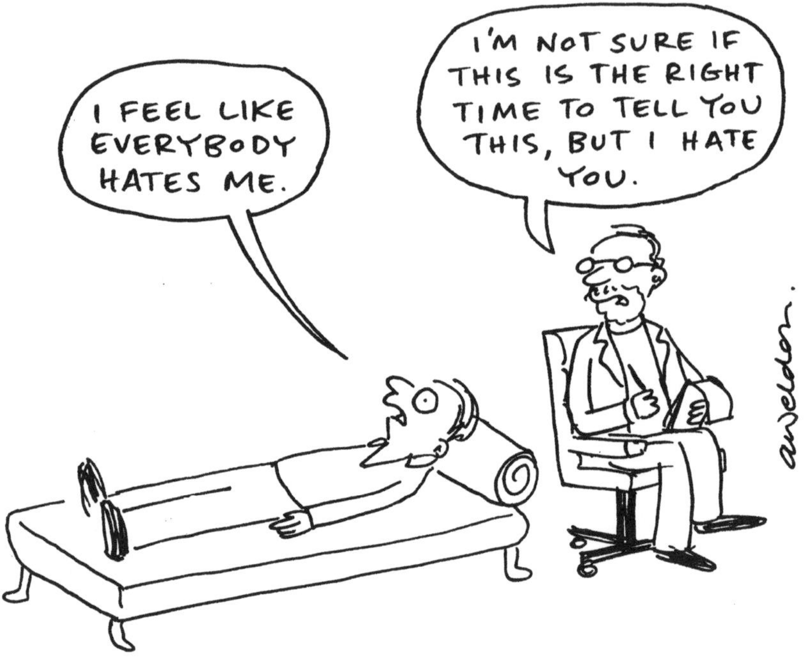
I FEEL LIKE EVERYBODY HATES ME.
I'M NOT SURE IF THIS IS THE RIGHT TIME TO TELL YOU THIS, BUT I HATE YOU.
aweldon.

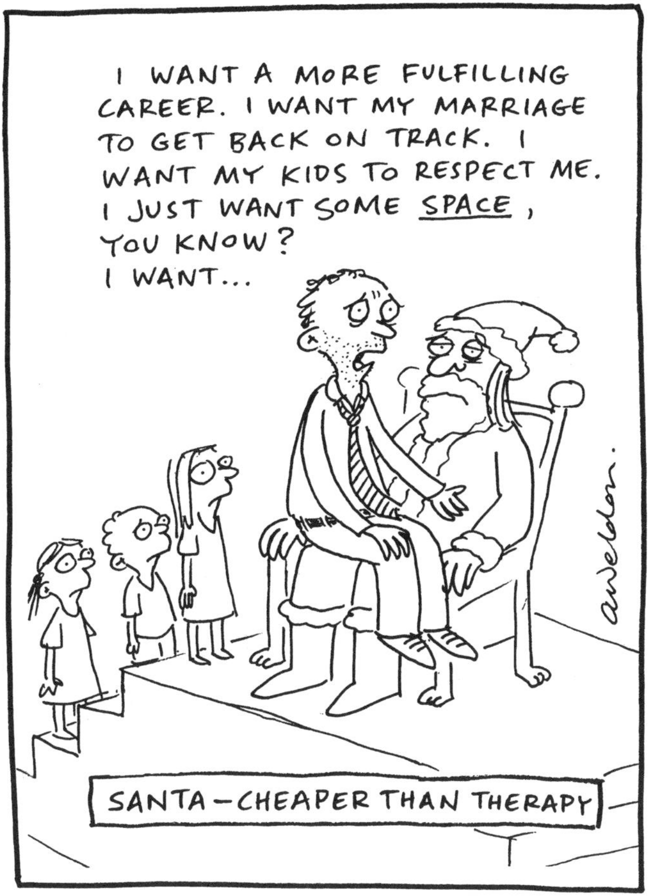
I WANT A MORE FULFILLING CAREER. I WANT MY MARRIAGE TO GET BACK ON TRACK. I WANT MY KIDS TO RESPECT ME. I JUST WANT SOME SPACE, YOU KNOW? I WANT...
SANTA—CHEAPER THAN THERAPY
aweldon.

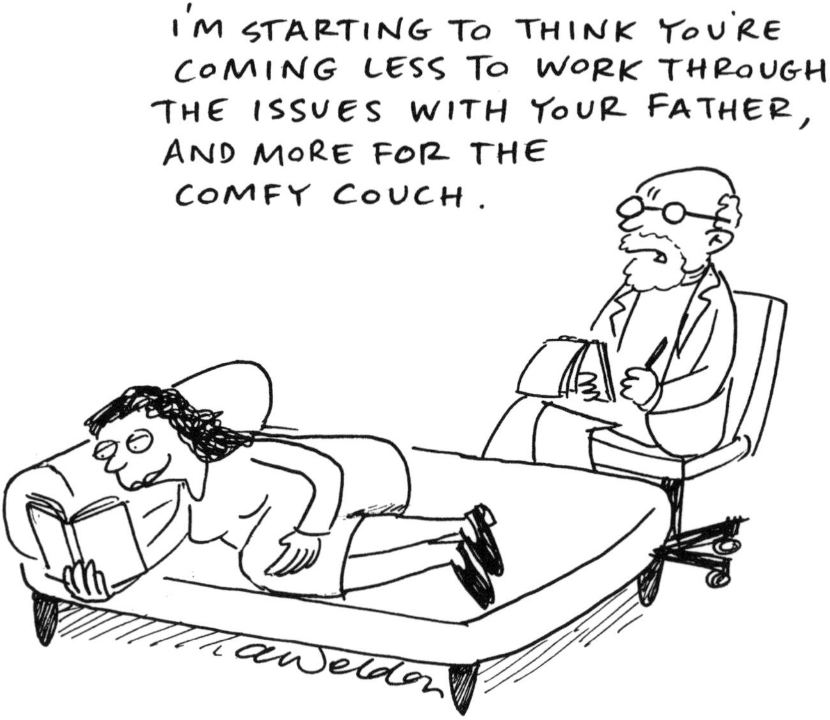
I'M STARTING TO THINK YOU'RE COMING LESS TO WORK THROUGH THE ISSUES WITH YOUR FATHER, AND MORE FOR THE COMFY COUCH.
aWeldon

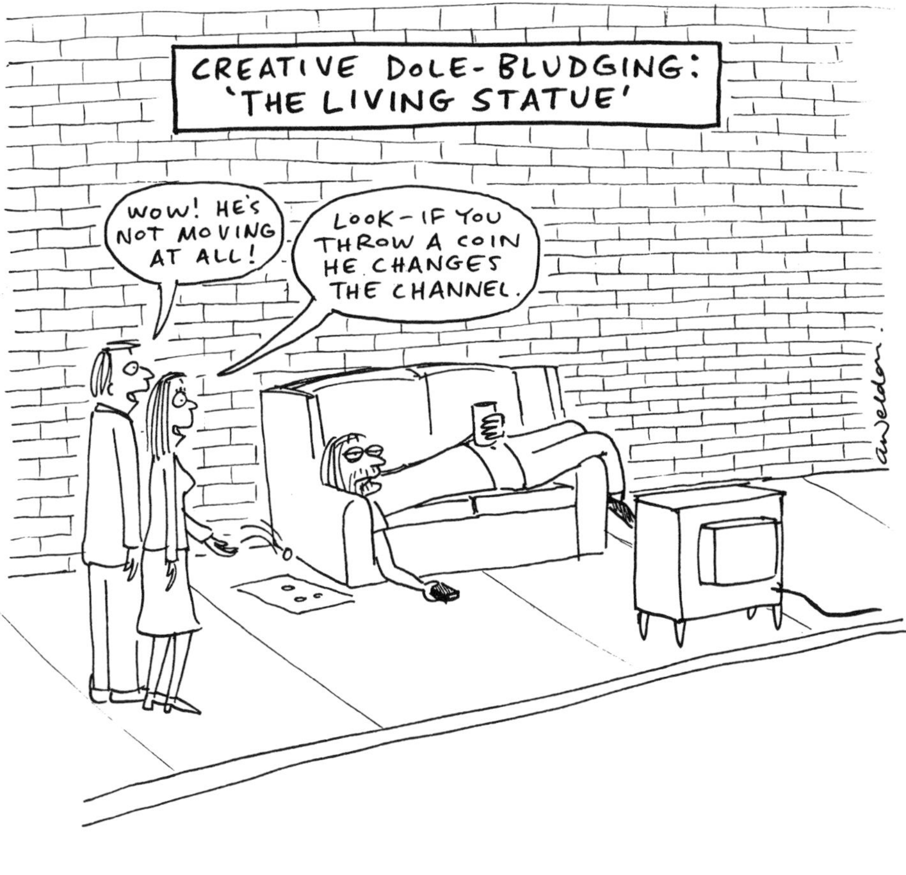
CREATIVE DOLE-BLUDGING: 'THE LIVING STATUE'
WOW! HE'S NOT MOVING AT ALL!
LOOK - IF YOU THROW A COIN HE CHANGES THE CHANNEL.
aweldon.

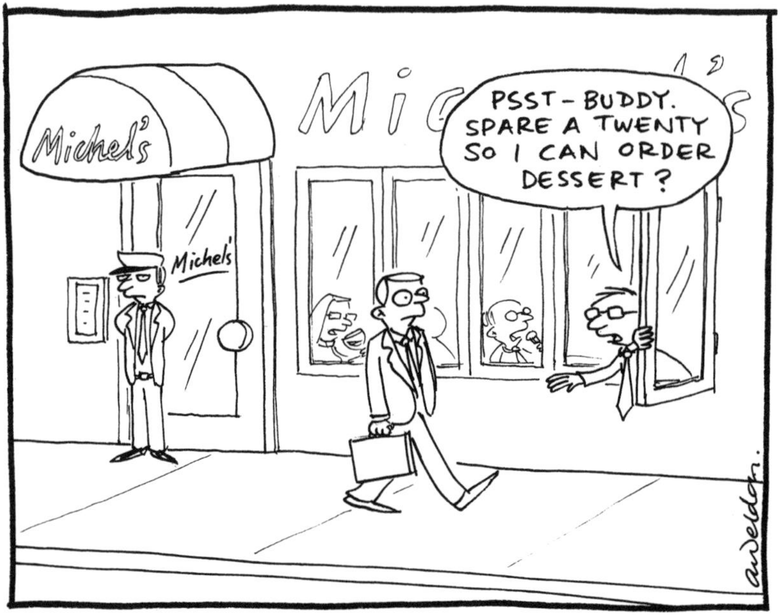
Michel's
Michel's
Michel's
PSST - BUDDY. SPARE A TWENTY SO I CAN ORDER DESSERT?
aweldon.

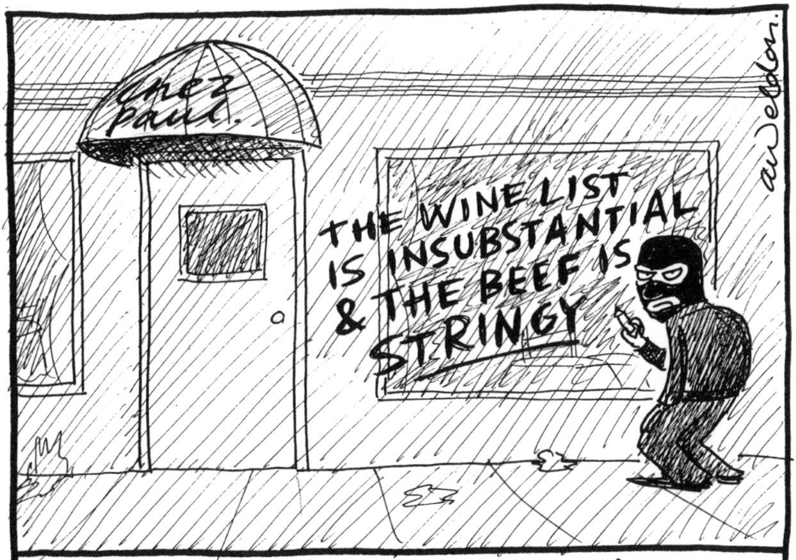
chez paul.
THE WINE LIST IS INSUBSTANTIAL & THE BEEF IS STRINGY
a weldon.
UNEMPLOYED RESTAURANT CRITIC GRAFFITI.

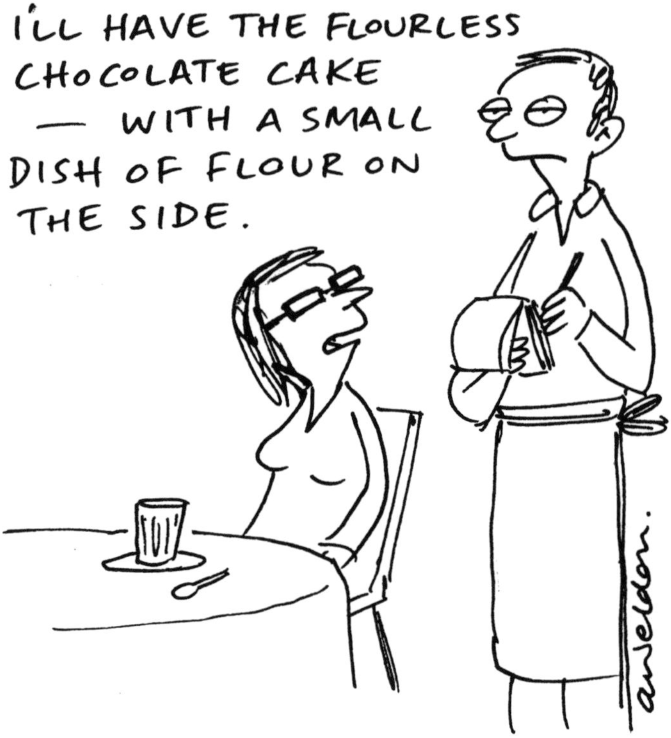
I'LL HAVE THE FLOURLESS CHOCOLATE CAKE — WITH A SMALL DISH OF FLOUR ON THE SIDE.

SPECIALS
NOT THAT GOOD
MENU
MENU
aweldon.

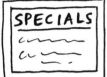

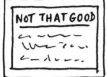

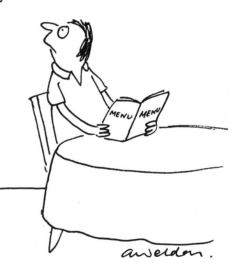

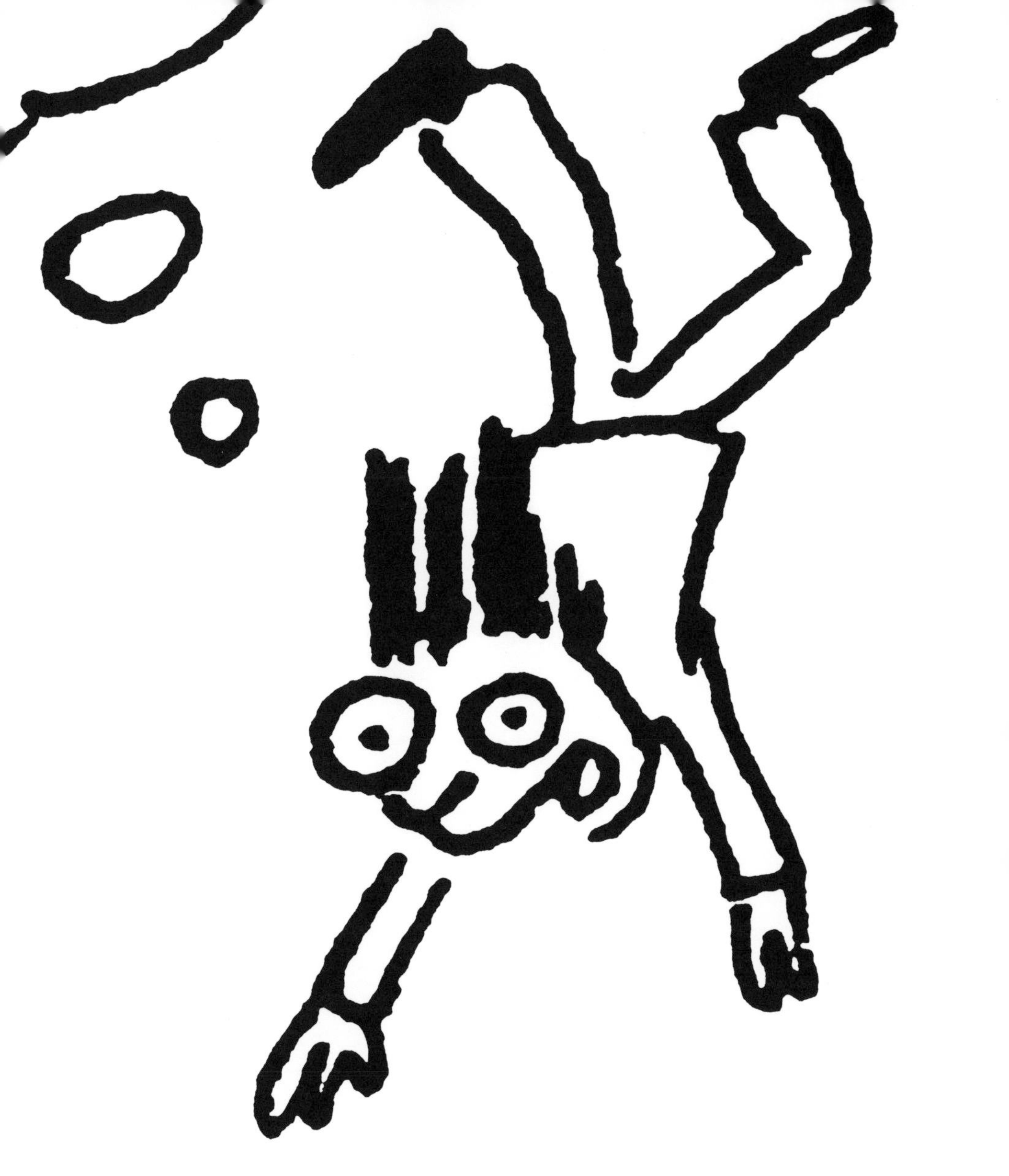

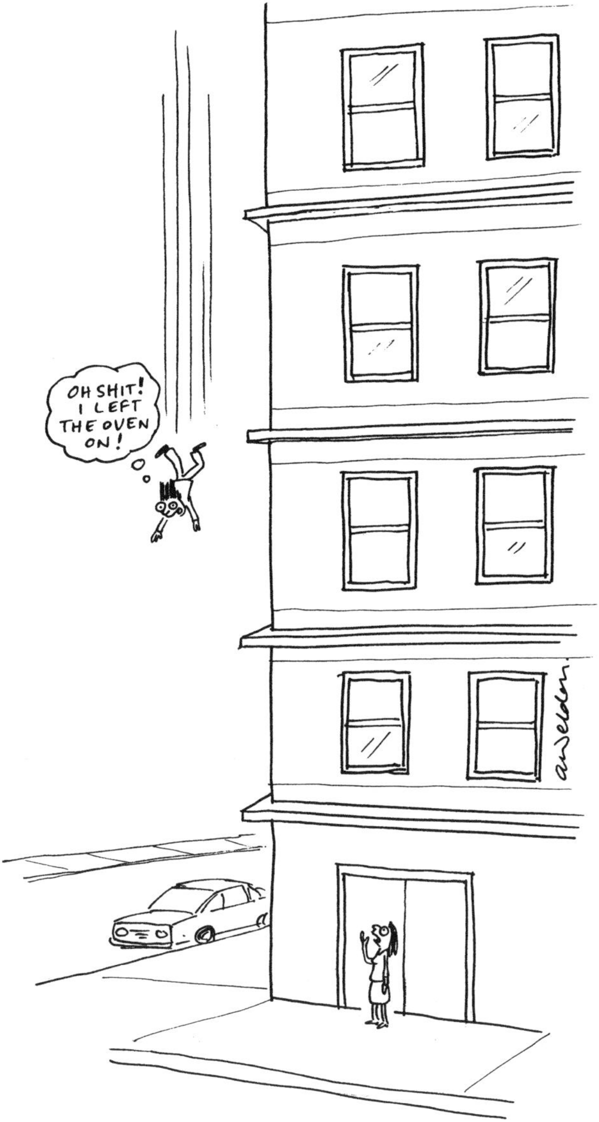
OH SHIT! I LEFT THE OVEN ON!
anselden

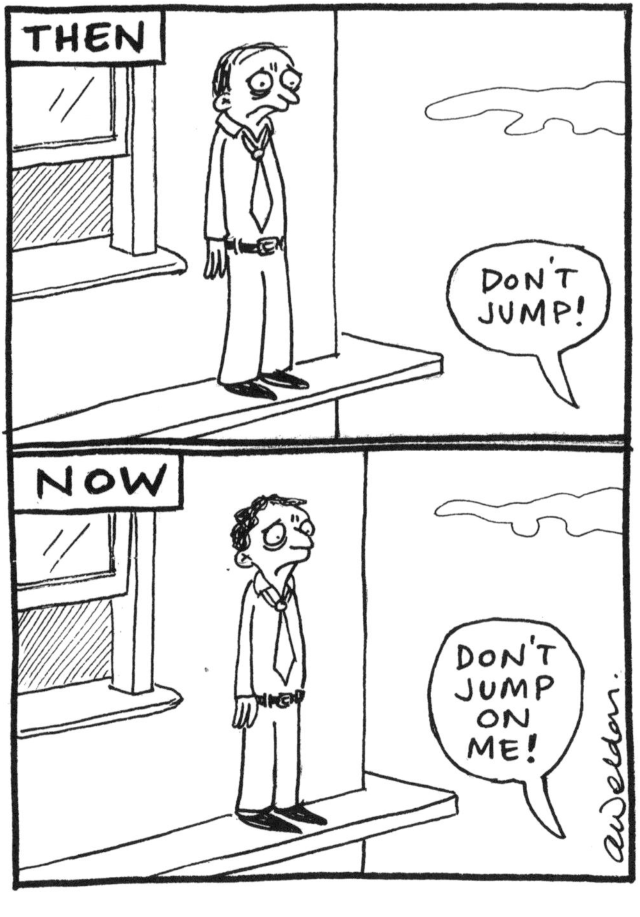
THEN
DON'T JUMP!
NOW
DON'T JUMP ON ME!
aWeldon

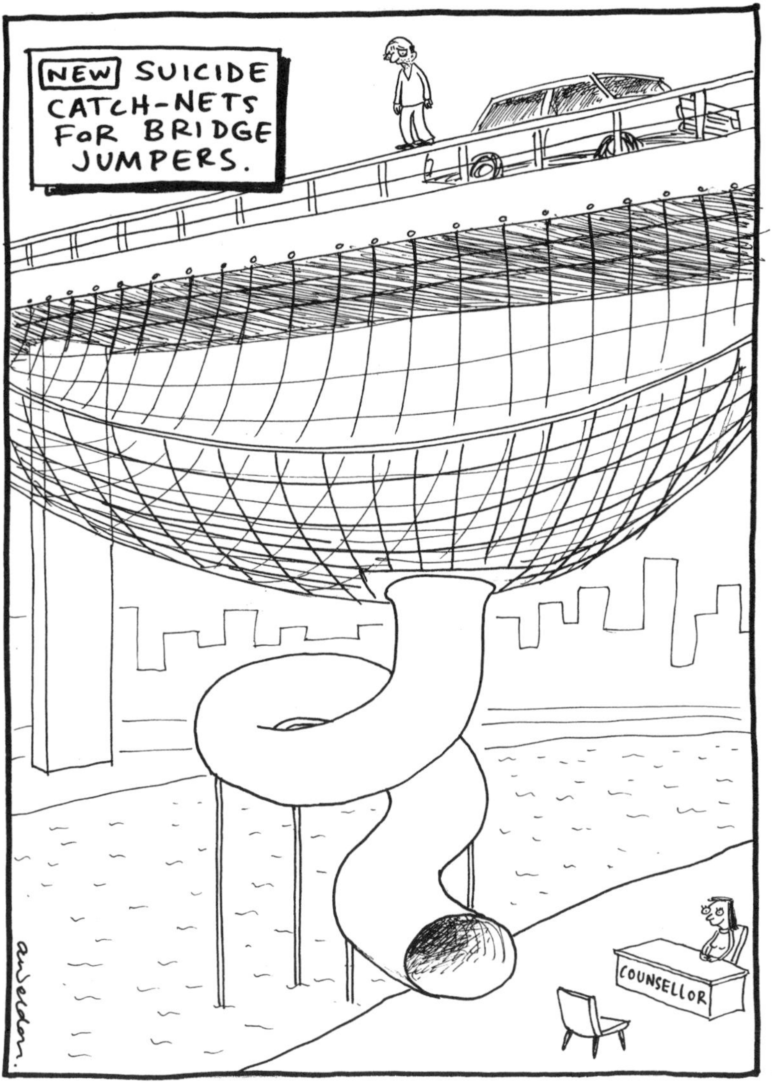
NEW SUICIDE CATCH-NETS FoR BRIDGE JUMPERS.
COUNSELLOR
aWeldon.

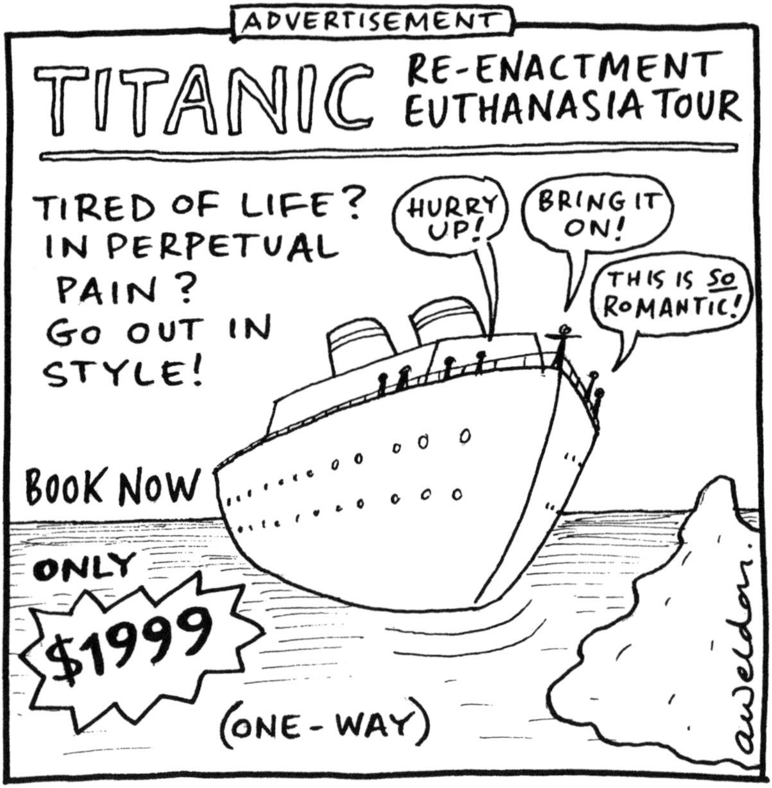
ADVERTISEMENT
TITANIC RE-ENACTMENT EUTHANASIA TOUR
TIRED OF LIFE? IN PERPETUAL PAIN? GO OUT IN STYLE!
HURRY UP!
BRING IT ON!
THIS IS SO ROMANTIC!
BOOK NOW
ONLY
$1999
(ONE-WAY)
aweldon.

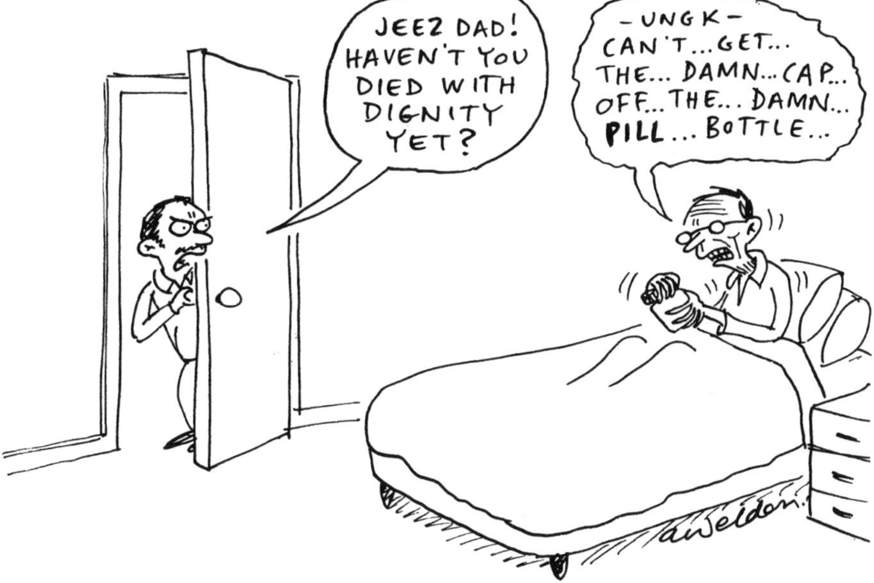
JEEZ DAD! HAVEN'T YOU DIED WITH DIGNITY YET?
-UNGK- CAN'T...GET... THE... DAMN...CAP... OFF...THE... DAMN... PILL... BOTTLE...
a weldon

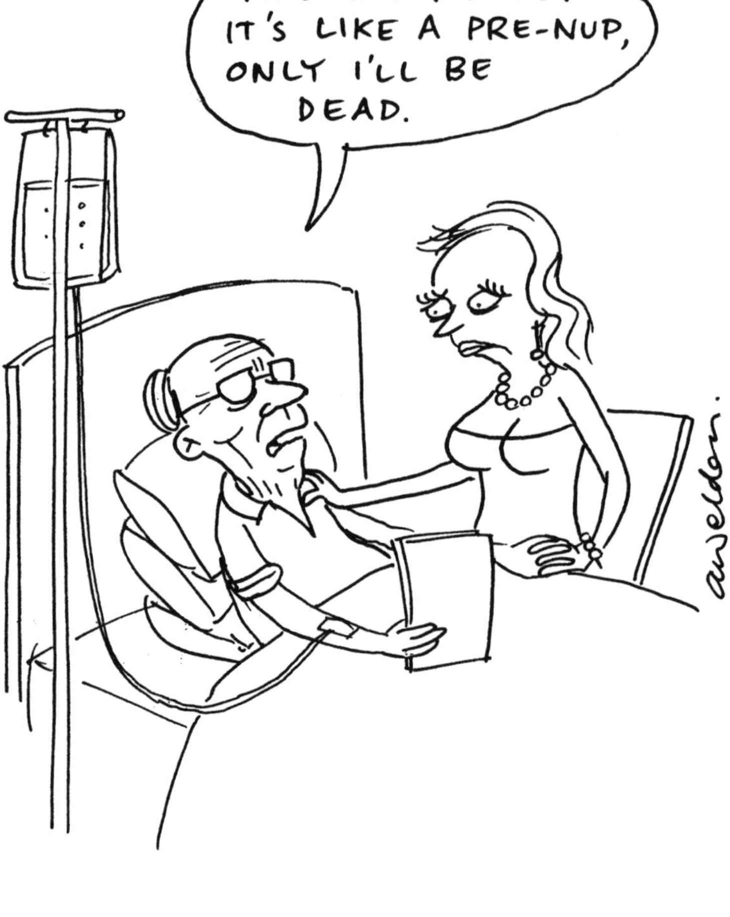
THIS IS MY WILL. IT'S LIKE A PRE-NUP, ONLY I'LL BE DEAD.
aweldon

IN ACCORDANCE
WITH HIS WISHES
BRIAN HAS BEEN CREMATED,
PATTED ON GOAT'S CHEESE,
AND NOW SERVED ON CRACKERS
TO LOVED ONES.

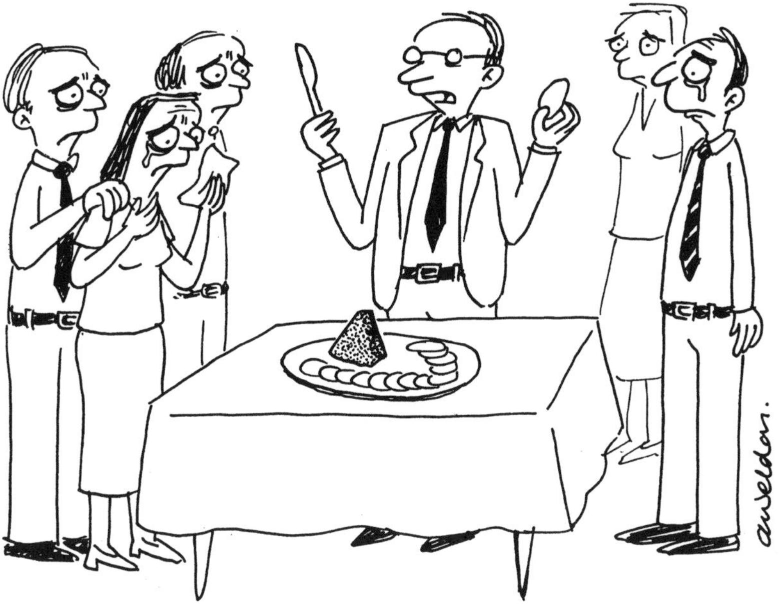
aweldon.

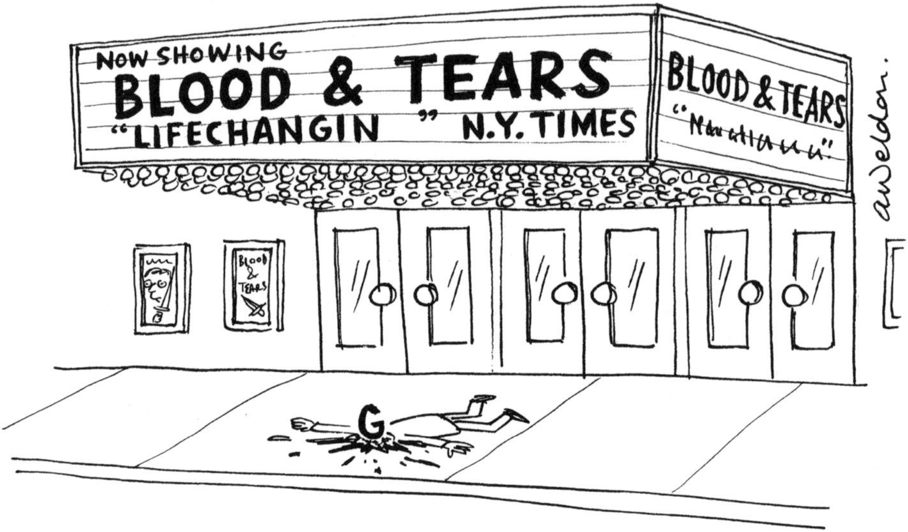
NOW SHOWING
BLOOD & TEARS
"LIFECHANGIN " N.Y. TIMES
BLOOD & TEARS
BLOOD & TEARS
G
aweldon.

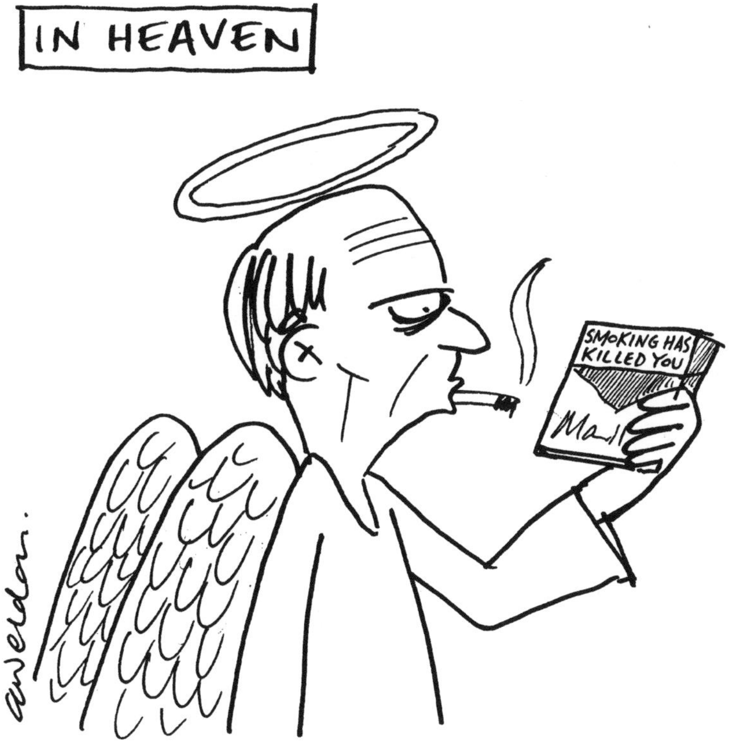
IN HEAVEN
SMOKING HAS KILLED YOU

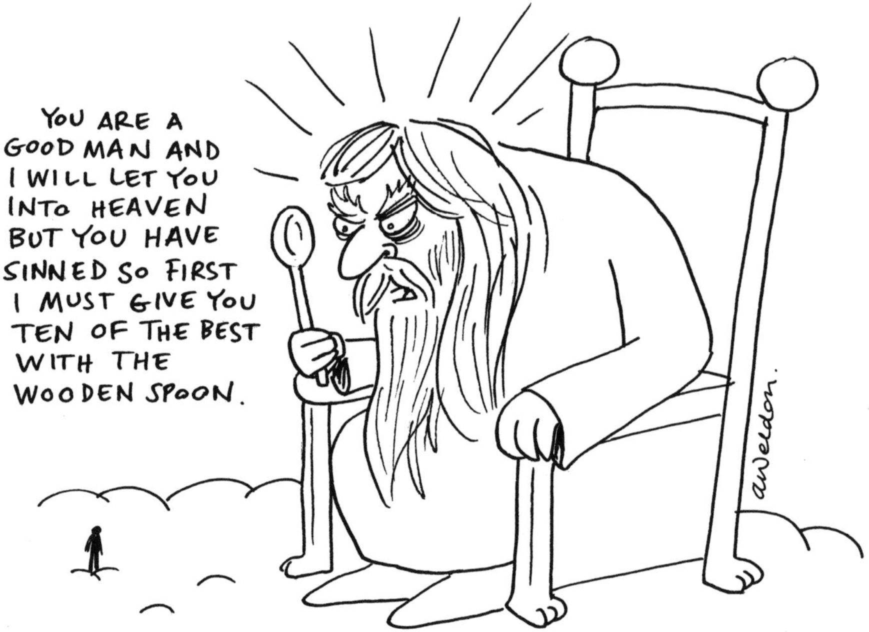
YOU ARE A GOOD MAN AND I WILL LET YOU INTO HEAVEN BUT YOU HAVE SINNED SO FIRST I MUST GIVE YOU TEN OF THE BEST WITH THE WOODEN SPOON.
a weldon.

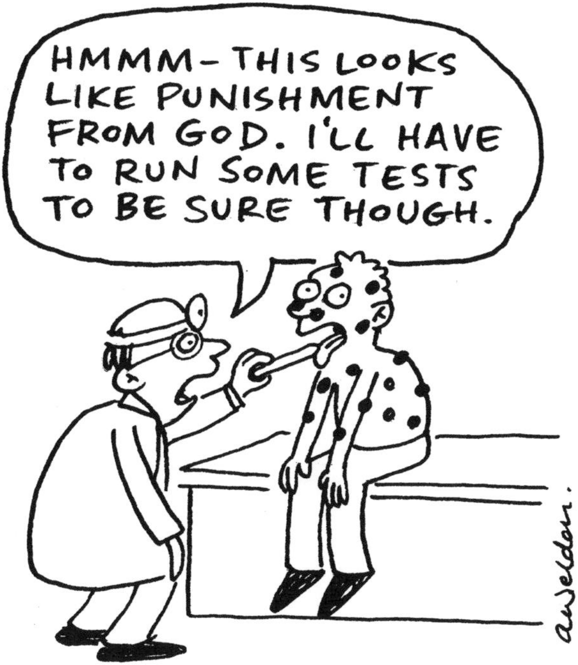
HMMM- THIS LOOKS LIKE PUNISHMENT FROM GOD. I'LL HAVE TO RUN SOME TESTS TO BE SURE THOUGH.
a weldon.

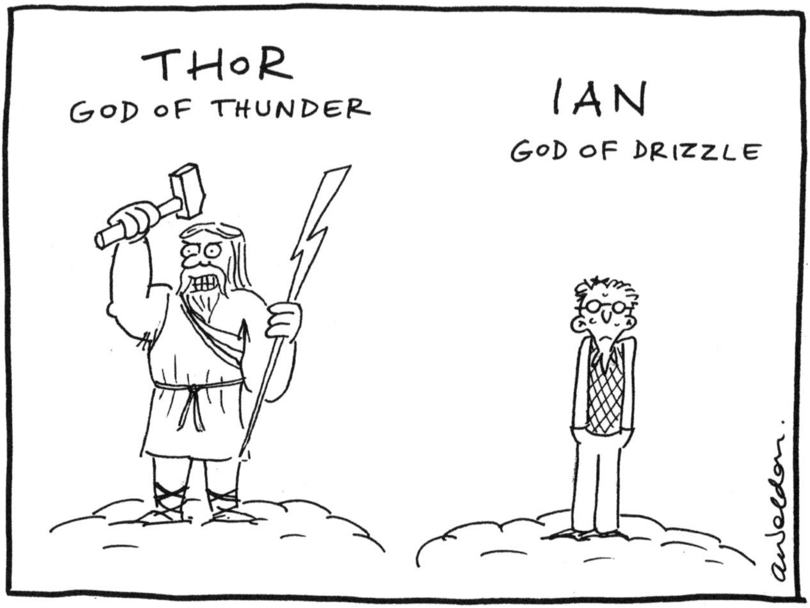
THOR
GOD OF THUNDER
IAN
GOD OF DRIZZLE
a weldon

SISTINE CHAPEL (ATHEIST'S VERSION)

THE MEEK INHERIT SOME EARTH.

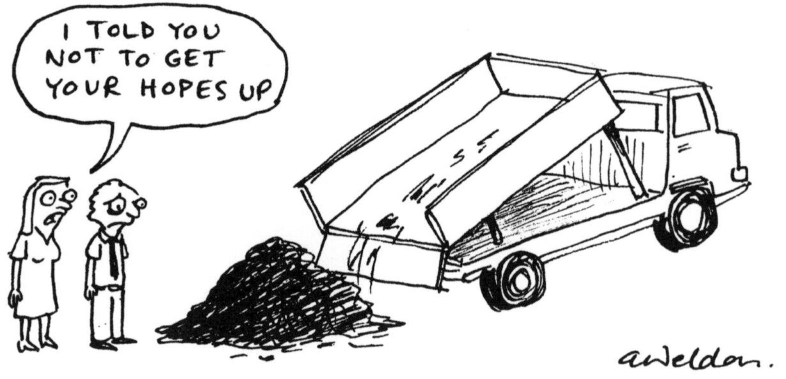
I TOLD YOU NOT TO GET YOUR HOPES UP

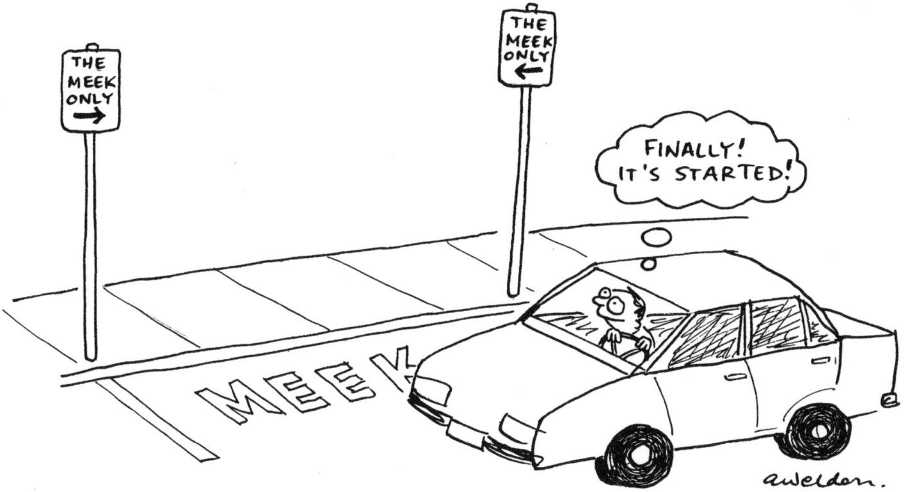
THE MEEK ONLY →
THE MEEK ONLY ←
FINALLY! IT'S STARTED!
MEEK
aweldon.

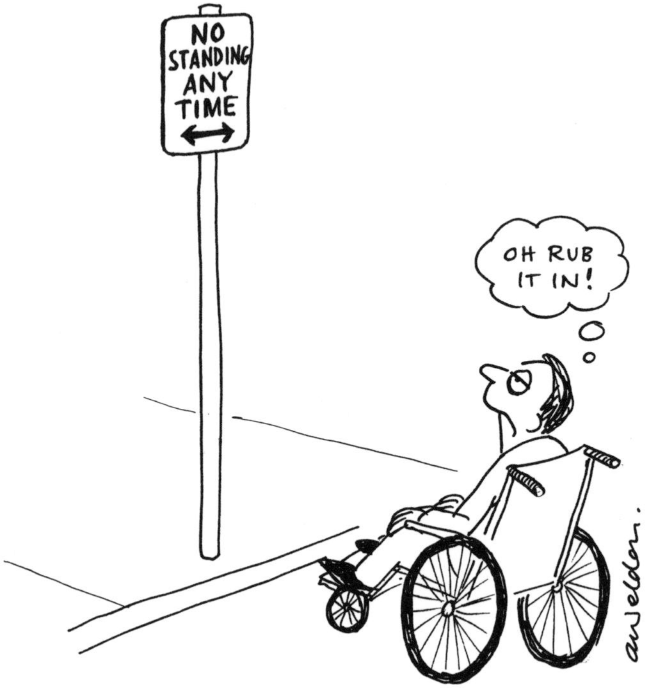
NO STANDING ANY TIME
OH RUB IT IN!
aweldon.

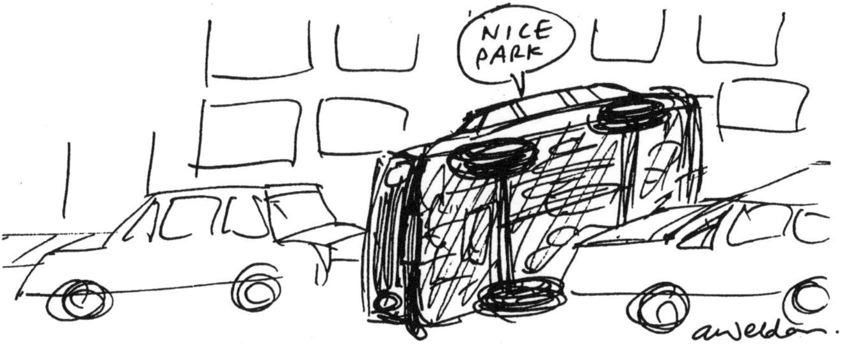
NICE PARK

DRIVERS PLATES
L
LEARNER
P
PROBATIONARY
B
BAD
D
DRUNK
aweldon.

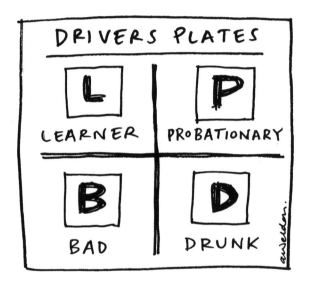

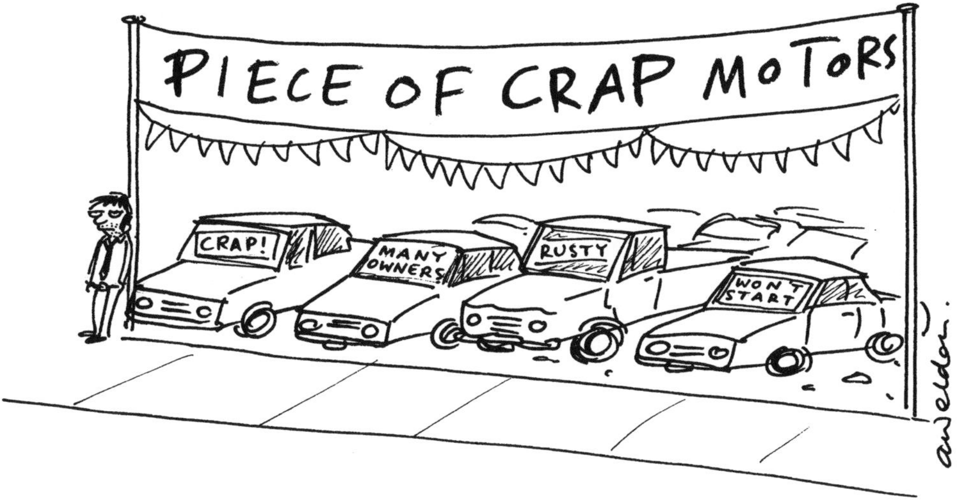
PIECE OF CRAP MOTORS
CRAP!
MANY OWNERS
RUSTY
WON'T START
aweldon.

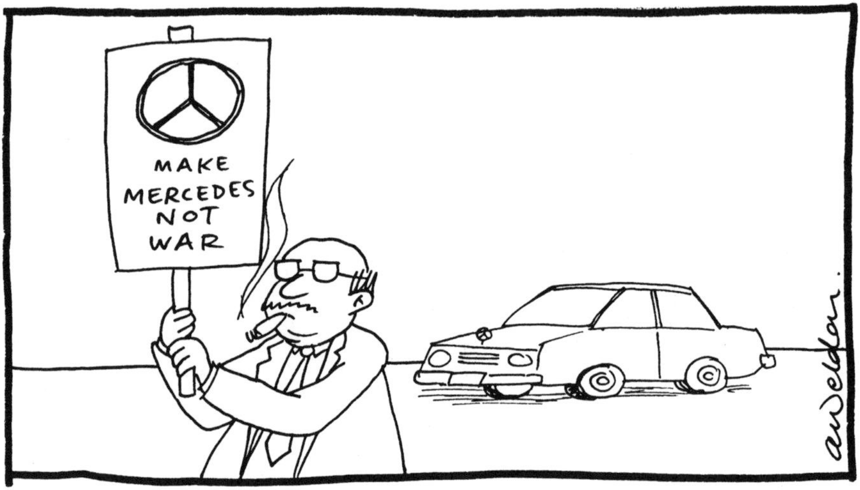
MAKE
MERCEDES
NOT
WAR

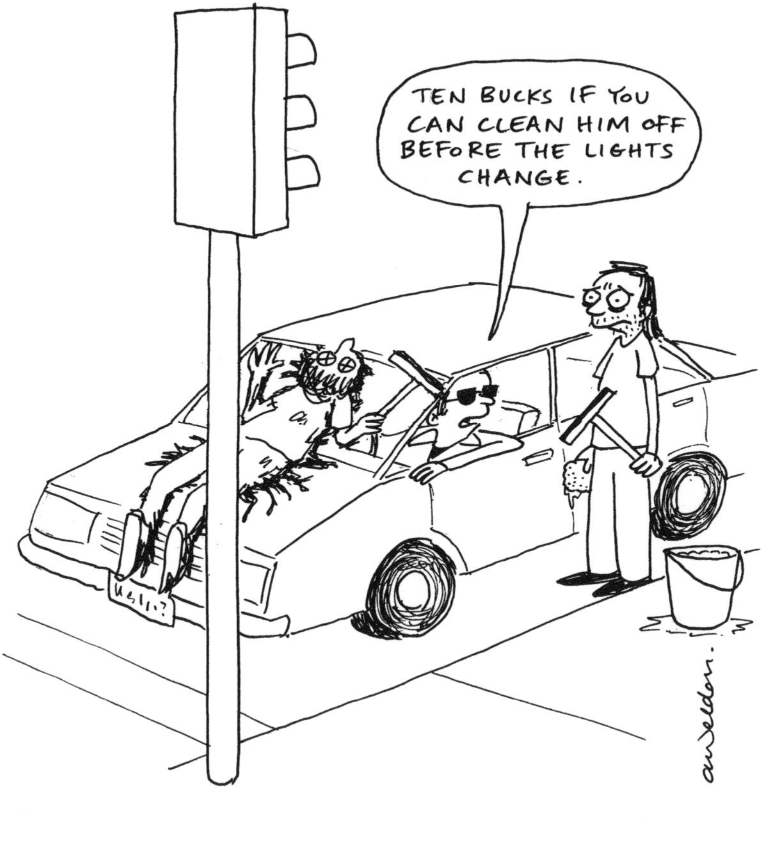
TEN BUCKS IF YOU CAN CLEAN HIM OFF BEFORE THE LIGHTS CHANGE.

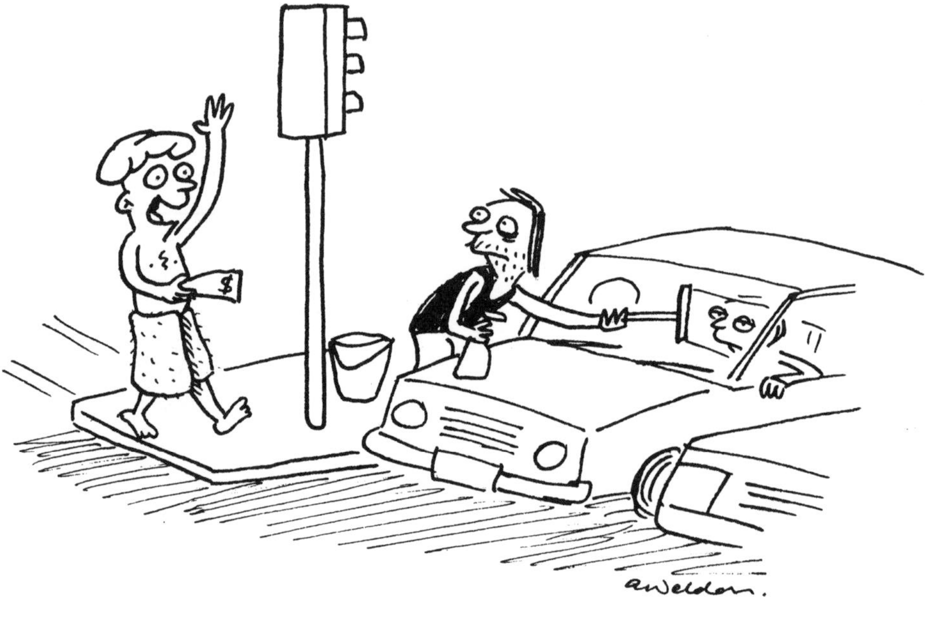
$
aWeldon.

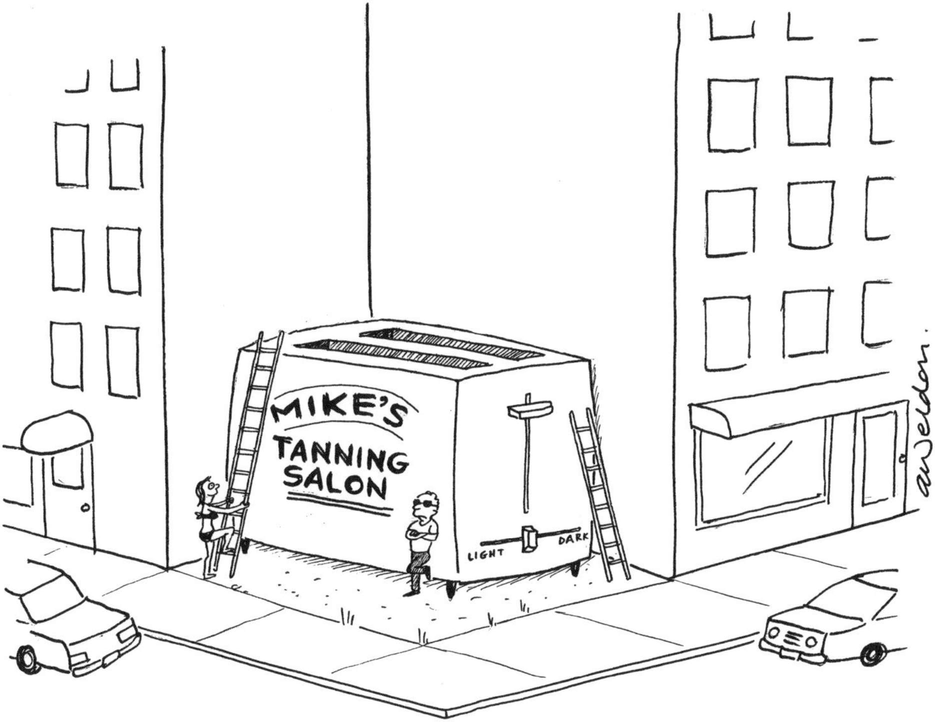
MIKE'S
TANNING
SALON
LIGHT
DARK
a weldon

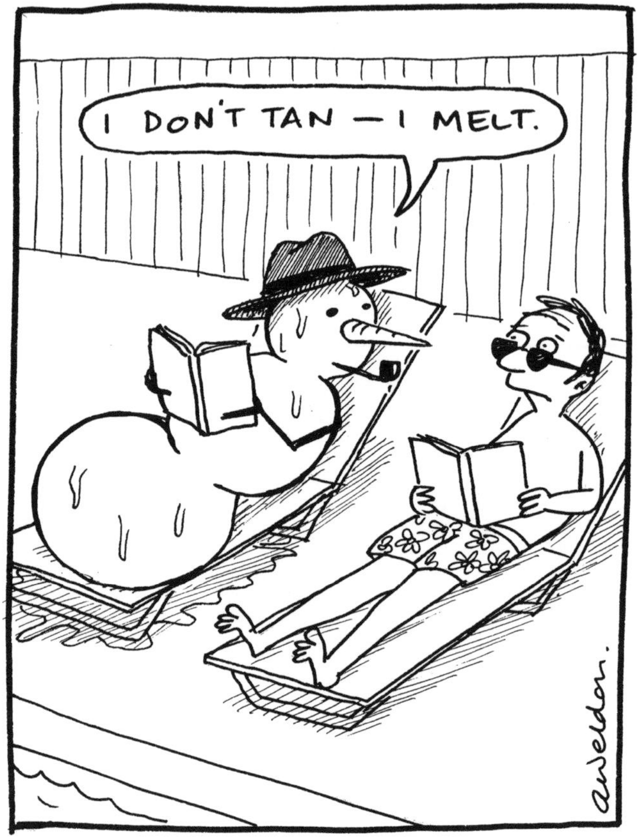
I DON'T TAN — I MELT.

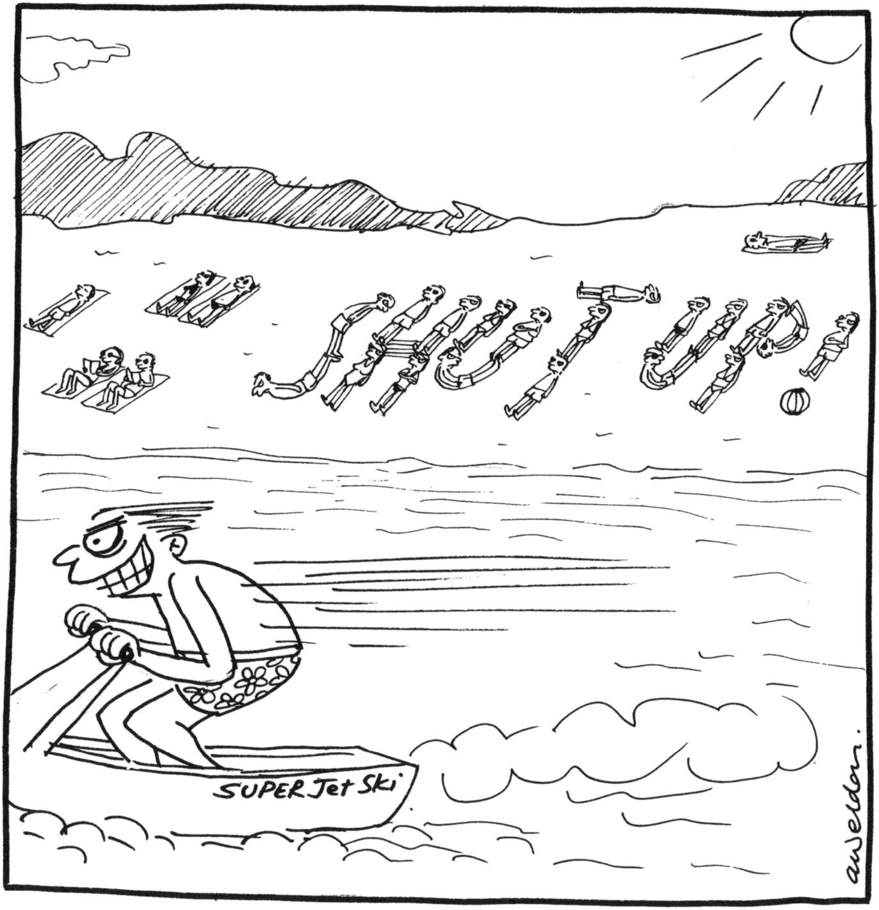
SHUT UP!
SUPER Jet Ski
aweldon.

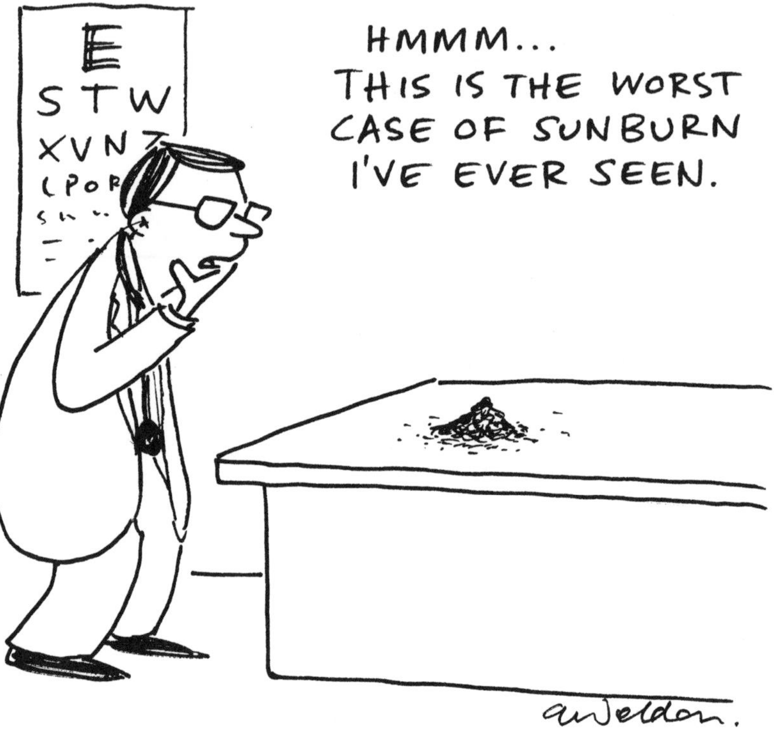
HMMM...
THIS IS THE WORST
CASE OF SUNBURN
I'VE EVER SEEN.

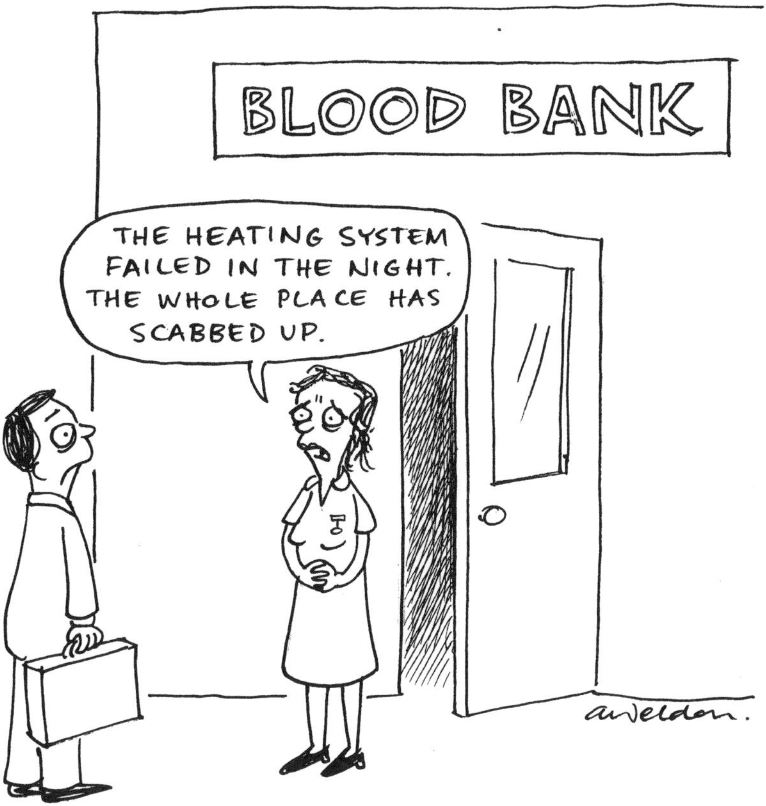
BLOOD BANK
THE HEATING SYSTEM FAILED IN THE NIGHT. THE WHOLE PLACE HAS SCABBED UP.
aweldon.

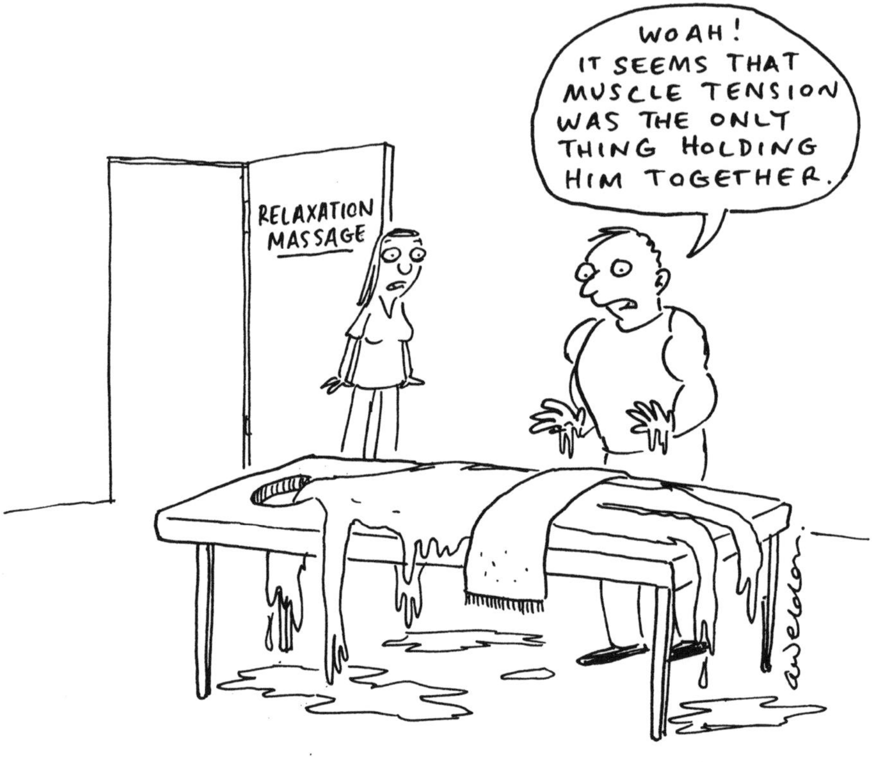
RELAXATION
MASSAGE
WOAH!
IT SEEMS THAT
MUSCLE TENSION
WAS THE ONLY
THING HOLDING
HIM TOGETHER.

POST-BOTOX COACHING.

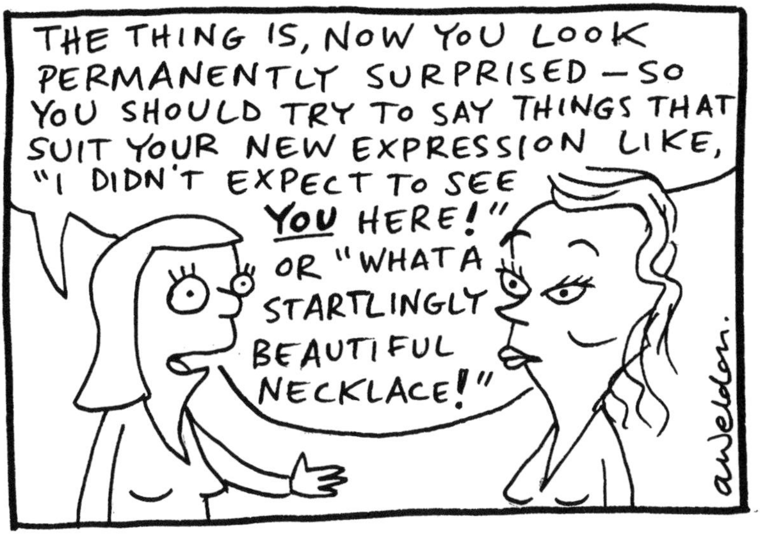
THE THING IS, NOW YOU LOOK PERMANENTLY SURPRISED — SO YOU SHOULD TRY TO SAY THINGS THAT SUIT YOUR NEW EXPRESSION LIKE, "I DIDN'T EXPECT TO SEE YOU HERE!" OR "WHAT A STARTLINGLY BEAUTIFUL NECKLACE!"
aweldon.

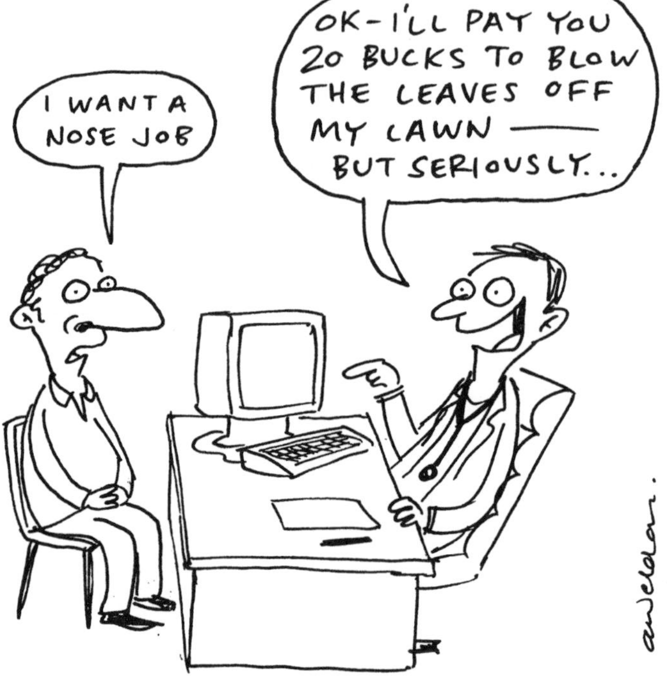
I WANT A NOSE JOB
OK-I'LL PAY YOU 20 BUCKS TO BLOW THE LEAVES OFF MY LAWN — BUT SERIOUSLY...

WISE-CRACKING PLASTIC SURGEON

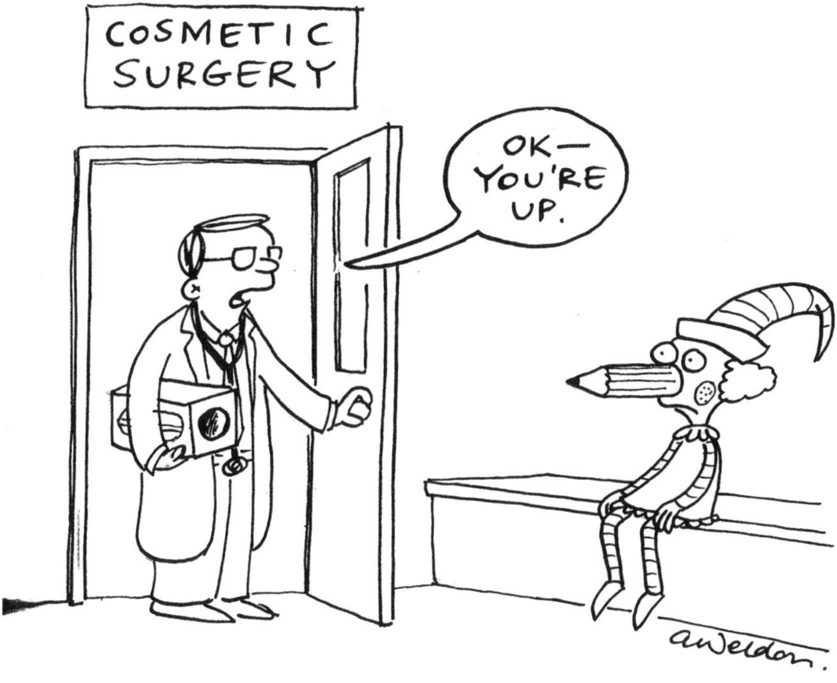
COSMETIC SURGERY
OK— YOU'RE UP.
aWeldon.

I JUST THOUGHT— IF I <u>HAVE</u> TO HAVE
FALSE TEETH, LET'S MAKE THEM SOME
KICK-ASS, GREAT-WHITE, THREE-LAYER
BAD BOYS. LET'S AT LEAST <u>ADD</u>
SOMETHING HERE, YOU KNOW
WHAT I MEAN?

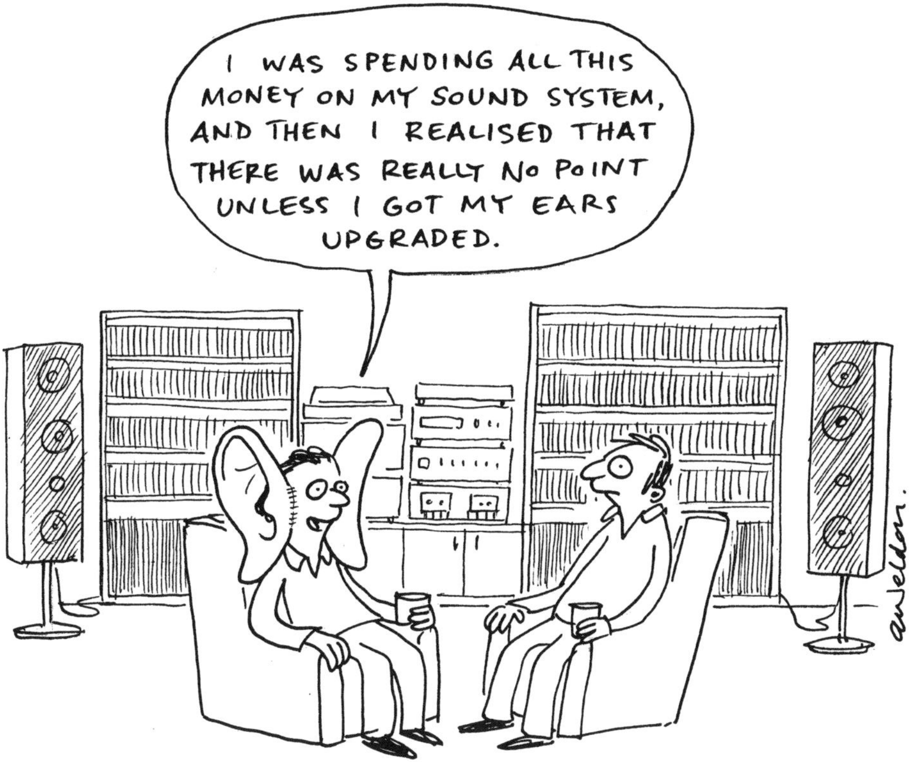
I WAS SPENDING ALL THIS MONEY ON MY SOUND SYSTEM, AND THEN I REALISED THAT THERE WAS REALLY NO POINT UNLESS I GOT MY EARS UPGRADED.
aweldon.

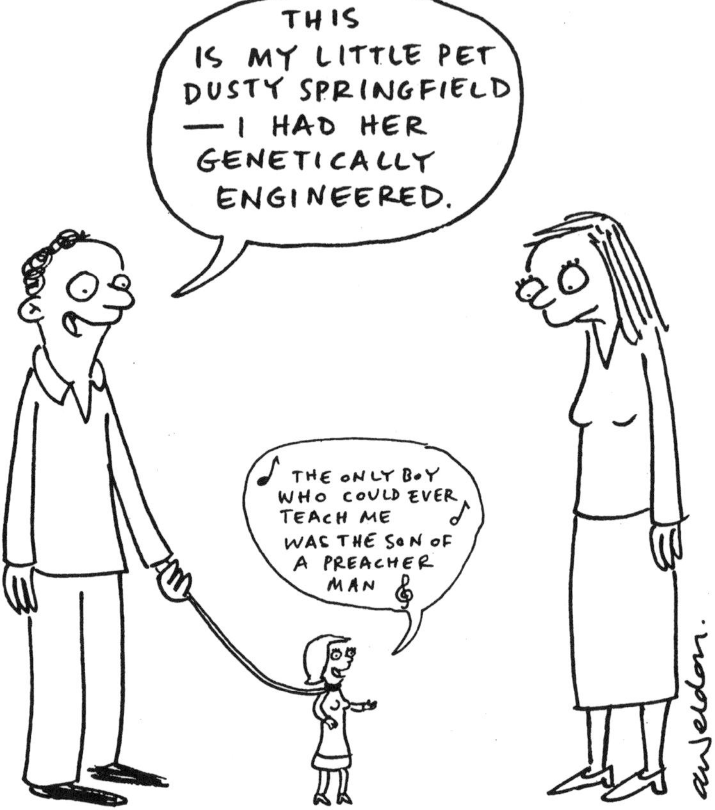
THIS IS MY LITTLE PET DUSTY SPRINGFIELD — I HAD HER GENETICALLY ENGINEERED.
THE ONLY BOY WHO COULD EVER TEACH ME WAS THE SON OF A PREACHER MAN
a weldon.

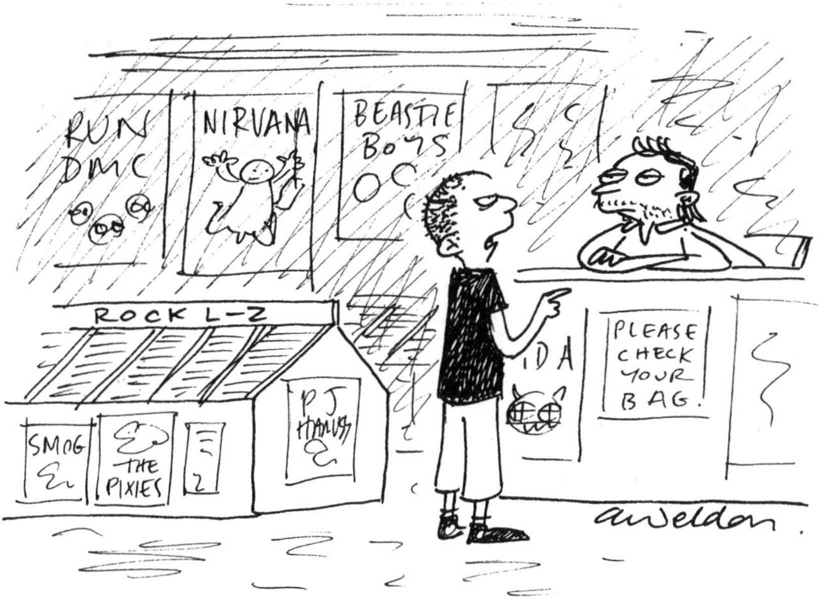
RUN DMC
NIRVANA
BEASTIE BOYS
ROCK L-Z
SMOG
THE PIXIES
PJ
IDA
PLEASE CHECK YOUR BAG!
aweldon.

"I'M AFTER SOMETHING THAT'S GOT THE EASY-LISTENING SMOOTHNESS OF SAY, KENNY G, BUT WITH THE EMINEM GAY-HATING THING AS WELL".

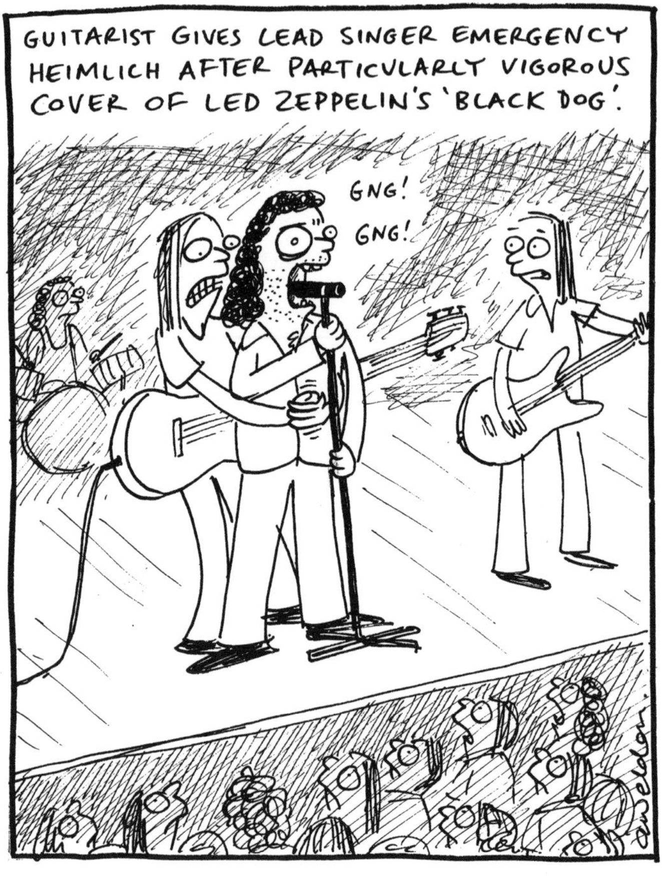
GNG!
GNG!
GUITARIST GIVES LEAD SINGER EMERGENCY HEIMLICH AFTER PARTICULARLY VIGOROUS COVER OF LED ZEPPELIN'S 'BLACK DOG'.

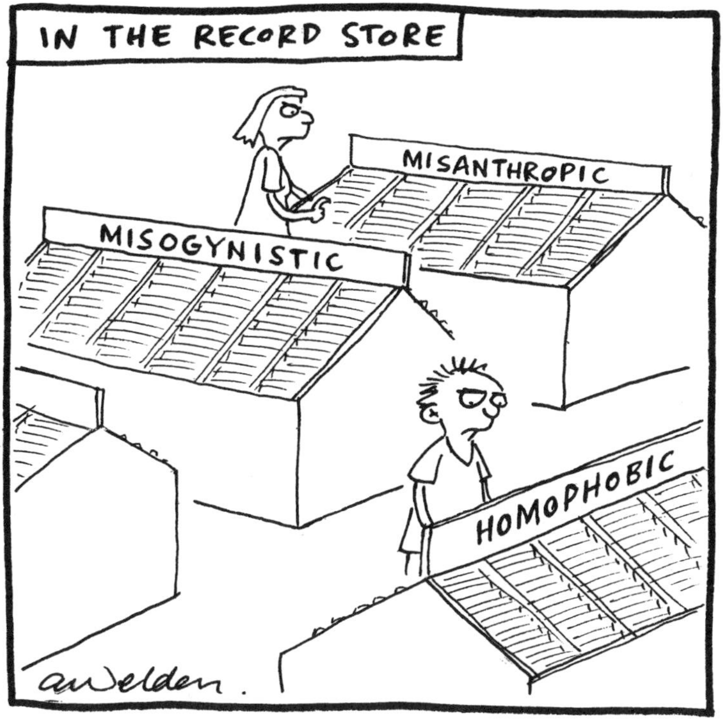
IN THE RECORD STORE
MISANTHROPIC
MISOGYNISTIC
HOMOPHOBIC
aWelden.

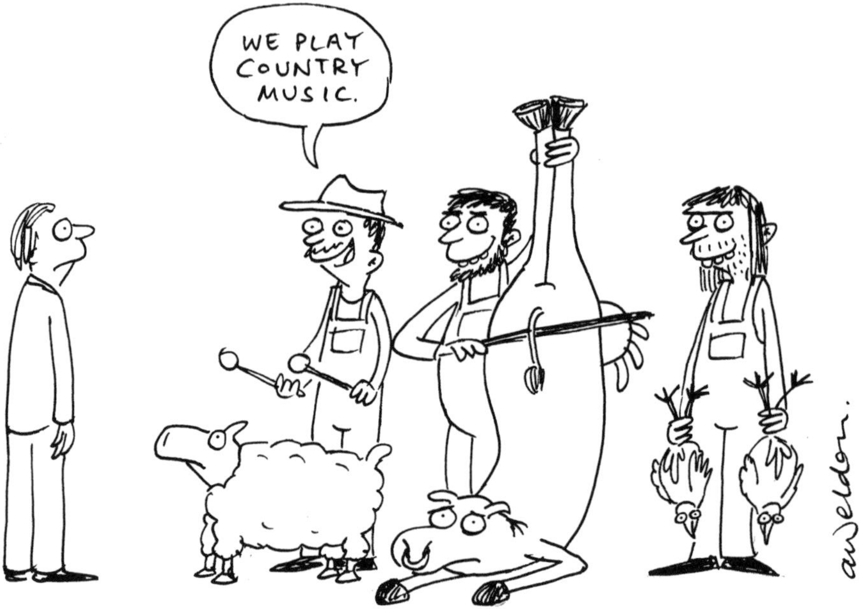
WE PLAY COUNTRY MUSIC.

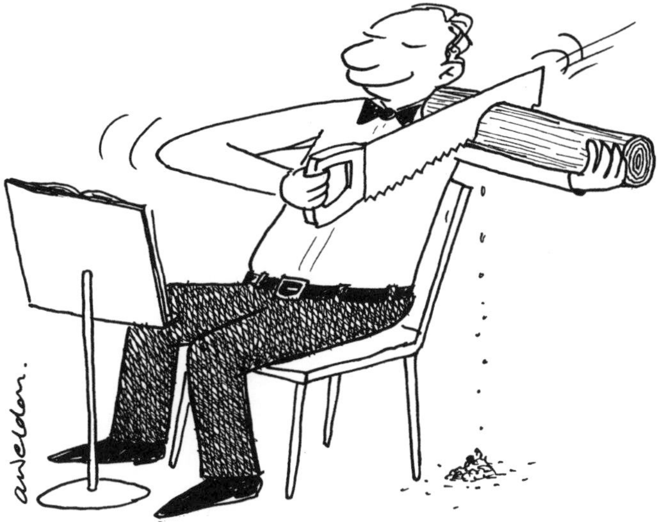

aweldon.

PRIOR TO THE GUILLOTINE

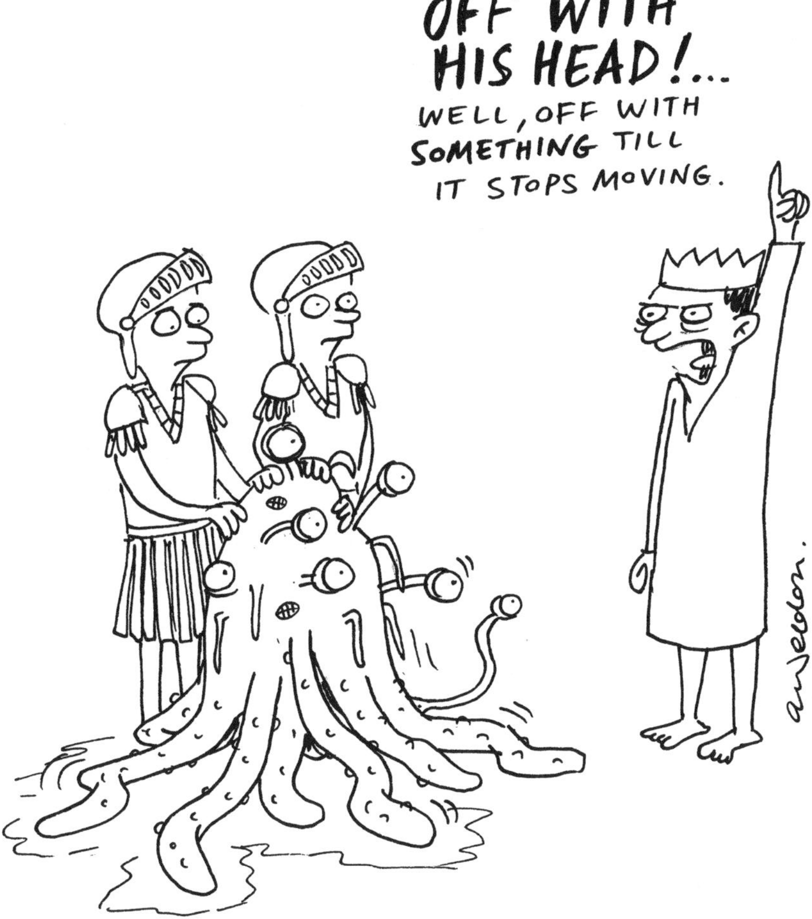
OFF WITH HIS HEAD!... WELL, OFF WITH SOMETHING TILL IT STOPS MOVING.
anderson.

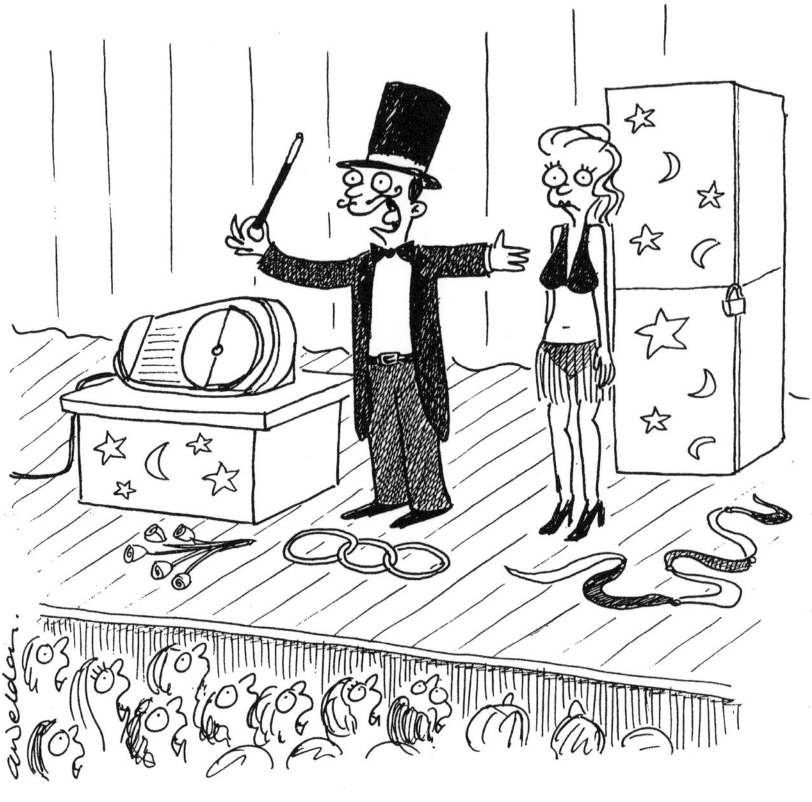
aweldon.

"AND NOW LADIES & GENTLEMEN, FOR YOUR ASTONISHMENT, I WILL CUT MY LOVELY ASSISTANT INTO FIFTEEN HUNDRED THIN SLICES WITH THIS DELICATESSEN-STYLE MEAT-SLICER..."

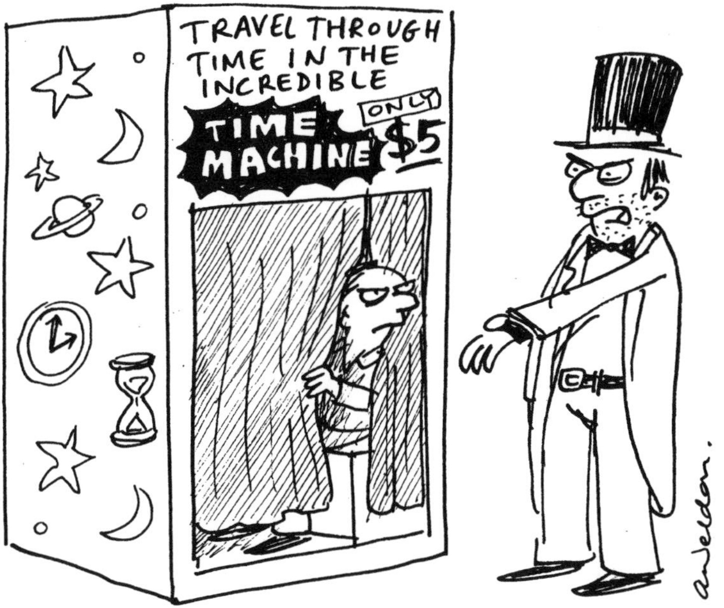
TRAVEL THROUGH TIME IN THE INCREDIBLE
TIME MACHINE
ONLY $5

"YOU GOT IN AT 4:32 AND NOW IT'S 4:34. THAT'S TRAVELLING THROUGH TIME! WHAT'S YOUR PROBLEM?"

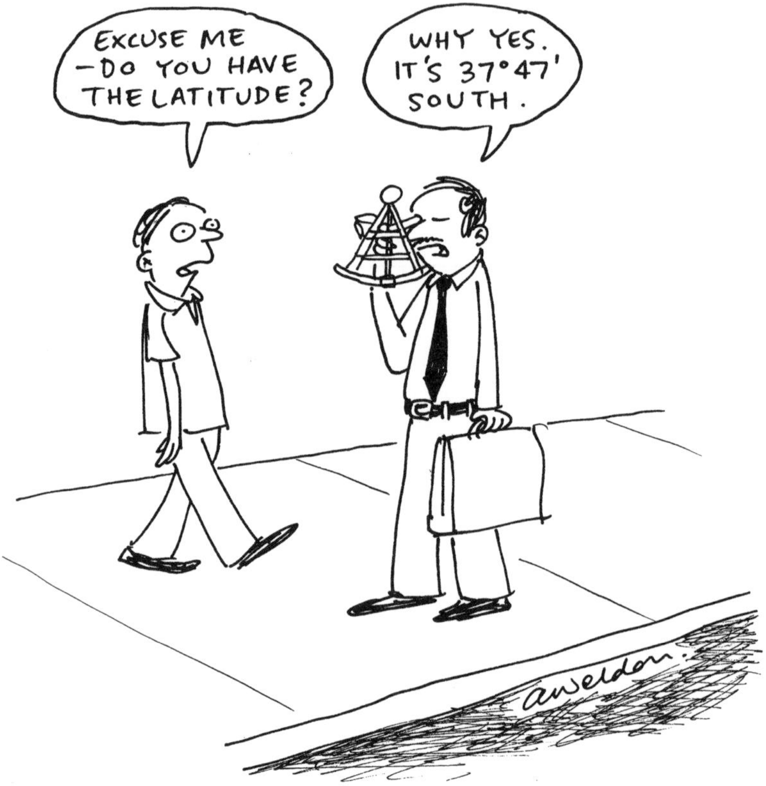
EXCUSE ME
—DO YOU HAVE
THE LATITUDE?
WHY YES.
IT'S 37°47'
SOUTH.
aweldon.

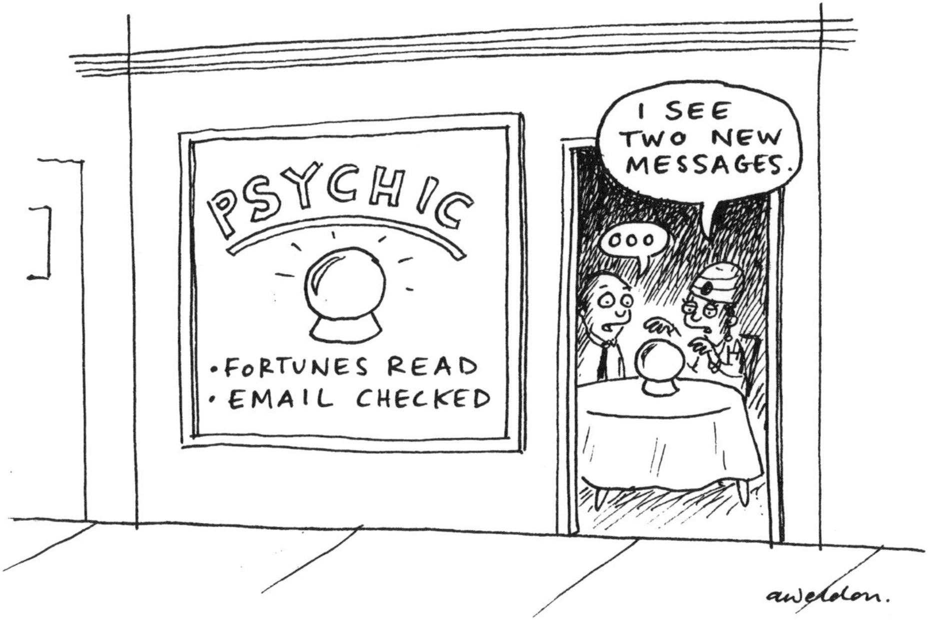
PSYCHIC
•FORTUNES READ
•EMAIL CHECKED
I SEE TWO NEW MESSAGES.
OOO
aweldon.

DONATIONS CAN
ALSO BE MADE
ONLINE AT
www.haveyougot
adollarI'vegotto
getfivebuckscos
Ilostmywallet
andIneedtoget
thetrain.com

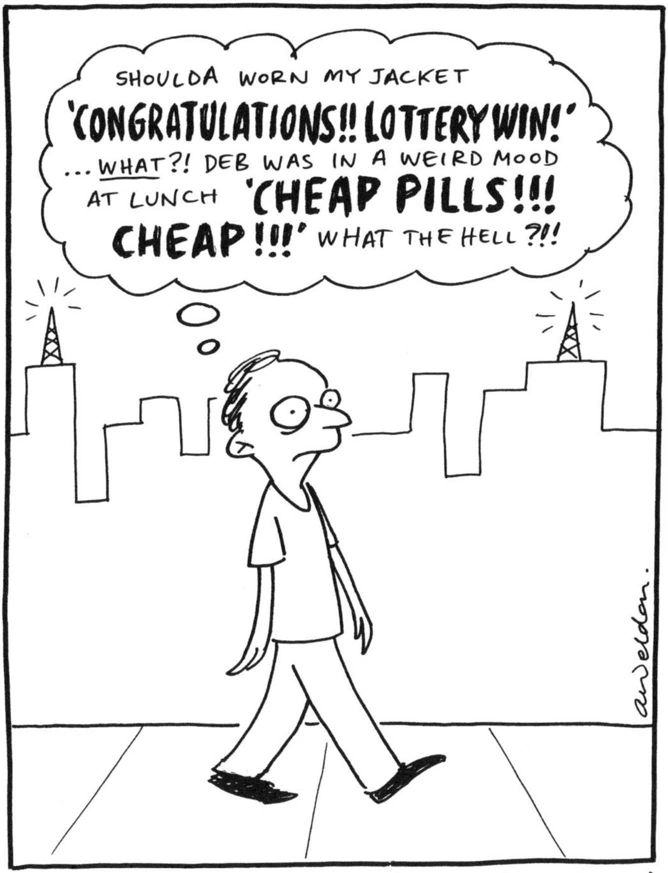
SHOULDA WORN MY JACKET
'CONGRATULATIONS!! LOTTERY WIN!'
... WHAT?! DEB WAS IN A WEIRD MOOD AT LUNCH 'CHEAP PILLS!!! CHEAP!!!' WHAT THE HELL ?!!
a weldon.

2014: EMERGENCE OF 'MENTAL SPAM'

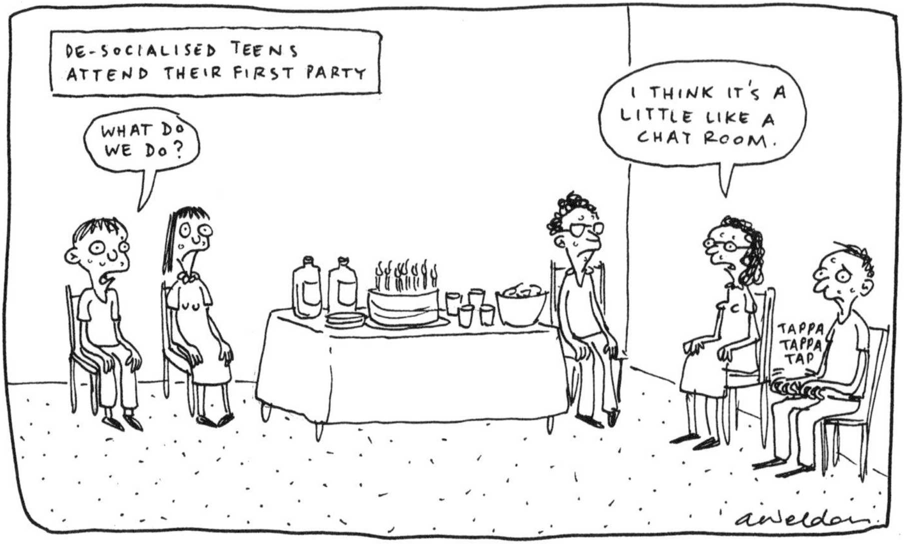
DE-SOCIALISED TEENS ATTEND THEIR FIRST PARTY
WHAT DO WE DO?
I THINK IT'S A LITTLE LIKE A CHAT ROOM.
TAPPA TAPPA TAP
aweldon

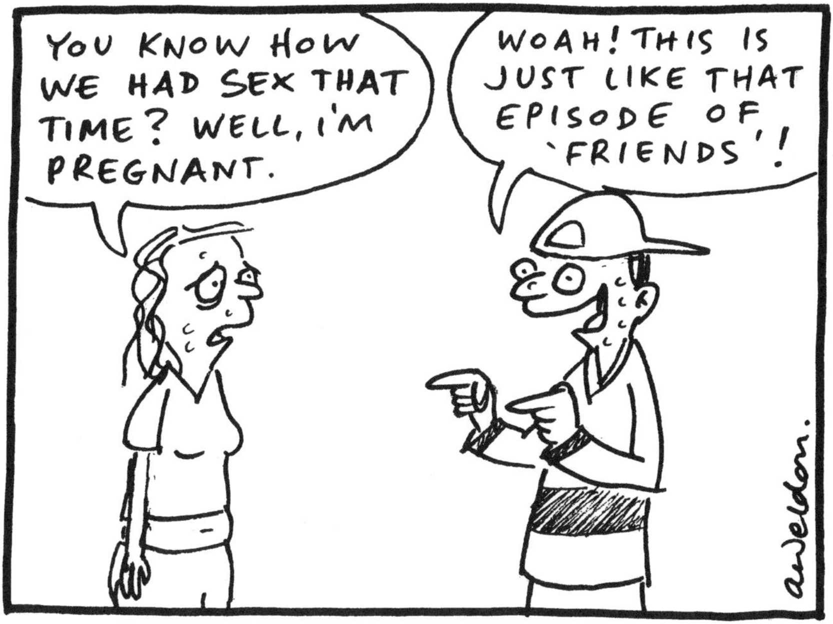
YOU KNOW HOW WE HAD SEX THAT TIME? WELL, I'M PREGNANT.
WOAH! THIS IS JUST LIKE THAT EPISODE OF 'FRIENDS'!
a weldon.

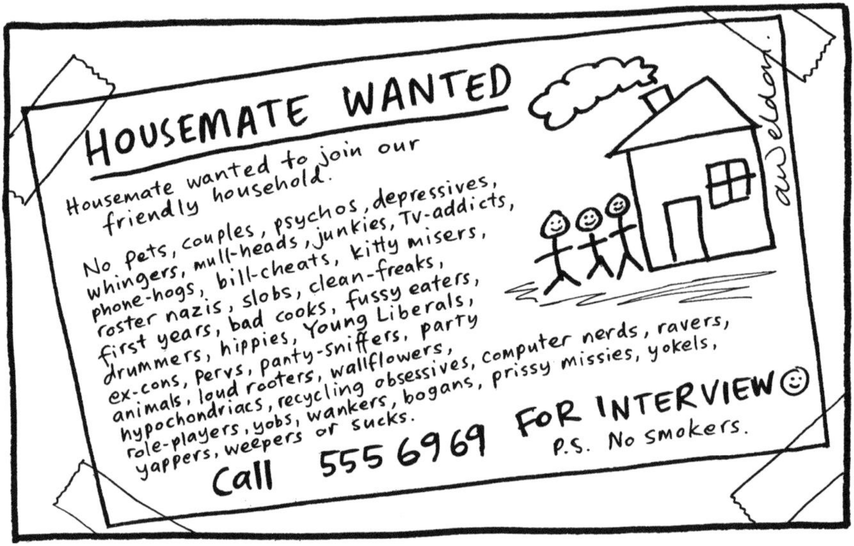
HOUSEMATE WANTED
Housemate wanted to join our friendly household.
No pets, couples, psychos, depressives, whingers, mull-heads, junkies, TV-addicts, phone-hogs, bill-cheats, kitty misers, roster nazis, slobs, clean-freaks, first years, bad cooks, fussy eaters, drummers, hippies, Young Liberals, ex-cons, pervs, panty-sniffers, party animals, loud rooters, wallflowers, hypochondriacs, recycling obsessives, computer nerds, ravers, role-players, yobs, wankers, bogans, prissy missies, yokels, yappers, weepers or sucks.
Call 555 6969 FOR INTERVIEW ☺
P.S. No smokers.
a weldon

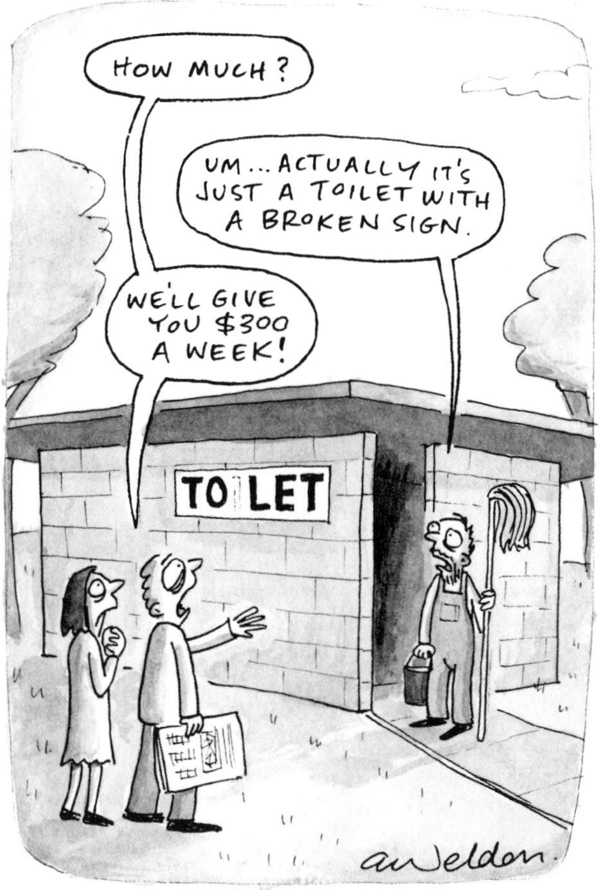
HOW MUCH?
WE'LL GIVE YOU $300 A WEEK!
UM... ACTUALLY IT'S JUST A TOILET WITH A BROKEN SIGN.
TO LET
a Weldon.

UNDER THE BRIDGE

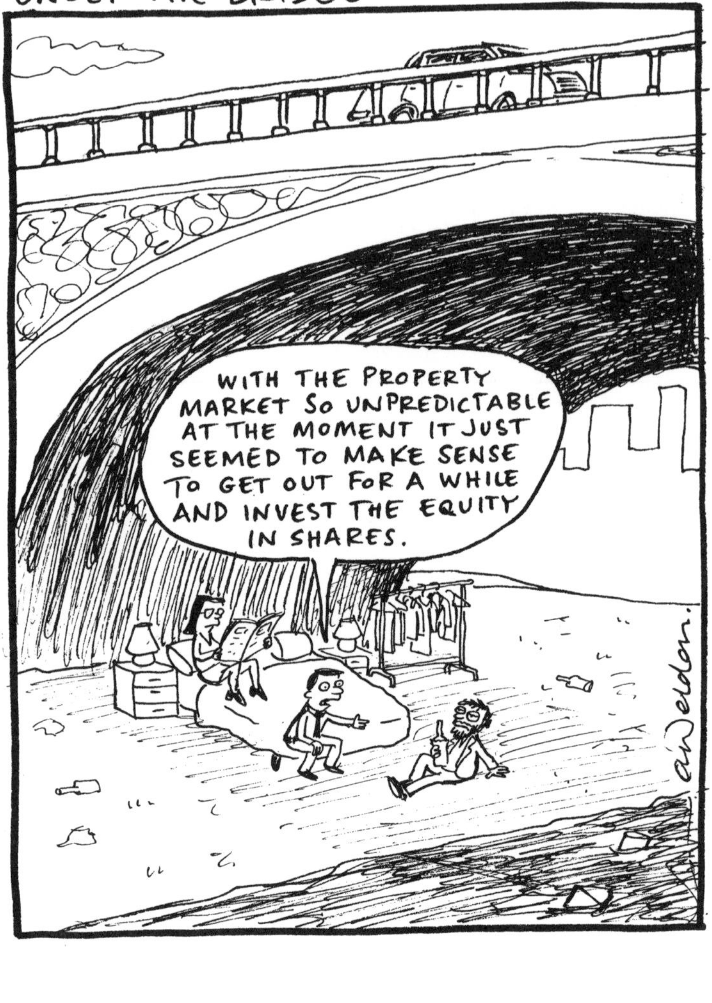
WITH THE PROPERTY MARKET SO UNPREDICTABLE AT THE MOMENT IT JUST SEEMED TO MAKE SENSE TO GET OUT FOR A WHILE AND INVEST THE EQUITY IN SHARES.
a weldon.

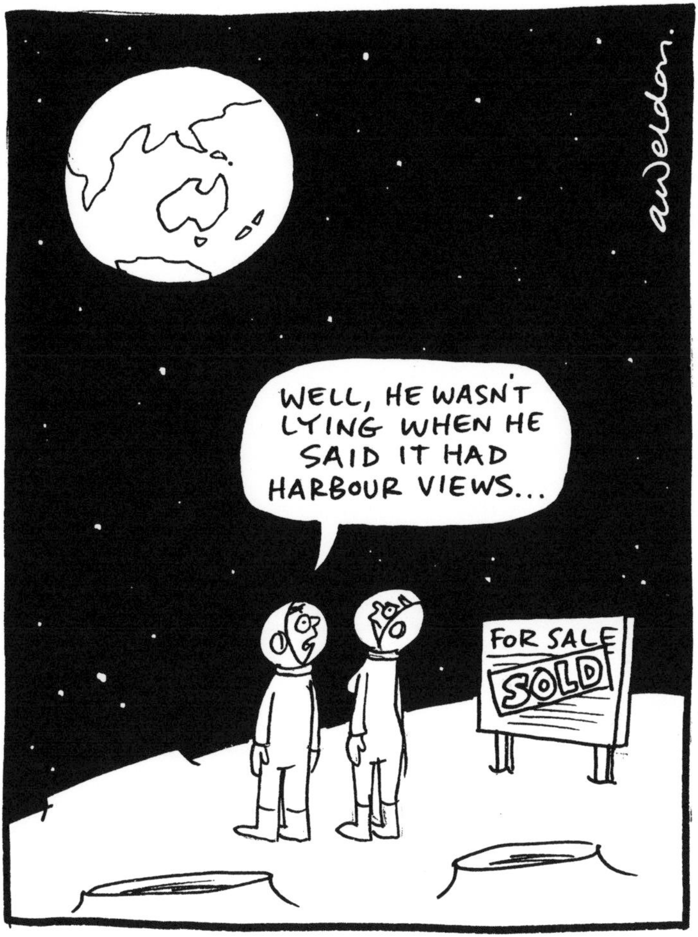
WELL, HE WASN'T LYING WHEN HE SAID IT HAD HARBOUR VIEWS...
FOR SALE
SOLD
aweldon.

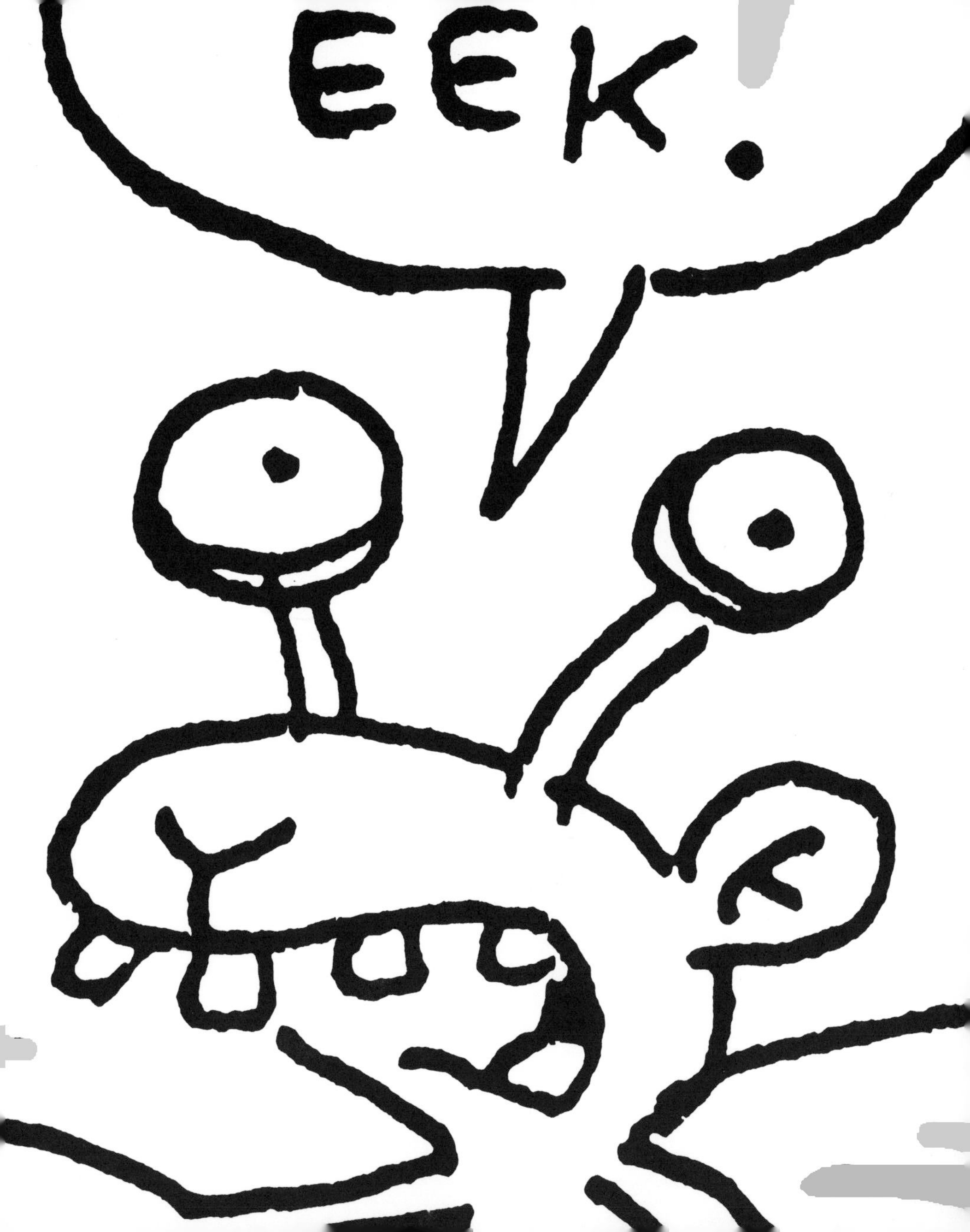
EEK.

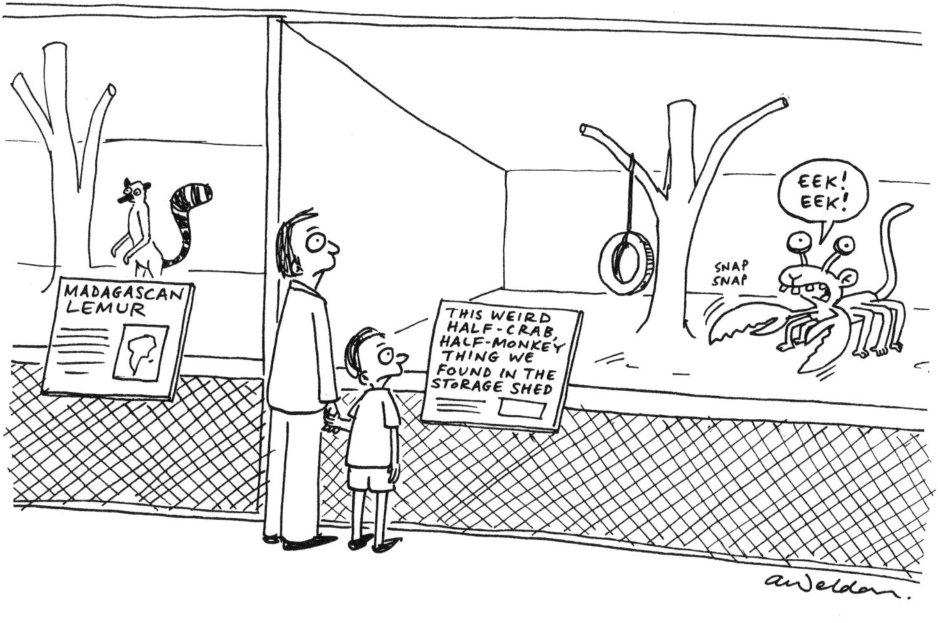
MADAGASCAN LEMUR
THIS WEIRD HALF-CRAB, HALF-MONKEY THING WE FOUND IN THE STORAGE SHED
SNAP SNAP
EEK! EEK!
aWeldon.

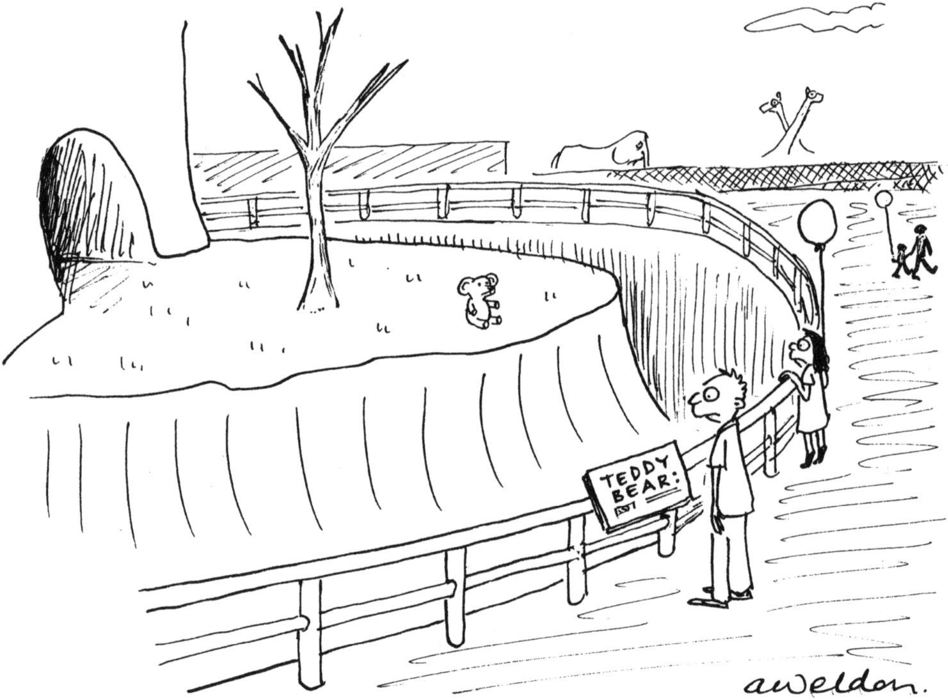
TEDDY BEAR:
aweldon.

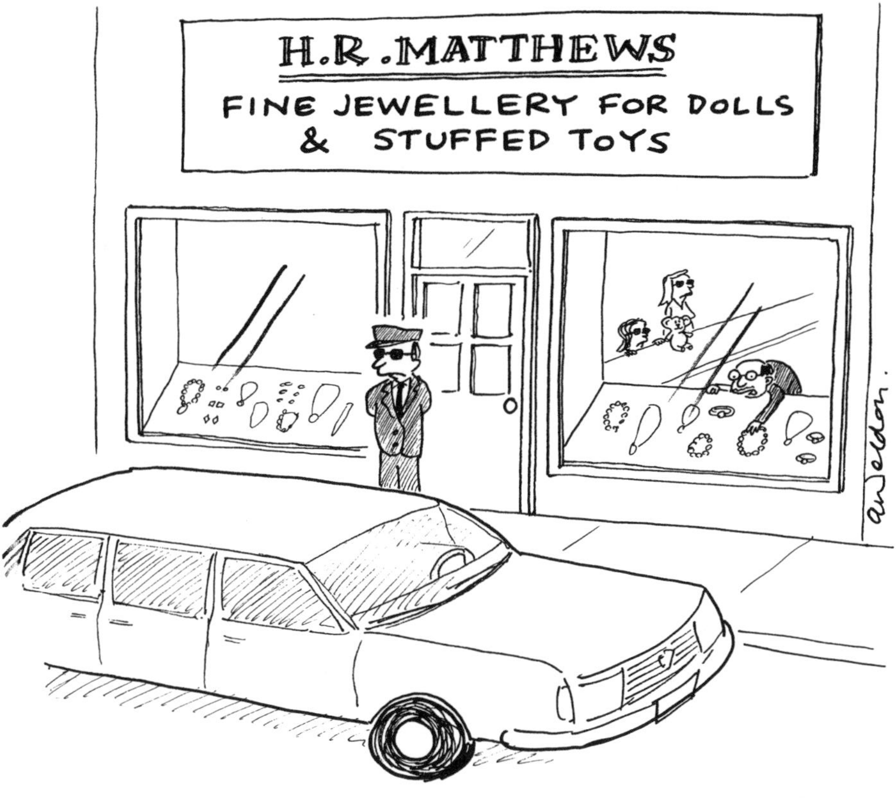
H.R. MATTHEWS
FINE JEWELLERY FOR DOLLS & STUFFED TOYS
anWeldon

"NOW HERE'S A DARLING LITTLE SAPPHIRE NECKLACE THAT I THINK TEDDY IS JUST GOING TO <u>LOVE</u>..."

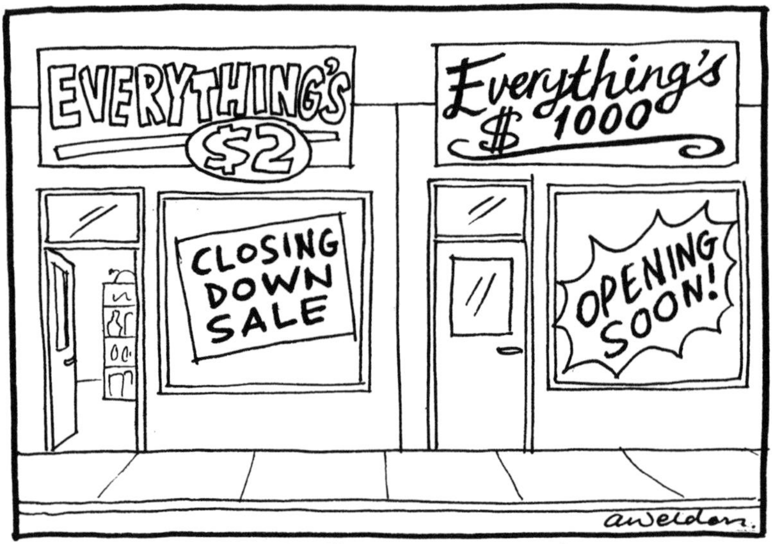
EVERYTHING'S
$2
Everything's
$ 1000
CLOSING
DOWN
SALE
OPENING
SOON!
aweldon.

GENTRIFICATION.

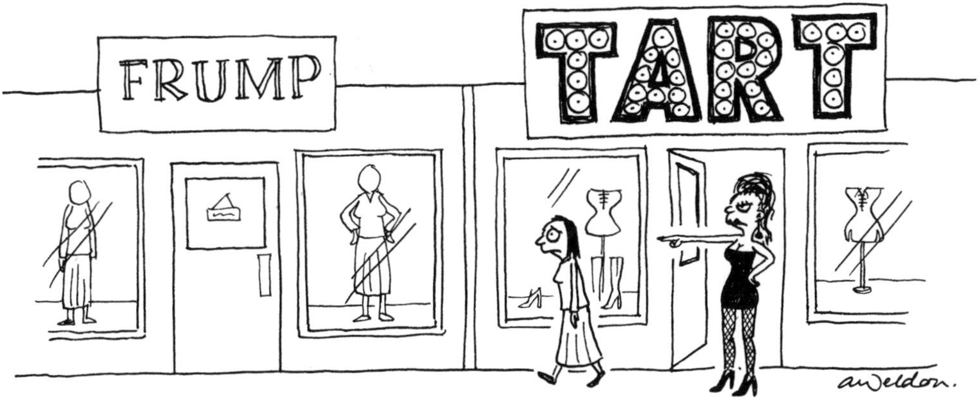
FRUMP
TART
aWeldon.

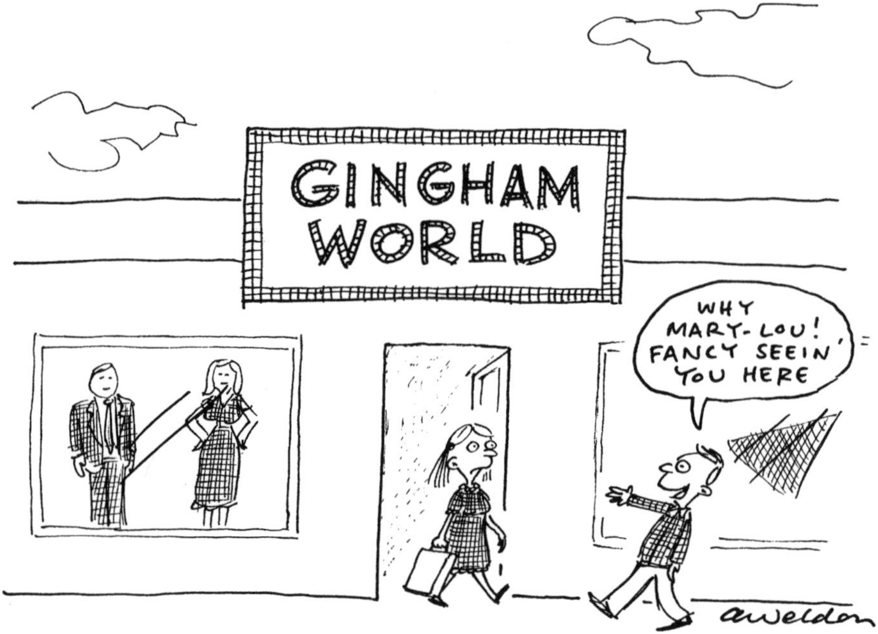
GINGHAM WORLD
WHY MARY-LOU! FANCY SEEIN' YOU HERE
aweldon

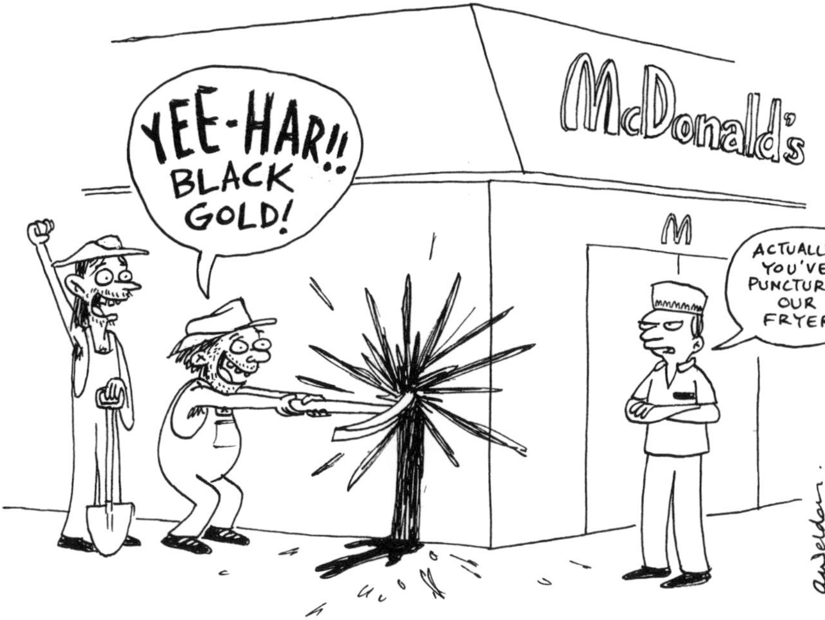
McDonald's
YEE-HAR!! BLACK GOLD!
ACTUALLY, YOU'VE PUNCTURED OUR FRYER.
aWeldon

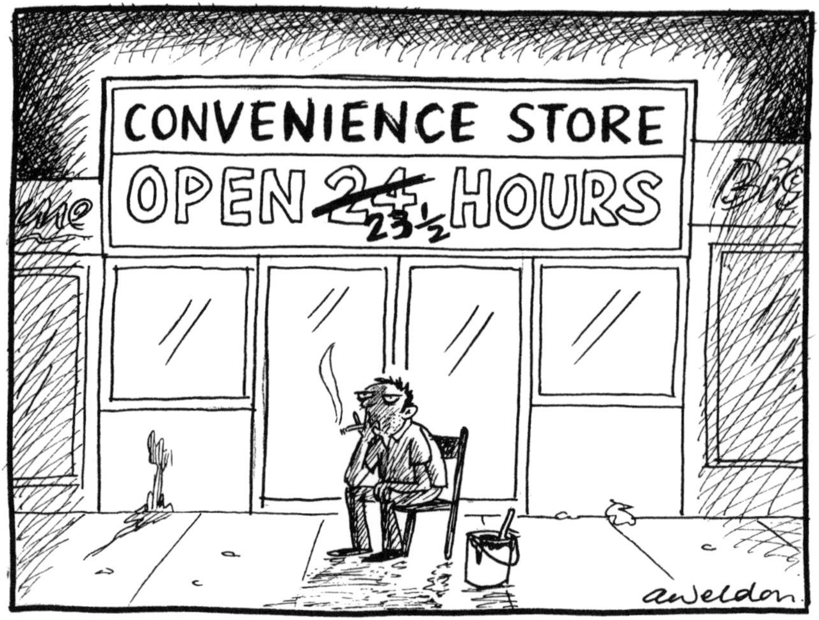
CONVENIENCE STORE
OPEN ~~24~~ 23½ HOURS
aweldon

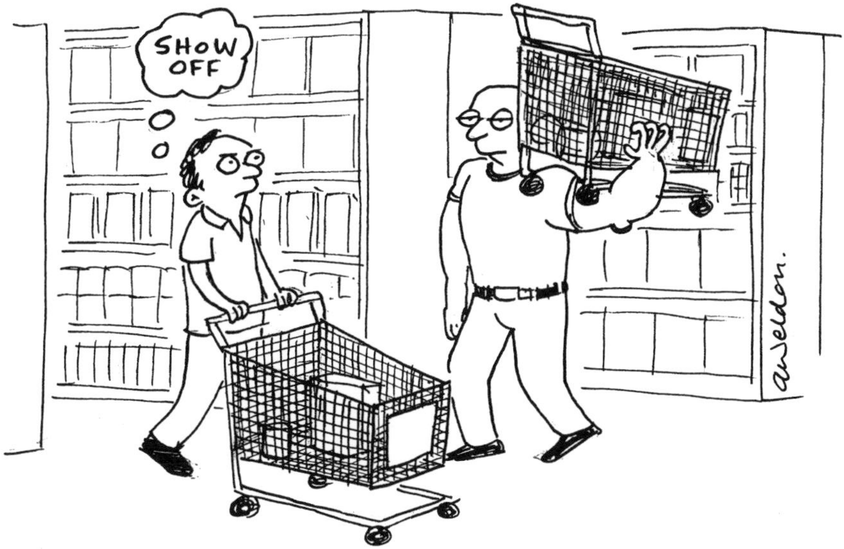
SHOW OFF
aweldon.

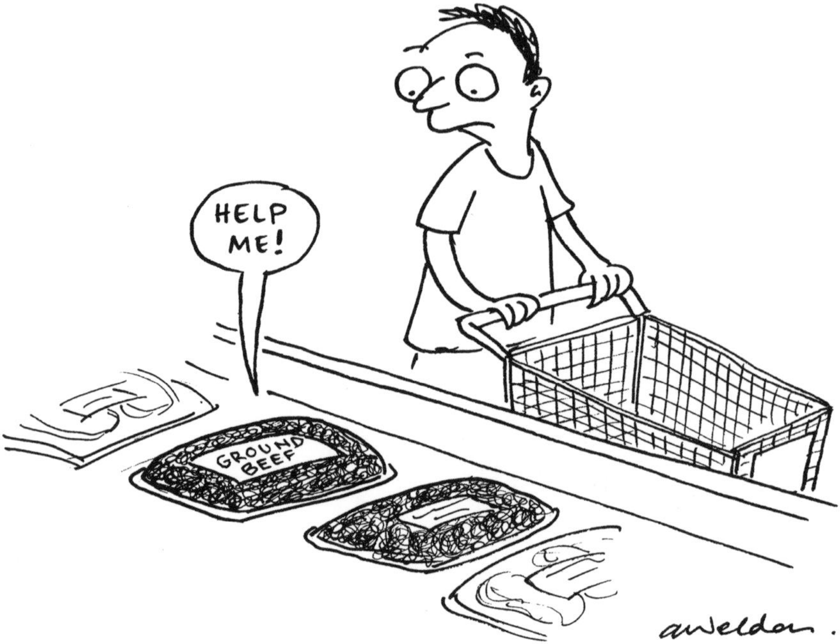
HELP ME!
GROUND BEEF
aweldon.

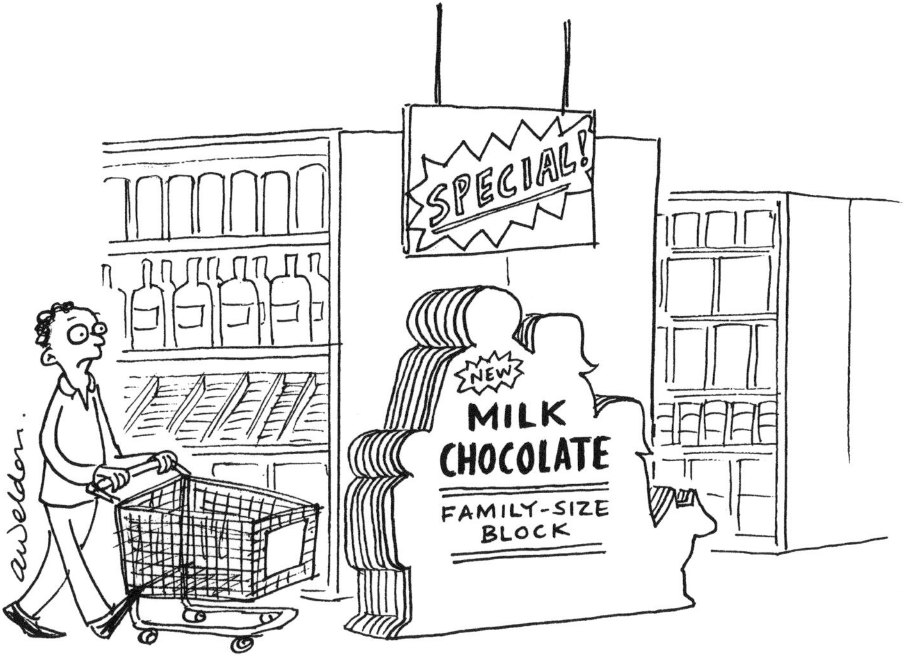
SPECIAL!
NEW
MILK
CHOCOLATE
FAMILY-SIZE
BLOCK
aweldon.

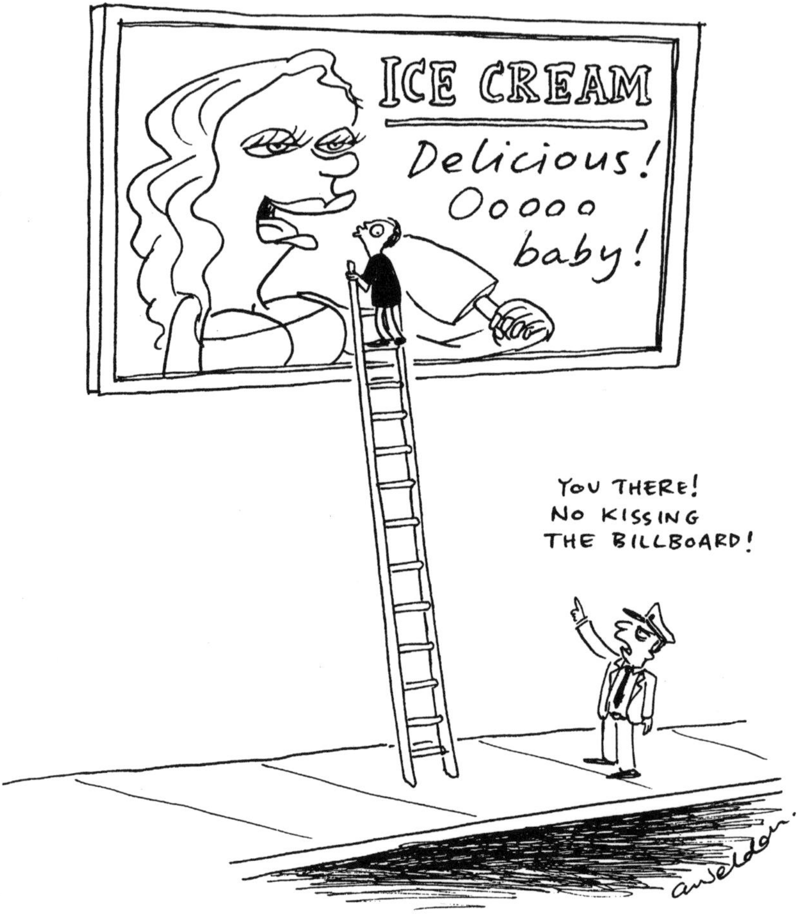
ICE CREAM
Delicious! Ooooo baby!
YOU THERE! NO KISSING THE BILLBOARD!

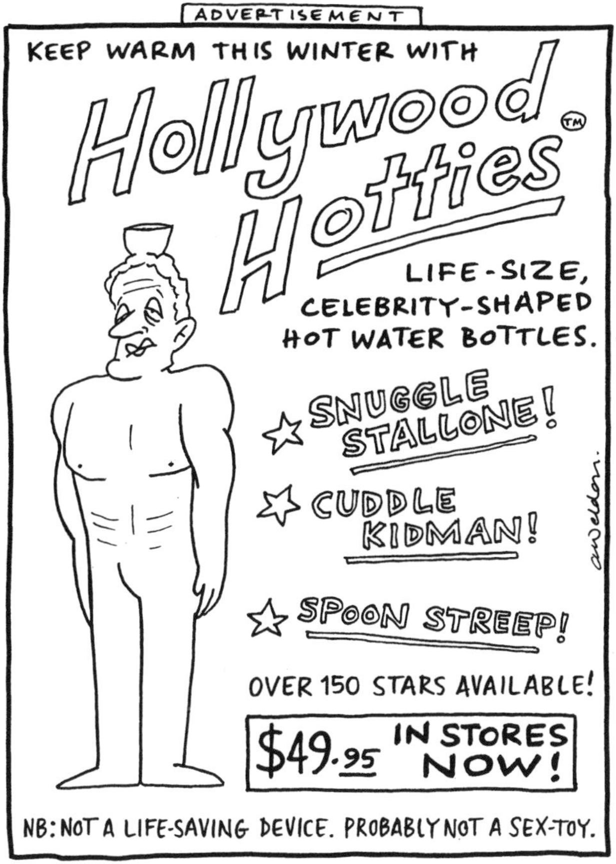
ADVERTISEMENT
KEEP WARM THIS WINTER WITH
Hollywood Hotties™
LIFE-SIZE, CELEBRITY-SHAPED HOT WATER BOTTLES.
★ SNUGGLE STALLONE!
★ CUDDLE KIDMAN!
★ SPOON STREEP!
OVER 150 STARS AVAILABLE!
$49.95 IN STORES NOW!
NB: NOT A LIFE-SAVING DEVICE. PROBABLY NOT A SEX-TOY.
a weldon.

AT THE HAIRDRESSER.

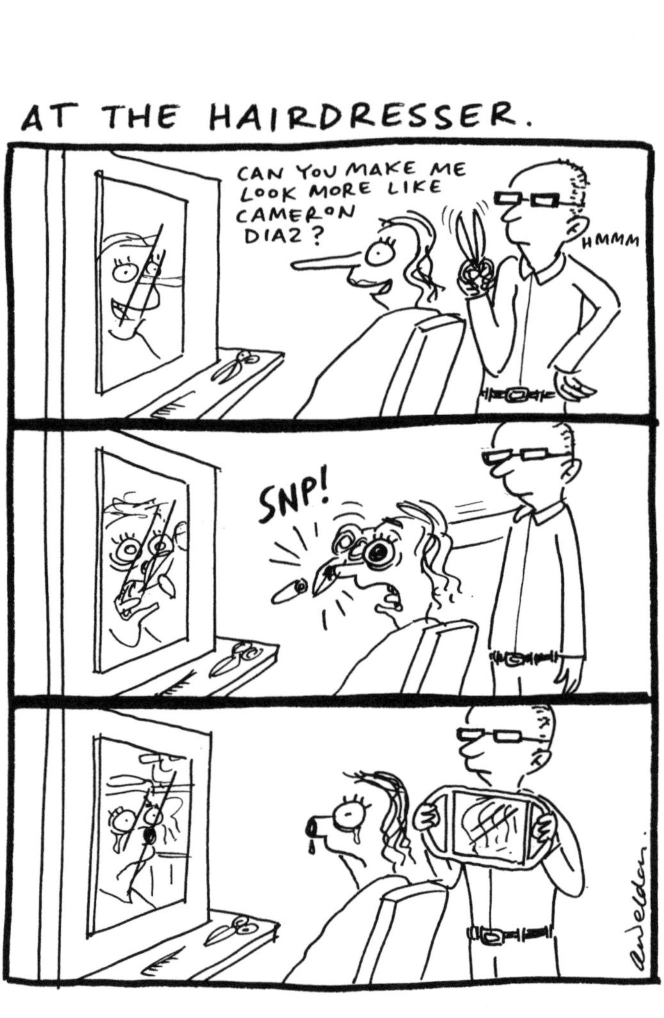
CAN YOU MAKE ME LOOK MORE LIKE CAMERON DIAZ?
HMMM
SNP!

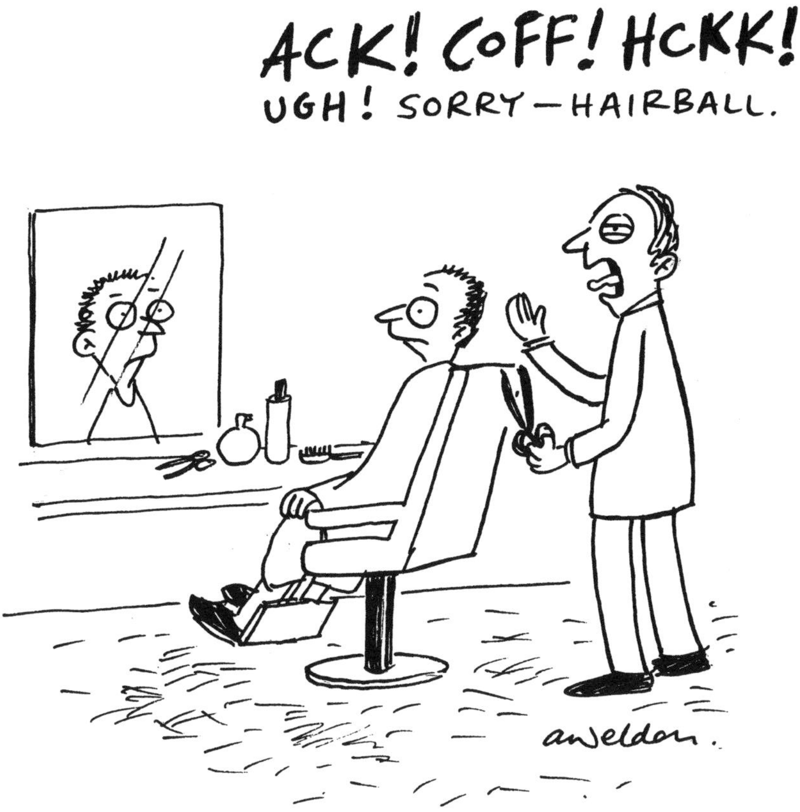
ACK! COFF! HCKK!
UGH! SORRY—HAIRBALL.
aweldon.

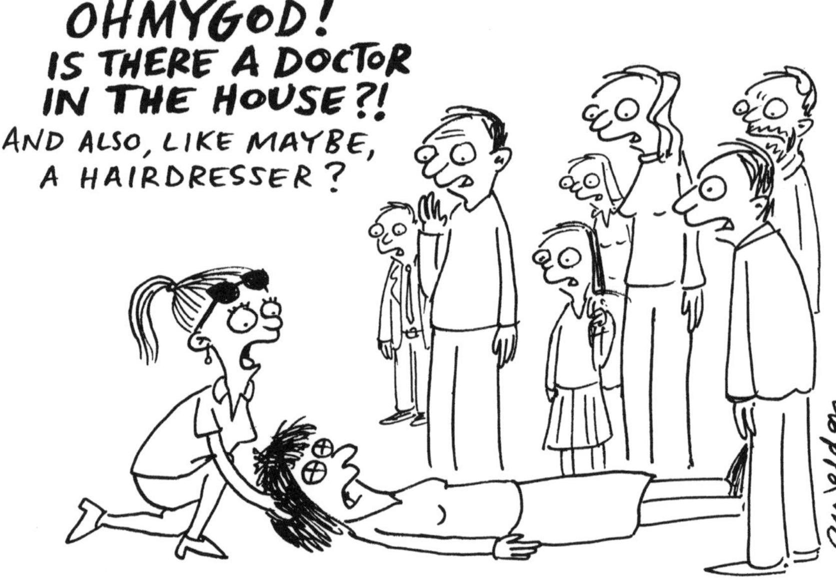
OHMYGOD!
IS THERE A DOCTOR
IN THE HOUSE?!
AND ALSO, LIKE MAYBE,
A HAIRDRESSER?
aweldon.

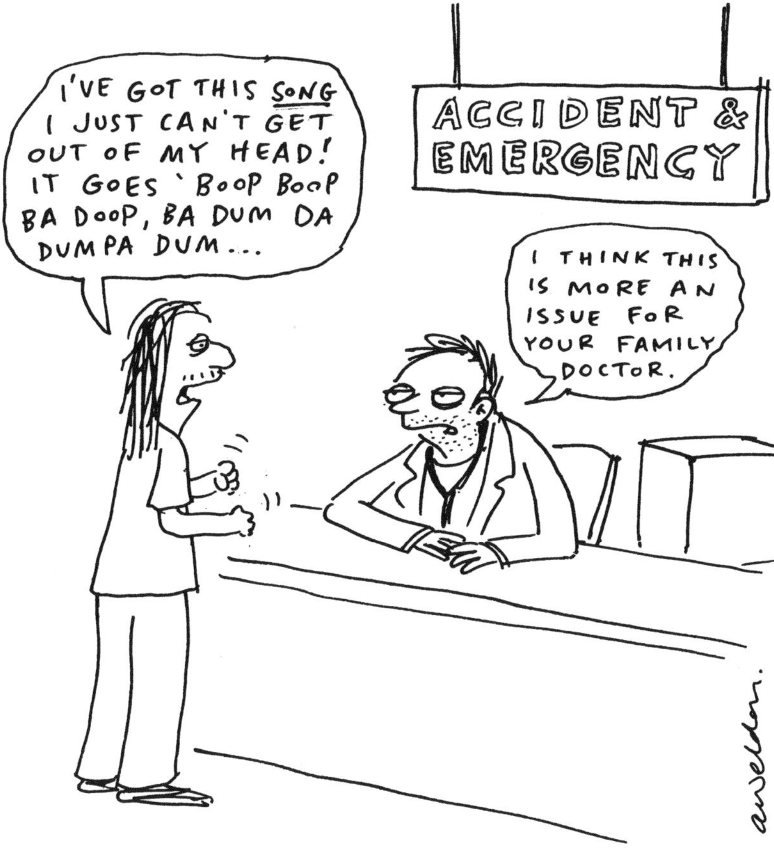
ACCIDENT & EMERGENCY
I'VE GOT THIS SONG I JUST CAN'T GET OUT OF MY HEAD! IT GOES `BOOP BOOP BA DOOP, BA DUM DA DUMPA DUM...
I THINK THIS IS MORE AN ISSUE FOR YOUR FAMILY DOCTOR.

TONE-DEAF MAN HUMS ALONG TO REFRIGERATOR.

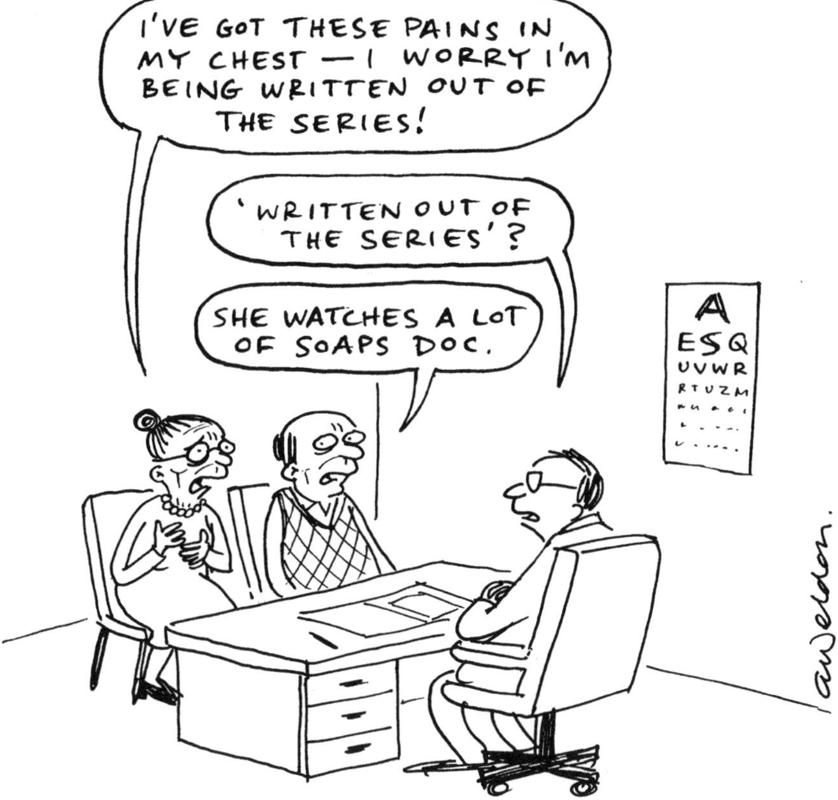
I'VE GOT THESE PAINS IN MY CHEST — I WORRY I'M BEING WRITTEN OUT OF THE SERIES!
'WRITTEN OUT OF THE SERIES'?
SHE WATCHES A LOT OF SOAPS DOC.

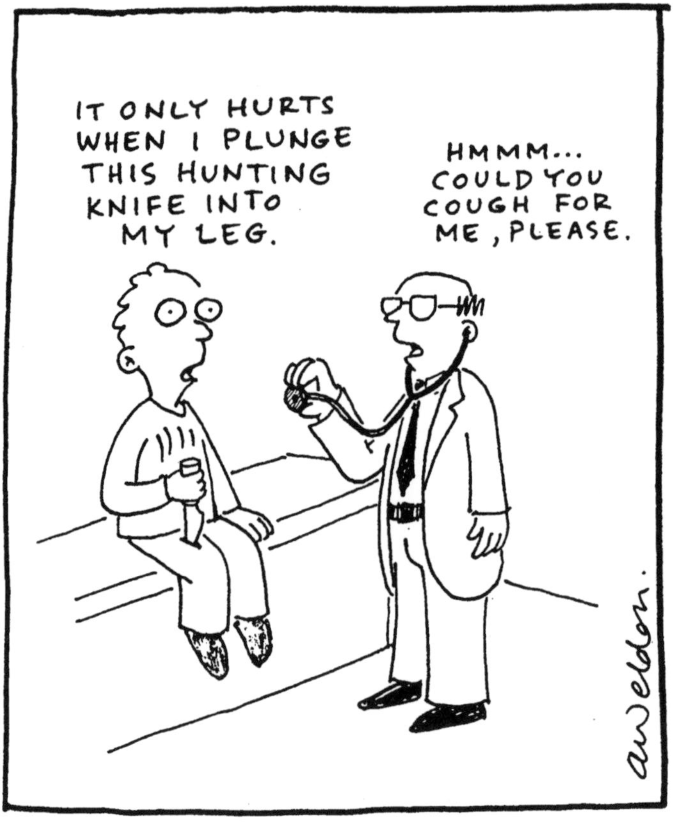
IT ONLY HURTS WHEN I PLUNGE THIS HUNTING KNIFE INTO MY LEG.
HMMM... COULD YOU COUGH FOR ME, PLEASE.
aweldon.

NO – THAT'S NOT ENVY,
THAT'S A FUNGAL
INFECTION.

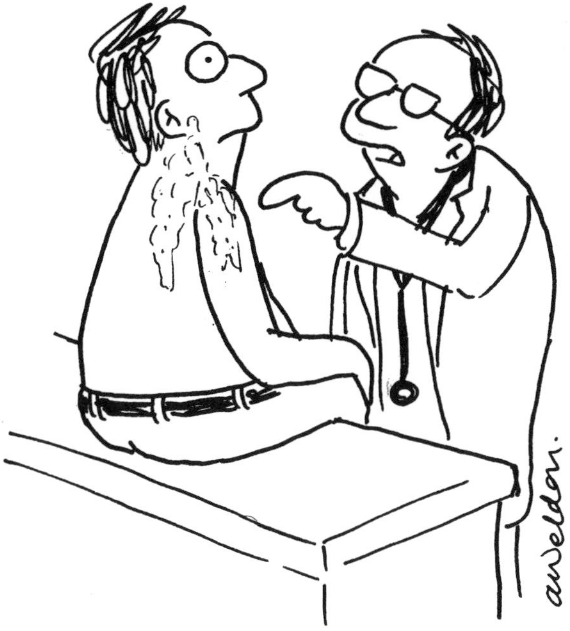
aweldon.

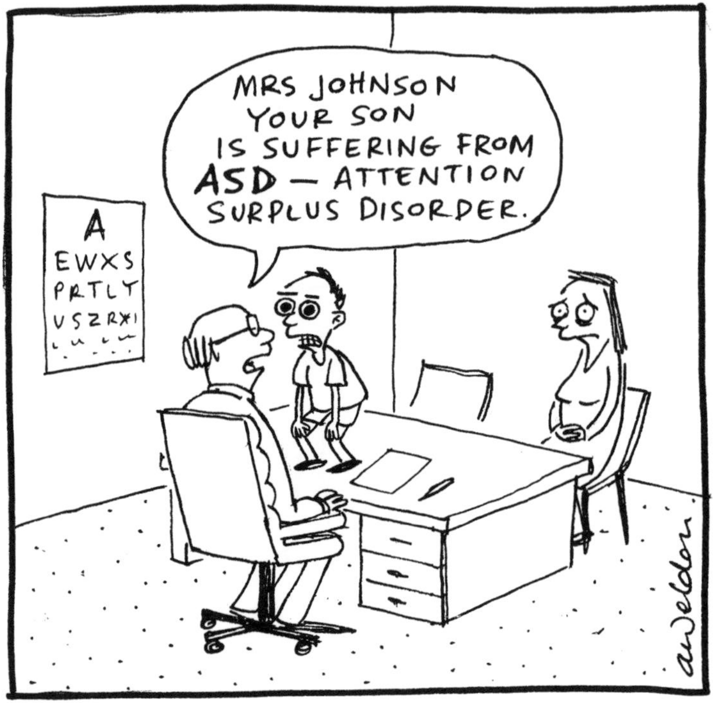
MRS JOHNSON YOUR SON IS SUFFERING FROM ASD — ATTENTION SURPLUS DISORDER.
A
EWXS
PRTLY
awe ldon

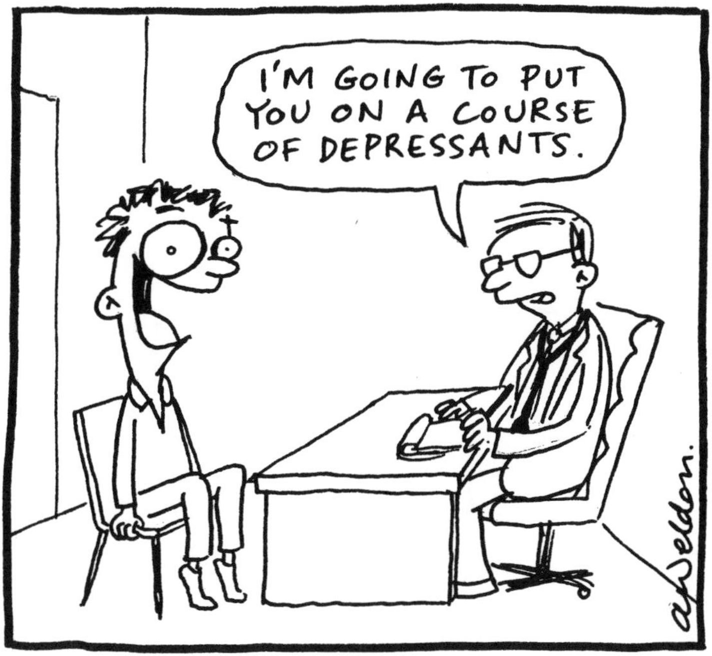
I'M GOING TO PUT YOU ON A COURSE OF DEPRESSANTS.
a Weldon.

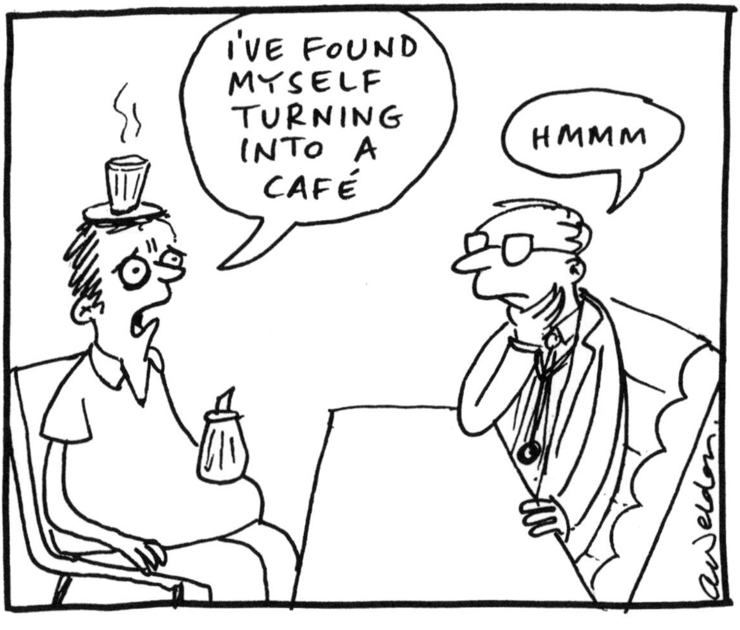
I'VE FOUND MYSELF TURNING INTO A CAFÉ
HMMM
aWeldon

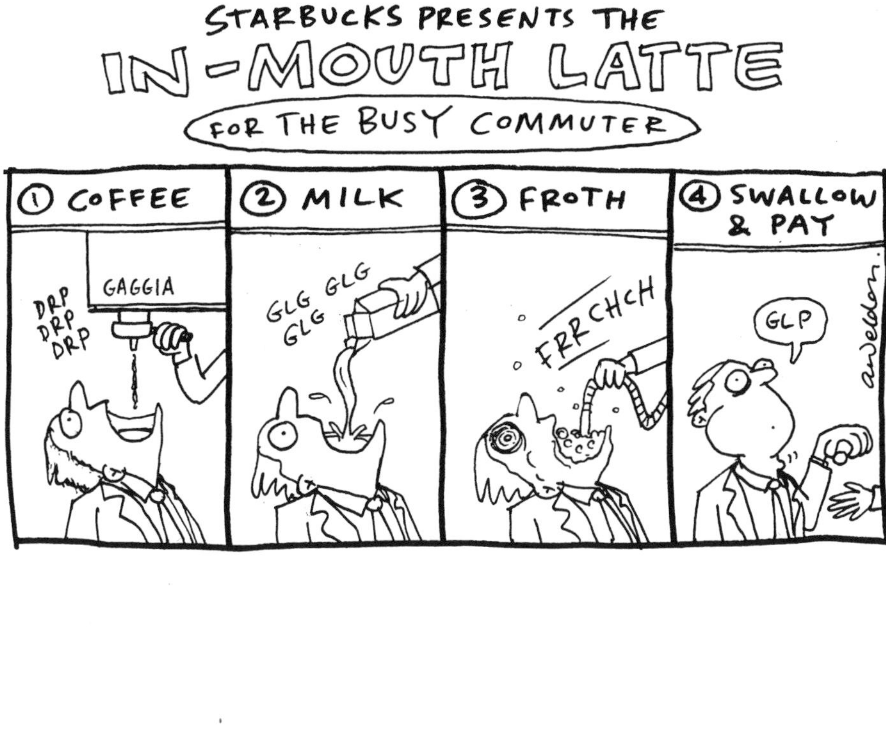
STARBUCKS PRESENTS THE
IN-MOUTH LATTE
FOR THE BUSY COMMUTER
1 COFFEE
GAGGIA
DRP DRP DRP
2 MILK
GLG GLG GLG GLG
3 FROTH
FRRCHCH
4 SWALLOW & PAY
GLP
aweldon

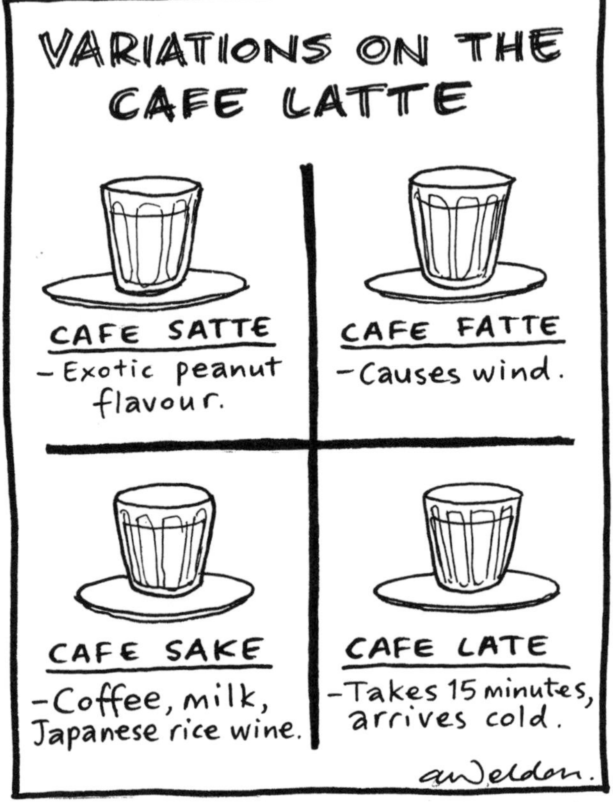
VARIATIONS ON THE CAFE LATTE
CAFE SATTE
-Exotic peanut flavour.
CAFE FATTE
-Causes wind.
CAFE SAKE
-Coffee, milk, Japanese rice wine.
CAFE LATE
-Takes 15 minutes, arrives cold.
aWeldon.

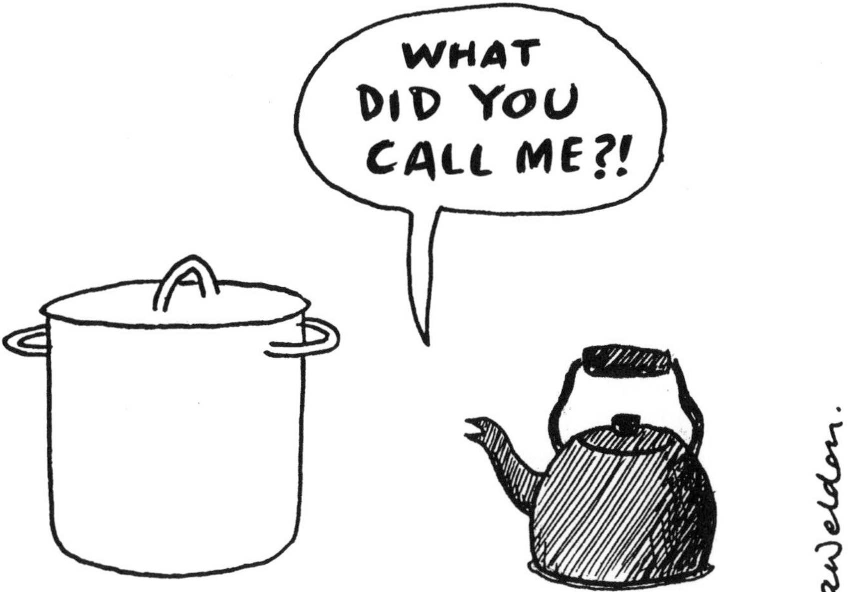
WHAT DID YOU CALL ME?!
aweldon.

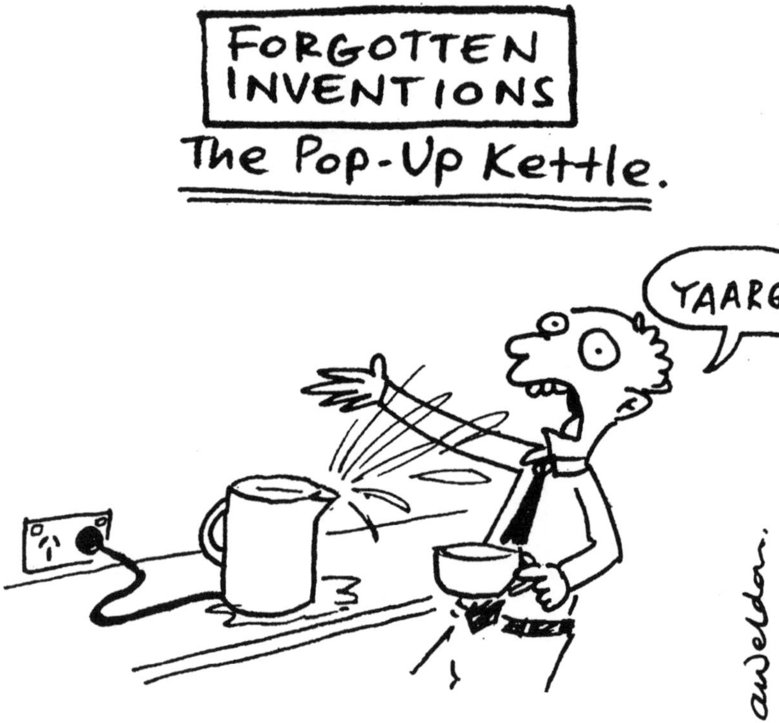
FORGOTTEN INVENTIONS
The Pop-Up Kettle.
YAARGH!
aweldon.

LOOK! I'VE
INVENTED
THE CHEESE
PLATTER!

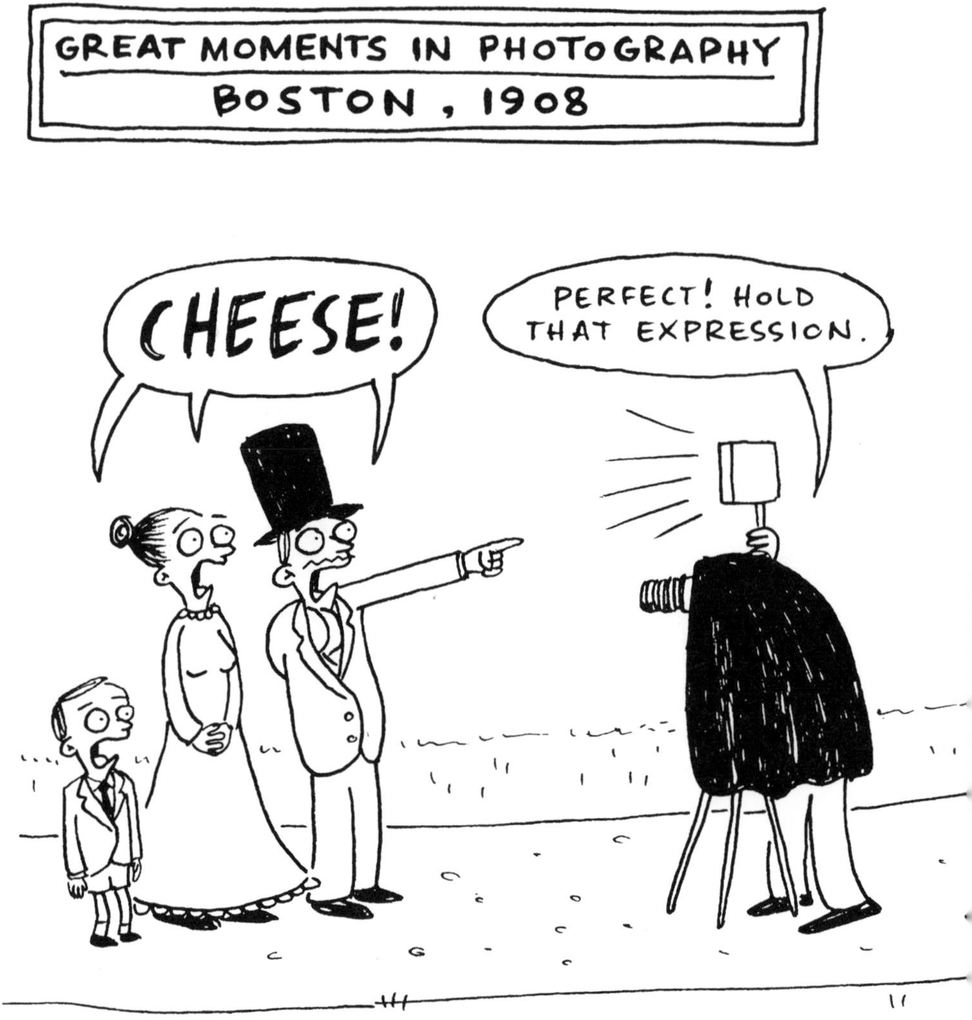
GREAT MOMENTS IN PHOTOGRAPHY
BOSTON, 1908
CHEESE!
PERFECT! HOLD THAT EXPRESSION.

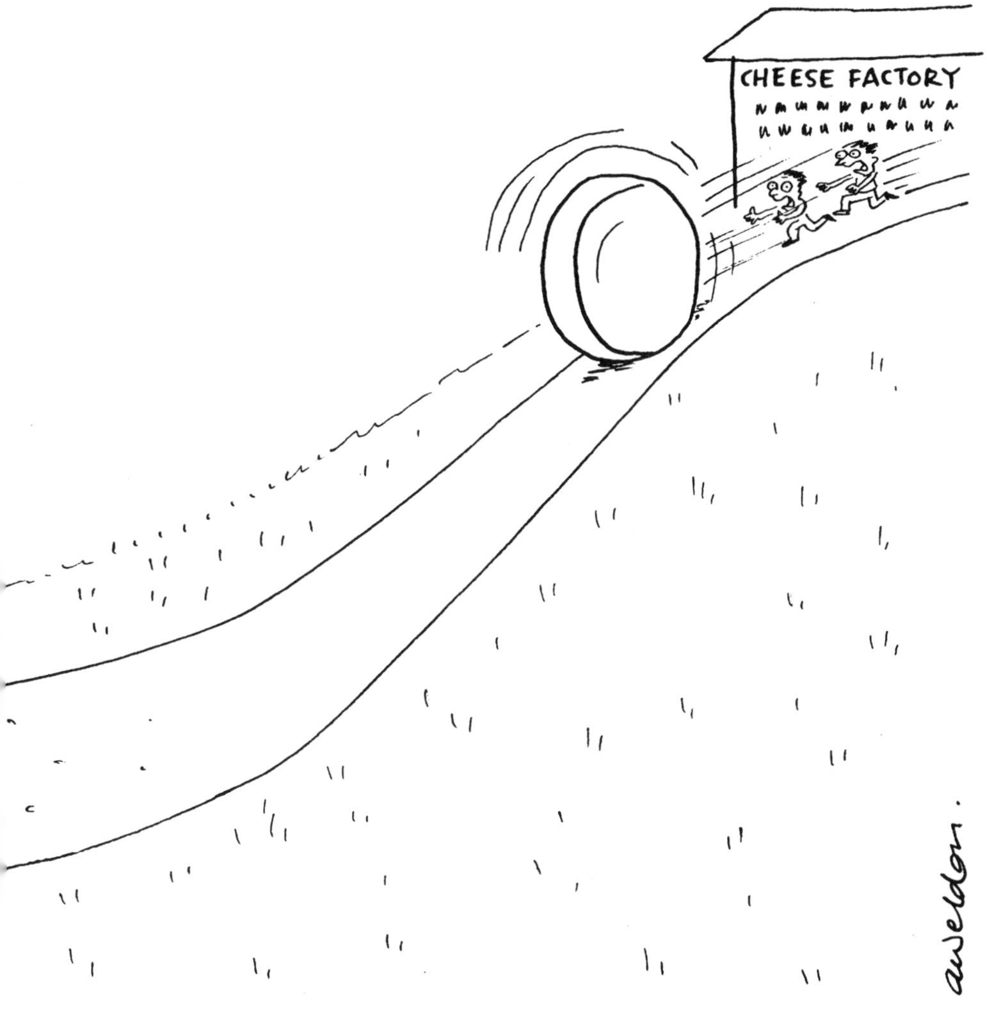
CHEESE FACTORY
aweldon.

Subject Index